Enlightenment and Romance

Robert P. Irvine

Enlightenment
and Romance

Gender and Agency in Smollett and Scott

PETER LANG

Oxford·Bern·Berlin·Bruxelles·Frankfurt am Main·New York·Wien

Die Deutsche Bibliothek – CIP-Einheitsaufnahme

Irvine, Robert P.:
Enlightenment and romance : gender and agendy in Smollett and Scott /
Robert P. Irvine. – Oxford ; Bern ; Berlin ; Bruxelles ; Frankfurt am Main ;
New York ; Wien : Lang, 2000
ISBN 3-906758-94-X

British Library and Library of Congress Cataloguing-in-Publication Data:
A catalogue record for this book is available from *The British Library,* Great
Britain, and from *The Library of Congress,* USA

Cover design: Thomas Jaberg, Peter Lang AG

ISBN 3-906758-94-X
US-ISBN 0-8204-5091-X

© Peter Lang AG, European Academic Publishers, Bern 2000
Jupiterstr. 15, Postfach, 3000 Bern 15, Switzerland; info@peterlang.com

Printed in Germany

Contents

Acknowledgements

Thanks go first and foremost to Cairns Craig, Penny Fielding, and Ian Duncan, whose ideas and example have influenced this study at every stage of its evolution. General thanks is also due to all who took part in the Sixth International Scott Conference, University of Oregon, July 1999, which was inspirational in so many ways. I am very grateful to Frances Dow, Dean of the Faculty of Arts at the University of Edinburgh, for the financial support that made this book possible. A shorter version of chapter 2 appeared in *Journal of Narrative Theory* 30.1 (Winter 2000) and I am grateful to the editors, Ian Wojcik Andrews and James A. Knapp, for permission to reprint that material here. Many thanks to Marie Campbell for proof-reading when she had much better things to do with her time. And finally, I cannot express how much this project has depended, from start to finish, on the endless support and patience of my parents, to whom a corresponding quantity of thanks is due.

Introduction

This is a study of the uses made of feminine-gendered language by two male novelists: Tobias Smollett and Walter Scott. It argues that the shifting relationship between authorship and gender in the late eighteenth and early nineteenth centuries can only be understood by placing it within a wider discursive context, and that, as far as Smollett and Scott are concerned, two developments in particular, both occurring from the middle of the eighteenth century, are crucial for understanding their novels: the rise of an enlightenment discourse of society, that is, of what would come to be known as the 'human sciences'; and the contemporaneous rise of feminine authority in the novel as a genre, as an extension and legitimation of the authority granted women in certain areas of private or domestic life. A more ambitious book than this could, I am sure, demonstrate how these two discursive events were in themselves related: my interest here is restricted to their interrelation in a selection of novels, in ways that established some of the possibilities of the form that were then developed by novelists later in the nineteenth century. My argument is that, by representing social institutions and political history as the products of economic circumstance, rather than the wills of individual statesmen; and, moreover, by understanding the 'manners', tastes and values of the individual subject as in turn shaped by those social institutions, the 'conjectural history' of the French and Scottish Enlightenments makes problematic the concept of human agency. Both Smollett and Scott address this problem in their novels by positing a space outside of historical determination thus conceived, in which the individual subject still has power to shape her life. I say 'her' life, because central to my case is that both Smollett and Scott imagined this self-determining subject as feminine. The generic resources developed by (mostly women) novelists to imagine a feminine subject capable of resisting the determining forces of patriarchy, principally in the heroine's choice of a husband, but also in their own limited autonomy as authors, were taken over by Smollett and Scott to imagine a subject that could escape the determining forces of history. The conventional romance plot as it is used by both novelists then takes on a new importance as the means whereby these two discourses are co-ordinated one with another. I want to suggest that it is the ability of romance, in Scott's hands in particular, to integrate a plausible representation of historical societies with a wish-fulfilling recovery of individual agency that gives the novel a new ideological importance at the beginning of the nineteenth century and which makes possible its Victorian apotheosis.

1. Michael McKeon and the history of the novel

In arguing thus, I hope to at least qualify the account of the development of the novel offered in Michael McKeon's *Origins of the English Novel*. McKeon's history of early-modern prose fiction culminates in and explains the work of Richardson and Fielding, in which, he argues, the novel form 'attains its institutional and canonic identity'.[1] The first section of McKeon's book traces the rejection of the epistemological idealism associated with romance narrative by the empirical location of truth in the material particularity of historical experience, and the subsequent dialectical incorporation and overcoming of both in an 'extreme skepticism' which argues 'the inescapability of romance in true history', the inevitable mediation of historicity by some set of conventions or other.[2] This epistemological stance, which claims a relation to historical reality without claiming to be an unmediated reproduction of it, is always in danger of slipping into one of the two older positions; but its adoption makes possible the achievement of Richardson and Fielding. However, in order to make this achievement, not simply the outcome of the discursive possibilities of a particular historical moment, but definitive of the discursive possibilities of the years to come, McKeon has to place it in a much wider discursive framework, namely the emergence of the aesthetic as a category of experience understood as autonomous from, and transcendent of, the world of historical reality.

---

1   Michael McKeon, *The Origins of the English Novel 1600–1740* (Baltimore: John Hopkins University Press, 1987) 21.
2   Ibid. 119.

The mediation of historical reality through fiction can then be legitimated by the participation of the medium involved in a truth higher than the merely historical:

> In the later eighteenth century, the rejuvenated Aristotelian notion of the universal truth of poetry will aid in the formulation of the modern belief in the autonomous realm of the aesthetic [...], the body of knowledge which in modern thought is designated as the last and lonely refuge of transcendent spirit, the sphere of artistic experience. Doctrines of literary realism, which rise from the ruins of the claim to historicity, reformulate the problem of mediation for a world in which spirituality has ceased to represent another realm to which human materiality has only difficult and gratuitous access, and has become instead the capacity of human creativity itself. [...] The idea of realism exists to concede the accountability of art to a prior reality, without seeming to compromise the uniquely modern belief that such reality as it is answerable to already is internalized in art itself as a demystified species of spirituality.[3]

As an account of the continuity of the novel form from its establishment by Richardson and Fielding, the vocabulary of this passage is oddly discontinuous with McKeon's discussion as a whole. The 'difficult and gratuitous access' of human materiality to 'spirituality' has not figured largely among the problems which the novel evolves to address; a 'reality' constituted by a 'demystified species of spirituality' is clearly 'real' in a very different sense to that 'realism' which arises from the ruins of historicity. This discontinuity is produced because that which mediates the historically particular within the aesthetic sphere as it is understood here is no longer a set of discursive conventions, a practice of representation particular to a society or a class, but 'human creativity' understood as transcendent of any particular social location. What McKeon is in fact doing here is assimilating the late eighteenth-century novel to late eighteenth-century poetry. To make this account continuous with his account of the origins of the novel, McKeon must then retrospectively turn Richardson's heroines, and Fielding's narrators, into prototype romantic poets, whose subjectivity in itself represents an historically transcendent 'truth':

> [...][B]oth the claim [to historicity] and its subversion end in the triumph of the creative human mind, a triumph already prefigured at the moment of the novel's

---

3   Ibid. 119–20.

emergence: in Richardson the triumphant mind is that of the protagonist; in Fielding it is that of the author.[4]

I will be arguing that, far from constituting a transcendent force mediating the realist novel's reference to history, 'human creativity' is figured in Scott's novels by a separate discursive element within the text, one defined *in opposition to* a discourse of history. The appearance of an autonomous aesthetic sphere in the late eighteenth century is after all the result of a more general fragmentation of the discursive land-scape; rather than the realist novel being contained within one of the fragments, as McKeon suggests, I shall argue that it develops by its capacity to contain within itself the various discourses produced.

To explain what I mean by discursive fragmentation in the late eighteenth century, let me consider briefly the problems that McKeon's account of the discourse of realism produces for his argument generally. Much of the power of McKeon's analysis comes from its deployment of an analogy between the dialectic relating three possible epistemologies – outlined above and discussed in section one of his book – with the dialectic relating three ideological positions. These are an aristocratic ideology, which finds its expression in romance idealism, but which is only formulated as such in dialectical opposition to a progressive ideology which appeals to empiricism; and a conservative ideology which transcends this opposition just as its epistemological equivalent, extreme skepticism, transcends idealism and empiricism. This analogy between 'questions of truth' and 'questions of virtue' are, argues McKeon, the defining problem-solving strategy of the novel as a form. One might then expect section two of *Origins of the English Novel*, which discusses these ideological questions, to end in an analogous way to section one: with a glance forward in time to see what becomes of these concepts in the ensuing decades.

This does not happen. Whatever role epistemological realism finds itself playing in the aesthetic sphere, it is not clear what kind of 'virtue' or ideology follows it there, or *can* follow it there, for the point about the aesthetic sphere is of course its claim to transcend the ethical, to transcend ideology: political questions are what it is supposed to be autonomous *from*. It is at this point that the whole analogical structure

---

4   Ibid. 418–19.

of McKeon's version of the novel is revealed as only working for a very specific historical period, one in which epistemology and ideology, knowledge and values, had become, under the pressure of the value-free natural sciences, distinct discursive spheres, but in which a profound sense of their interconnectedness still remained. In such a transitional period, *analogies* between 'questions of truth' and 'questions of value' have immense explanatory power. But a challenge to this power arises as soon as ideology itself becomes an object of knowledge, when the value-free rhetoric of empirical science is turned on social reality itself. This happens in the year before *Pamela*, the year before McKeon's survey ends:

> In every system of morality, which I have hitherto met with, I have always remark'd, that the author proceeds for some time in the ordinary way of reasoning, and establishes the being of a God, or makes observations concerning human affairs; when of a sudden I am surpriz'd to find, that instead of the usual copulations of propositions, *is*, and *is not*, I meet with no proposition that is not connected with an *ought*, or an *ought not*. This change is imperceptible; but is, however, of the last consequence. For as this *ought*, or *ought not*, expresses some new relation or affirmation, 'tis necessary that it shou'd be observ'd and explain'd; and at the same time that a reason should be given, for what seems altogether inconceivable, how this new relation can be a deduction from others, which are entirely different from it.[5]

For Hume, knowledge about the world, what *is*, and moral judgement, what *ought*, belong to two distinct language games. The enlightenment disenchantment of the world, its withdrawal of ethical or religious categories from the grammar of knowledge, produces a split between the epistemological and the ethical, between facts and values, that spells the end of the cultural utility of the analogies that McKeon finds in the early novel. The novel remains a crucial form of discourse for just the reason that McKeon explains: namely, its ability to solve otherwise intractable categorial problems. But in the early modern period, on McKeon's account, those problems were of instability in epistemological or social categories, and the analogy between the two spheres allowed by the novel gave it this problem-solving capacity. By the later eighteenth century, the gap between the two spheres of knowledge and ethics has

---

5   David Hume, *A Treatise of Human Nature* (1739; Oxford: Clarendon Press, 1978) 469–70.

become precisely the problem that needs to be solved. By the last decade of the century, this gap has become for Kant a 'great gulf', between the sensible world of knowledge and the supersensible world of Freedom in which ethics is possible:

> Albeit, then, between the realm of the natural concept, as the sensible, and the realm of the concept of freedom, as the supersensible, there is a great gulf fixed, so that it is not possible to pass from the former to the latter [...], just as if they were so many separate worlds, the first of which is powerless to exercise influence on the second: still the latter is *meant* to influence the former—that is to say, the concept of freedom is meant to actualize in the sensible world the end proposed by its laws; and nature must consequently also be capable of being regarded in such a way that in the conformity to law of its form it at least harmonizes with the possibility of the ends to be effectuated in it according to the laws of freedom.[6]

Kant's project in the third Critique is of course to bridge this gulf precisely by means of an account of the aesthetic autonomous from both knowledge and ethics: a third, aesthetic realm will 'harmonize' the other two. That the aesthetic has some relation to the ethical in this sense McKeon acknowledges. Looking forward to the dangers spotted by Mackenzie, Barbauld and others in sentimentalism, he comments:

> In these apprehensions lie the seeds of the Brechtian insight that art in the modern period seeks to replace not only religious spirituality but responsible action. With the triumph of 'aesthetic truth' over naive empiricism, literary fictions are able to have a value without laying claim to being 'real', and the end of literature has become not teaching goodness but being 'good' in itself.[7]

What McKeon misses is the extent to which it is enlightenment conceptions of knowledge that make it *necessary* to replace 'responsible action' with something or other to begin with. For what the separation of 'is' and 'ought' makes possible, among other things, are discourses which construct human societies and human history as interrelated objects of scientific knowledge, that is, a knowledge whose ostensible purpose does not include the validation of ethical categories. Taking our cue from Kant, one might then expect the aesthetic, not to replace or mediate reference to historical or social reality as McKeon suggests, but

---

6   Immanuel Kant, *The Critique of Judgement*, trans. J.C. Meredith (1790; Oxford: Clarendon Press, 1952) 14.
7   McKeon 126.

to 'harmonize' it in some sense with that which such reference now excludes: the ethical, ideology, or 'virtue'. This is precisely the function filled, as we shall see, by romance plot in Scott's *Guy Mannering*. While McKeon is right to see romance as being assimilated to some such autonomous aesthetic sphere, he misses that enlightenment historiography and social science both mediated the revival of interest in romance itself (by turning traditional narrative forms into objects of inquiry), and called up romance narrative forms as their counterweight. To understand the place of the novel within an ideology of the aesthetic, it is thus necessary to work out the novel's relationship to enlightenment itself.

2. Enlightenment, history, and gender

The enlightenment with which I am concerned here is the emergence, in the second half of the eighteenth century, in Scotland and France, of a 'Science of Man', and particularly the 'Conjectural History' of Montesquieu, Turgot, Smith, Ferguson and Millar which provided the framework for that science.[8] I am taking the object of this science as 'society' rather than 'Man', both to avoid confusion with the invention of 'man' that Foucault locates in the more institutionalised disciplines of sociology and anthropology, linguistics and economics that only emerge in the nineteenth century;[9] and because my interest here is in the construction of the social *totality* in its historical specificity (this specificity organised in four historical stages of hunter-gatherer, pastoral, agricultural, and commercial societies) as the object of this discourse rather than any universal human *nature* which might be abstracted out of it.

---

8   The former phrase is Hume's (*Treatise* xv), the latter Dugald Stewart's: 'An Account of the Life and Writings of the Adam Smith, LL.D.', in Adam Smith, *Essays on Philosophical Subjects*, Adam Smith, *Essays on Philosophical Subjects* (Strasburg: F.G. Levrault, 1799) xlvii.

9   I leave to one side the fraught question of the epistemic relation of the earlier discourse to the later disciplines: see Michel Foucault, *The Order of Things* (London: Tavistock, 1970) chapters 9 and 10.

The rhetoric of 'science' in this context evokes the methods of Newtonian physics: 'the methodological history of the human sciences before 1800', writes John Christie, '[...] was a history of attempts to appropriate, transfer and apply natural science methodological canons to the human world.'[10] Thus, social institutions (property relations, laws, 'manners') are understood as the *effects* of *causes* (climate, population, and, above all, the 'modes of sustenance' just listed) which it is the task of the scientist to discover: 'everything in society and history, just like everything in the physical realm, was bound together by an intricate concatenation of causes and effects.'[11] Two specific aspects of this rhetoric require elaboration. Clearly, these causes must all be understood in temporal or historical terms. There is no space here for divine intervention or Providence as an explanation for social effects: at least in its Scottish form, conjectural history offers no comforting *telos* towards which humanity is moving, in which history will ultimately fulfil human desire.[12] In one sense, thus, this enlightenment discourse makes human beings *agents* as never before, precisely by banishing God as a possible explanation of their social arrangements: society was now to be understood as produced by human needs and desires and not as the product of some divine master-plan. This discovery that humanity invents itself finds its clearest theoretical articulation in the idea of the social contract, whereby pre-social individuals *choose* to surrender their primal freedom in order to enjoy the goods that follow from life in a social group. However, the writers of the Scottish Enlightenment tend to be critical of social contract theories, from an underlying scepticism about the extent to which individual intentions can be responsible for conventions and institutions that constitute society. The most famous statement of this principle comes from Adam Ferguson:

---

10   John Christie, 'The human sciences: origins and histories', *History of the Human Sciences* 6.1 (1993): 3.

11   Ronald L. Meek, *Social Science and the Ignoble Savage* (Cambridge: Cambridge University Press, 1976) 1.

12   'Now it should be noted that this developmental history is not at all teleological. It is described in terms of the original sources that prompt it, not backward from its conclusion. It issues from the springs of human action, whose impetus is undirected by the supposed destiny of mankind's moral development.' Robert Wokler, 'Anthropology and Conjectural History in the Enlightenment', in Christopher Fox, Roy Porter, and Robert Wokler, eds., *Inventing Human Science: Eighteenth-Century Domains* (Berkeley: University of California Press, 1995) 39.

> Every step and every movement of the multitude, even in what are termed enlightened ages, are made with equal blindness to the future; and nations stumble upon establishments, which are indeed the result of human action, but not the execution of any human design. [...] [Communities] admit of the greatest revolutions where no change is intended, and [...] the most refined politicians do not always know whither they are leading the state by their projects.[13]

As David Carrithers notes, this is quite consistent, throughout eighteenth-century thought, with a '"sociological" conviction that causal patterns can be discovered in the social realm':

> Such convictions of unintended consequences—whether in Vico's Providential formulation, or in Mandeville's transformation of private license into public gain, or in Smith's conception of 'an invisible hand'—need not undermine belief in lawfulness and pattern. Such theories merely exclude the conscious design of individuals from being considered the true agents creating those patterns that exist.[14]

The model of the natural sciences in this way obscures 'the fundamental difference between human actors possessing free will and natural objects obeying fixed laws'.[15] Historical agency thus lies with 'human nature', with a set of needs and desires shared among what Ferguson calls 'the multitude', rather than with the designs of any particular subject.

However, if social institutions develop independently of human design, those institutions nevertheless shape the character of the subject who lives under those institutions. A problem might then be expected to arise concerning the status of that subject as a source of moral judgement, for its ethics will be shaped, as its tastes and manners are shaped, by the current institutions of its society. Conjectural history thus tends to turn values into social facts available for explanation in terms of mode of subsistence and so on. Within the framework of this type of human science, not only is *political* agency withdrawn from the subject, but there seems little room for an account of how moral considerations

---

13   Adam Ferguson, *An Essay on the History of Civil Society*, ed. Duncan Forbes (1767; Edinburgh: Edinburgh University Press, 1966) 122.
14   David Carrithers, 'The Enlightenment Science of Society', *Inventing Human Science* 246–7.
15   Ibid. 239–40.

could ground a critique of social institutions. Once again, this contrasts with social contract theory, whose explanation of social institutions is also an explanation of their legitimacy, to which citizens can appeal when the state breaks the terms of the contract. The discourse of science deployed by conjectural history attends to questions, not of legitimacy, but of necessity, and the free choice of the human subject thus has only a subordinate role in its explanations.

And yet for all that, the writers of the Scottish Enlightenment (to go no further) perceived of their own social role in ethical terms. Nicholas Phillipson has brought out this tension in an essay on Adam Smith. Contrasting his own approach to those who understand these philosophers in terms of their introduction of the methods of natural science, he writes: 'I prefer to think of them as practical moralists who had developed a formidable and complex casuistical armoury to instruct young men of middling rank in their duties as men and as citizens of a modern commercial polity.'[16] That last point is crucial, of course: the *Theory of Moral Sentiments* is *not* 'an account of moral behaviour in general, but [...] an account of the peculiar moral constraints which are placed on the citizens of a commercial society', and is 'redundant outside the context of a commercial society with a complex division of labour'.[17] To discover what a commercial society is, we must turn to the conjectural history of the *Lectures on Jurisprudence*; to understand the division of labour, to the *Wealth of Nations*. One can then choose to see, with Phillipson, Smith's 'scientific' discourse as enclosed within and serving the ends of an overall moral purpose, or on the contrary choose to see his ethics as ultimately reducible to merely prudential maxims for the subjects of a commercial polity; but either move constitutes jumping one way or the other over the gap between 'is' and 'ought' described by Hume.[18]

---

16   Nicholas Phillipson, 'Adam Smith as Civic Moralist', in Istvan Hont and Michael Ignatieff, eds., *Wealth and Virtue* (Cambridge: Cambridge University Press, 1983) 179.
17   Ibid. 188, 182.
18   This tension in 'Scottish Philosophy' between its rhetoric of scientific objectivity and its claim to play an ethical role within its society is one missed, I think, by Clifford Siskin. For Siskin, the 'scientificity' of the Scottish Enlightenment is indeed shaped within 'Scottish imperatives of common-ness'; but this 'common-ness' turns out to name, apparently unproblematically, *both* the co-ordination of

In offering advice for living in a modern society Smith is continuing 'a discussion about the principles of practical morality which had begun with Addison and Steele's *Tatler* and *Spectator*'.[19] Indeed, one could suggest that within the terms of Smith's overall project, the place of ethics is taken by that of 'politeness', of a mutually improving sociability that can unite gentlemen (in Smith's scheme of things, at least: see below) in a sphere independent of the economics and politics of a commercial society even if they are what make it possible. This is suggested by David Allan's *Virtue, Learning and the Scottish Enlightenment*, which sees the prioritisation of the social and the moral in these writers as rooted not in the contemporary social imperatives of an imperial-commercial state, but in their continuing debt to renaissance humanism.[20] What has been lost in the transition is clearly just that sense of political agency whose absence from enlightenment writing I have been discussing. For where Buchanan had a prince for his student, and the other historians discussed by Allan tried to harangue a fractious and decadent aristocracy into their civic responsibilities and the transformation of the Scottish state, Smith has only a lecture hall of the sons of the 'middling sort'. The latter cannot hope to transform the state to their own design (not least, of course, because there is no longer any Scottish state to transform), only to accommodate themselves to it and, by their industriousness and politeness, be the unintentional causes of unknown political effects. In consequence, the modern historian or moral philosopher cannot hope to gain the sort of political agency through their pupils that the role of Ciceronian orator granted their renaissance predecessors. This replacement of a political virtue with 'polite' values is, however, a process that is also worked out in England in the context of an openly political struggle; and this is the context which informs, I will argue in chapter 1, Smollett's *Roderick Random*.

It is David Hume rather than Adam Smith who most famously, as Phillipson notes in the essay quoted above, abandoned the overtly

---

disciplines within the single project, *and* its 'common accessibility' to an educated audience. *The Work of Writing: Literature and Social Change in Britain, 1700–1830* (Baltimore: John Hopkins University Press, 1998) 96.

19 Phillipson 188.

20 David Allan, *Virtue, Learning, and the Scottish Enlightenment: Ideas of Scholarship in Early Modern History* (Edinburgh: Edinburgh University Press, 1993).

scientific enterprise of the *Treatise of Human Nature* to write instead polite essays for more general consumption in the manner of Addison and Steele. One can indeed argue that Hume is already engaged in this sort of writing at particular moments of the *Treatise* itself. The passage quoted above, establishing the logical gap between matters of fact and matters of value, continues thus:

> But as authors do not commonly use this precaution, I shall presume to recommend it to the readers; and am persuaded, that this small attention wou'd subvert all the vulgar systems of morality, and let us see, that the distinction of vice and virtue is not founded merely on the relations of the objects, nor is perceiv'd by reason.[21]

'I shall presume to recommend it to the readers': Hume takes his philosophical point and applies it to his reader's experience of reading. His audience is imagined here as a group united by reading the same books, and, now, united in reading them in the same and improved way. Hume is here already adopting the stance of a contributor to the *Spectator*, eager to share an 'observation' that may 'be found of some importance', alerting his readers as it does to a potential 'vulgarity'. But if Hume is here on an Addisonian mission to improve, what is the logical or grammatical status of that mission? For in the course of this passage, Hume surely commits exactly the solecism that he identifies in others: he himself proceeds from an 'is', an 'observation', a statement of grammatical or logical fact, to an 'ought', in the recommendation of one reading practice over another. Hume only escapes self-contradiction if the imperative implied in this recommendation is *not* a *moral* imperative, since it is clear from the context that it is only a moral 'ought' that cannot be derived from statements of fact. But what then *is* the status of that recommendation? 'Politeness', if that is in effect what is being recommended in this alert reading practice, seems not to be a moral category after all, in the sense in which the moral is defined within the terms of Hume's new 'science of man'.

Similarly, one of Hume's essays, 'Of the Rise and Progress of the Arts and Sciences', begins by seeming to define that most crucial of categories for his enlightenment science, that of *cause*: 'Nothing requires greater nicety, in our enquiries concerning human affairs, than to distinguish exactly what is owing to chance and what proceeds from

---

21   Hume, *Treatise* 470.

causes.'[22] The next paragraph appeals to just that enlightenment principle, already mentioned in the case of Ferguson, that the agent of history available to scientific analysis is humanity in the mass, the multitude, rather than the individual: '*What depends on a few persons is, in a great measure, to be ascribed to chance, or secret and unknown causes: what arises from a great number, may often be accounted for by determinate and known causes.*'[23] The bulk of the essay will consider the types of government under which trade on the one hand or learning on the other is likely to arise. But this first paragraph has already, like the shift from observation to recommendation in the *Treatise,* enclosed the rhetoric of science within a hermeneutic imperative for polite readers:

> [N]or is there any subject, in which an author is more liable to deceive himself by false subtilties and refinements. To say that any event is derived from chance, cuts short all further inquiry concerning it, and leaves the writer in the same state of ignorance with the rest of mankind. But when the event is supposed to proceed from certain and stable causes, he may then display his ingenuity in assigning these causes; and [...] he has thereby an opportunity of swelling his volumes, and discovering his profound knowledge of what escapes the vulgar and ignorant.[24]

Once again, we move very fast from an epistemological question into its implications for the reading practices of Hume's polite audience; from science to its discursive situation, one structured by the vulgarity of the author who claims a false authority, and his address to a vulgar readership who can demonstrate their politeness by finding him out.

In passages like this the place of Hume himself is thus one of the things at stake. Its effect is to (perhaps disingenuously) distinguish between an authorial practice marked by vanity and pretence, and Hume's own, which by implication is one much closer to 'the same state of ignorance with the rest of mankind'. His position is indeed sufficiently removed from this ignorance to be able to point out the difference, but once again this is an observation that his readers will themselves now be able to make in their own reading practice. Hume's polite discourse, that is, implies a degree of *equality* between author and

---

22   Hume, 'Of the Rise and Progress of the Arts and Sciences', in *Selected Essays* (Oxford: Oxford University Press, 1993) 56.
23   Hume, *Essays* 57.
24   Hume, *Essays* 56.

reader; and that equality is imagined as a *conversation*: Hume begins his essay-journalism with a self-description 'as a kind of resident or ambassador from the dominions of learning to those of conversation'.[25] Within what Lawrence Klein calls 'the culture of politeness', this is a conventional presupposition.

> This discursivity was the crux of politeness, and the model for discursivity was conversation, the locale from which its vocabulary and strategies radiated. Conversation was a structure of mutuality and equality. It addressed subject matter of mutual relevance, but was at the same time disinterested. Propriety and decorum reined in self-concerned impulses.[26]

– impulses such as those, perhaps, which tempted authors to pretend to a greater understanding than they actually enjoyed.

However, the Addisonian mode to which Hume turns in the essays carries with it a very particular role for *gender*: for the abandonment of the technically philosophical mode is also an abandonment of a strictly *masculine* readership for a mixed one. Addison's desire to bring philosophy 'out of Closets and Libraries, Schools and Colleges', predominantly masculine retreats, and 'to dwell in Clubs *and* Assemblies, at Tea-Tables, *and* in Coffee-Houses' (my italics), that is, into a range of public spaces where the exclusively masculine ones are balanced by others to which women have access.[27] Richard Steele had already made the same point: 'I shall take it for the greatest Glory of my Work, if among reasonable Women this Paper may furnish *Tea-Table Talk*.'[28] However, not only is the discourse of the *Spectator* going to be available for use in feminine conversation, feminine conversation provides a model for its whole enterprise. For if polite journalism of this sort sets out to refine the manners and broaden the culture of its readers

---

25   Hume, 'Of Essay Writing', *Essays* 2.

26   Lawrence Klein, *Shaftesbury and the Culture of Politeness: Moral discourse and cultural politics in early eighteenth-century England* (Cambridge: Cambridge University Press, 1994) 119.

27   *The Spectator* ed. Donald S. Bond (Oxford: Clarendon Press, 1965) 10 (March 12, 1711) vol. I, p.44. This point is made by Lawrence Klein in 'Gender, conversation and the public sphere in early eighteenth-century England', in Judith Still and Michael Warton, eds., *Textuality and Sexuality: Reading Theories and Practices* (Manchester: Manchester University Press, 1993) 109.

28   *The Spectator* 4 (March 4, 1711) vol. I, p.21.

male *and* female, this is exactly what polite women are imagined as doing in conversation with men:

> Had our Species no females in it, Men would be quite different Creatures from what they are at present; their Endeavours to please the opposite Sex, polishes and refines them out of those Manners which are most natural to them [...]. In a word, Man would not only be an unhappy, but a rude unfinished Creature, were he conversant with none but those of his own Make.[29]

And once again we find Hume, in 'Of Essay Writing', following suit, and extending his political metaphor in which the essay-writer was ambassador,

> it would be altogether inexcusable in me not to address myself with a particular respect to the fair sex, who are the sovereigns of the empire of conversation.
> [...] I am of the opinion that women, that is, women of sense and education (for to such alone I address myself) are much better judges of all polite writing than men of the same degree of understanding [...].[30]

Although Hume goes on to qualify this, the gender dynamic involved here between masculine author and feminine judge underpins much of Hume's writing, and has been thoroughly explored by Jerome Christensen. The male author has lost his political agency within the state, which survives in his writing only as a source of metaphors to describe his relation to a feminine authority of taste by which his productions will be judged. Christensen concludes, 'There are two criteria of modernity for Hume: the ascendancy of the woman as sovereign and the emergence of the man of letters as the successor of the classical orator.'[31]

The female reader now appears in the polite discourse that Hume shares with the *Spectator* as the site of both moral and aesthetic judgement, and feminine conversation as that space within a commercial culture where the moral agency no longer possible in the political world can still be exercised. This idea will go through a series of transformations in the course of the eighteenth century, most importantly in

---

29 *The Spectator* 433 (July 17, 1712) vol. IV, p.21.
30 Hume, 'Of Essay Writing', *Essays* 3.
31 Jerome Christensen, *Practicing Enlightenment: Hume and the Formation of a Literary Career* (Madison: University of Wisconsin Press, 1987) 105.

Richardson's novels, where the improving female conversationalist is turned into the improving female *writer* (*Pamela*), and the feminine conversation turned into a feminine epistolary correspondence (*Clarissa*) in novels which 'envisage a responsive feminine sensibility as the best embodiment of social instinct'.[32] I will discuss these developments, and the cultural situation they created for women novelists, in chapter 2.

Let me note one other consequence of the rise of this discourse of politeness: its effacement of party-political conflict, understood as part of that public historical world from which feminine conversation offered refuge. Party loyalty, like religious enthusiasm, is associated in Addisonian discourse with the violence of seventeenth-century controversy, as a potential fracture line in the hegemony of landed and trading interests that 'politeness' was designed to make possible. Party politics was now, of course, a matter of print-polemic and literary satire rather than open warfare: in chapter 1 we will find, even in a novel as resolutely impolite as *Roderick Random*, the discourse of satire contained and defused by a narrative pattern with a feminized discursive realm at its centre; and *Humphry Clinker* acts out the replacement of satire with two complementary discourses, enlightenment science as the new, objective discourse of the public world, and feminine virtue as the governing principle of the private world.

3. Scott, gender, and the novel

If the confidence of a writer like Richardson in the interpretive strategies of his audience is eroded, however, the very privacy of the reading experience can also have the effect of making 'the reader' an opaque category as never before. The relationship between Clarissa and Anna Howe can stand in for the relationship between author and reader because authors in the 1740s are still able to imagine readers, as Hume does, as versions of themselves: cultivated, polite, leisured, genteel.

---

32 John Mullan, *Sentiment and Sociability: The Language of Feeling in the Eighteenth Century* (Oxford: Clarendon, 1990) 4.

'Politeness' in this sense allows the continuation by other means of the political orator's (or the satirist's) 'public address', for although polite readers are dispersed and atomised in their privacy, they are conjured into a homogeneous group by the socialising rhetoric of the text as much as any senate by the eloquence of the statesman. By Scott's time, however, that intimate relation between author and reader imagined by Addison and Hume has been undermined by, on the one hand, the spread of literacy and the resulting mass-market for books, and on the other by anxieties about the stability of the hegemony of polite culture produced by the French Revolution. The representation of the social heterogeneity of public spaces in the novels of both Smollett and Scott reflects an anxiety that a mass readership was similarly heterogeneous, rendering the meaning of these texts radically contingent on an unknowable reception. Jon Klancher notes how '[t]he English Romantics were the first to become radically uncertain of their readers' and certainly had 'no single, unified "reading public"' to address.[33] Klancher discusses how the writers of all sorts of prose, from periodical articles to theories of poetry, tried to shape an audience for themselves, and contrasts their efforts with those who benefited from the change:

> The phenomenon of the *un*sought mass audience [...] first appeared in the early nineteenth century: Lord Byron and Walter Scott awakened to something hardly imaginable to the writers who thought and wrote in terms of a deliberately formed compact between writer and audience.[34]

With the loss of that compact, the author loses the last vestige of political agency (if one could still call it that) that had been preserved within the republic of polite letters; and indeed, the post-revolutionary context opens the possibility that the texts, falling into the wrong hands, may have political effects quite opposite to the intentions of their authors. In chapter 3, we will find this return of politics to a discursive world from which it had appeared excluded, figured in the secret life of Diana Vernon, in Scott's *Rob Roy*.

In place of the moral agency made possible by an imaginable readership, Scott's novels make a claim to be a means of knowing the

---

33   Jon Klancher, *The Making of English Reading Audiences 1790–1832* (Madison: University of Wisconsin Press, 1987) 3.
34   Klancher 172.

historical world, understood as a totality determining human action; that is, understood in the terms of enlightenment conjectural history. For a long time, critical discussions of Scott's relation to enlightenment historical and social writing assumed a fairly unproblematic adoption by Scott of conjectural history as his master narrative.[35] But this cognitive claim does not in itself replace the social (although socially exclusive) commonality that had been a structuring feature of prose culture in the previous century. Lyotard uses the expression 'narrative knowledge' to name the social practices passed on by means of stories in traditional societies, stories that, to some extent, the audience always already knew. But the contrast that he draws between this socially constitutive narrative act and an enlightenment scientific knowledge is just the one I wish to draw between scientific discourse and the tales that united the dispersed but genteel tribe of novel readers in the eighteenth century:

> Scientific knowledge requires that one language game, denotation, be retained and all others excluded. [...] Scientific knowledge is in this way set apart from the language games that combine to form the social bond. Unlike narrative knowledge, it is no longer a direct and shared component of the bond. [...] The relation between knowledge and society [...] becomes one of mutual exteriority.[36]

The gap that I identified earlier between a science of society and its moral function in the hands of Adam Smith is, I want to suggest, internalised in the social-realist novel as the tension between its denotative function as social representation and its function as providing a social bond equivalent, in some way, to the mutually improving conversation of Addison and his readers, or the sentimental union between Clarissa and Anna Howe.

---

35 See, for the basic connections, Duncan Forbes, 'The Rationalism of Sir Walter Scott', *Cambridge Journal* 7 (1953): 20–35; then P.D. Garside, 'Scott and the Philosophical Historians', *Journal of the History of Ideas* 36.3 (1975): 497–512 for the sources of this influence in Scott's education and reading; then, for more detailed discussion, David Brown, *Walter Scott and the Historical Imagination* London: Routledge and Kegan Paul, 1979) chapter 10; Graham McMaster, *Scott and Society* (Cambridge: Cambridge University Press, 1981) chapter 2; and, with particular reference to *Waverley*, Avrom Fleishman, *The English Historical Novel* (Baltimore and London: John Hopkins University Press, 1971) 37–46.
36 Jean-François Lyotard, *The Postmodern Condition: A Report on Knowledge,* trans. Geoff Bennington and Brian Massumi (Manchester: Manchester University Press, 1984) 25.

Many critics have indeed commented on the disjunction between the seriousness with which Scott takes the accurate representation of history and society in his novels, and his disingenuous disavowal of any serious intention governing the design of his plot. George Levine, in *The Realistic Imagination*, gives as an example the bathetic ending of *Old Mortality*, where Peter Pattieson, the fictional author of the *Tales of My Landlord*, describes how he consulted with Miss Martha Buskbody, over the tea-table, about how he should end his story. One of Scott's grimmest portrayals of failed revolution, which gives a detailed picture of the social, political, and cultural conditions behind the Covenanters' revolt of 1679, ends with the recommendation of a happy ending from 'a young lady who has carried on the profession of mantua-making at Gandercleugh and in the neighbourhood, with great success, for about forty years'.[37] 'The sequence is actually funny at the expense of popular taste but it is also embarrassingly incongruous. It implies Scott's radical lack of interest in his own plot, and reminds us again of the severe disjunction between the imagined and the real that marks his narratives.'[38] So long as Scott rigorously separates fiction from reality in this way, argues Levine, he cannot make meaningful that which is nevertheless essential to the novel as a novel, namely, the plot. More recently, Homer Brown has noted Scott's praise for Defoe and Austen's realism on identical grounds: that is, an understanding of that realism as a lack of what he calls a 'story', equated with romance.[39]

Can we make a connection between the problematic status of plot-structure in Scott's novels, and the problematic status of agency in enlightenment discourse? The connection has, of course, already been made for us, in the thinking about the novel of Northrop Frye and those who have developed his ideas. Where Ian Watt, and after him Michael McKeon, understand the difference of the novel from previous narrative forms primarily in terms of its cognitive claims, Frye uses the extent of the agency which the hero of a tale enjoys as a generic index. For example, romances, whether Homeric epic or medieval quest romance,

37   Walter Scott, *The Tale of Old Mortality*, ed. Douglas S. Mack (1816; Edinburgh: Edinburgh University Press, 1993) 349.

38   George Levine, *The Realistic Imagination: English Fiction from Frankenstein to Lady Chatterley* (Chicago: University of Chicago Press, 1981) 91.

39   Homer Brown, 'The Institution of the English Novel: Defoe's Contribution', *Novel: A Forum on Fiction* 29.3 (Spring 1996): 307.

have as their protagonists human characters who nevertheless enjoy powers greater in degree than any mortal; in the 'low mimetic' novel, on the other hand, we find characters as powerless as ourselves.

> [T]he mimetic tendency itself, the tendency to verisimilitude and accuracy of description, is one of the two poles of literature. At the other end is [...] a tendency to tell a story which is in origin a story about characters who can do anything, and only gradually becomes attracted toward a tendency to tell a plausible or credible story [...].[40]

Frye then adopts *romance* as the name for narrative form *per se*, for example in his discussion of narrative archetypes in the third essay of the *Anatomy*. A genre, defined at first in terms of the agency of its protagonist, has become the principle of narrative form in any type of story whatsoever. This is more than just a play on Greek words: for underlying Frye's project is a psychology which locates the function of narrative in its ability to imagine for us a world in which someone, at least, *was* in control, and narrative form itself remains an order which has been imposed on meaningless, chaotic reality, even when there is no longer a mythic or romance hero in the story to whom this control can be ascribed.

Although Frye's schema is, far from being historical, itself a modernist recovery of literary history as romance, nevertheless it has proved possible to put it to historical use. For Frederic Jameson, what Frye shows is that no matter how committed to reproducing social reality a narrative might be, its narrative form necessarily offers the prospect of something better, however muted this hope.[41] In this utopian moment, every narrative is to some extent critical of the social reality

---

40   Northrop Frye, *The Anatomy of Criticism* (1957; Harmondsworth: Penguin, 1990) 51–2.

41   For Jameson, the paradigm case of this function of narrative is the late nineteenth-century romance revival that feeds into modernism: '[M]odernism – far from being a mere reflection of the reification of late nineteenth-century social life – is also a revolt against that reification and a symbolic act which involves a whole Utopian compensation for increasing dehumanization on the level of daily life.' *The Political Unconscious: Narrative as a Socially Symbolic Act* (London: Methuen, 1981) 42. I am arguing that eighteenth-century romance revival can be understood in a similar way: romance narrative is always a psychic compensation for a 'dehumanization' of the world of some sort, in this case the effacement of human agency in historical narrative.

that it represents. To see how this works in individual texts, it is necessary to turn Frye around, and instead of pulling from a text an ahistorical narrative essence called romance, see just how romance is expressing the utopian aspiration to self-determination against the particular historical circumstances of the narrative's production. Romance, for Jameson, is always historically situated and politically effective; replacing Frye's Blakean psychology as the source of our longing is the alienation and fragmentation of life under capitalism. Jameson is the theorist who most directly lies behind Ian Duncan's study, *Modern Romance and Transformations of the Novel* (1992), a work with which I will be in sporadic dialogue throughout this study.

George Levine suggests, as we have seen, that Scott neglected the potential for meaning in his plots, and left this potential to his Victorian successors to develop. Duncan argues instead that the use of plot to bring an extra-realistic principle to bear on the novel's realistic contents is precisely what Scott bequeathed to the Victorians. And looking in the other direction, this function of plot was one that Scott himself inherited from the eighteenth-century romance revival and specifically from the Gothic novel. Duncan's description echoes both Frye and Jameson:

> Romance is the essential principle of fiction: its *difference* from a record of 'reality', of 'everyday life' [...]. [E]ven as the novel began to totalize its mimetic range it reasserted fiction, and not mimesis, as its critical principle, in an elaborate commitment to plot. Fiction in these novels is the effect above all of plot, conspicuous as a grammar of formal conventions, that is, a shared cultural order distinct from material and historical contingency. To read a plot – to take part in its work of recognition – is to imagine a transformation of life and its conditions, and not their mere reproduction [...].[42]

The plot is in and of itself non-mimetic; but rather than being simply irrelevant to the novel's realist purpose, the plot *gives* that realism its purpose, mediating between the imitated world and the reader by giving the reader a sense of that world's inherent possibilities, possibilities that *transcend* the realist content of the text. This transforming interaction between historical content and romance form is, in Duncan's view,

---

42   Ian Duncan, *Modern Romance and Transformations of the Novel: The Gothic, Scott, Dickens* (Cambridge: Cambridge University Press, 1992) 2.

Scott's great gift to his successors, rather than the inclusion of historical-realist content alone.

Duncan goes further than this, however, in ways that bring us back to my concern with the relation of agency to *gender* in enlightenment culture: romance, as it appears in the novels of the late eighteenth and early nineteenth centuries, is gendered *feminine*. The writer most responsible for this is Ann Radcliffe, who

> defines a feminine principle of private subjectivity in antithetical relation to history, which appears as a synchronic public domain of patriarchal coercion. [...] Radcliffe's female subjectivity holds (in its very separation from narrative agency) the secret dialectical power to transform – to reduce and colonize – the antagonistic realm of historical patriarchy.[43]

It is thus due to Radcliffe that the very power of romance structure to transform historical reality is available to Scott when he begins writing historical novels. Duncan argues that despite Scott's gender, this transforming power remains, in *Waverley* for example, a *feminine* one. Scott puts his hero, Edward Waverley, through the same *agon* as that which Radcliffe imposes on her heroines, but the gender of this narrative form does not change when it is a male author deploying it. The gender of the authors, of Scott or of Radcliffe, does not seem to be important.

This might seem a trivial point in the context of Duncan's overall argument, if it were not for two things. The first is the way that this suspension of the authors' gender is made possible by his description of femininity as it is constructed within the novels themselves. 'Female subjectivity' can overcome the vagaries of historical contingency 'in its very separation from narrative agency': within the fiction, feminine subjectivity, whether that of Radcliffe's heroines or Waverley himself, is *powerless*. It is the plot itself that manifests a feminine will-to-power that can guarantee the transformation of patriarchy. In Radcliffe, for example, 'The heroine's grace lies in a passive sensibility, rather than in an active desire, a will to agency. We read, instead, a romance rhetoric in which desire is sublimated to drive the plot without a visible agent, by a tropological saturation of the narrative.'[44]

---

43   Ibid. 13.
44   Ibid. 38.

When Duncan considers *active* female characters in the novels, he is inevitably hampered by his construction of romance as an *impersonal* authority behind the plot. In *Guy Mannering*, for example, while recognising that Sophia Mannering's manipulation of her daughter constitutes 'a variant of the female-quixote motif', Duncan does not recognize the possibility that Sophia or Julia might constitute autonomous authorities within the novel, but conflates their (unambiguously feminine) narrative power with (nominally feminine, but in effect genderless) romance.[45] The gender of Sophia Mannering's plot-making is raised:

> In India, Mannering's wife spins a web of female-quixotic delusion,

assimilated to romance:

> in a deadly parody of 'the wonderful effects' her daughter has seen 'the romances of the East produce upon their hearers.'

and then forgotten:

> This is a version of Scott's favourite figure of the artist, not as Prospero but as sorcerer's apprentice, entangled within the fabric *he* has woven: the dupe of his own fictions, not source but object of the power *he* has invoked. [my italics][46]

What romance does to its protagonists, it does also to the author: that which leaves hero or heroine powerless over his or her fate within the fiction, is that which similarly appears to the novelist as a given, a set of inherited conventions over which (s)he has no control. Authorship in both cases is ascribed to romance, and not to any particular individual. And not ascribing authority to any particular individual means not having to consider their particular *gender*.

This effect of Duncan's elision of gender, both within the novels and in the question of authorship, produces the second problem with his thesis on the Waverley novels, namely their place in literary history. The other way, besides his development of social realism, in which Scott's novels created 'the enabling environment for the form itself of the nineteenth-century novel', was by making it again a genre that

---

45   Ibid. 121.
46   Ibid. 124.

31

deserved the attention of an educated, privileged, and above all *male* readership, and thus made possible its reappropriation by male writers.[47] In the three decades or so before *Waverley* appeared in 1814, the novel had been largely written by women and, although it is hard to be sure about such things, read by women. Scott himself, in his essay on Charlotte Smith for *Ballantyne's Novelists Library*, comments, 'We cannot but remark the number of highly talented women, who have, within our time of novel-reading, distinguished themselves advantageously in this department of literature.' He lists Burney, Edgeworth, Austen, Opie, Inchbald and Susan Ferrier alongside Smith and the female Gothics like Ann Radcliffe, Clara Reeve and Mary Shelley, before adding, 'we think that it would be impossible to match against these names the same number of masculine competitors, arising within the same space of time.'[48] After Scott's own fiction, the novel was no longer gendered feminine in this way. Scott remasculinized the novel; in doing so he raised its cultural status in a way that made possible the genre's centrality to Victorian culture. And it was his own gender as a man that made this possible; that which makes him different as an author from Radcliffe, and that which Duncan tends to elide.

The most comprehensive study of this cultural effect of the Waverley novels is Ina Ferris's *The Achievement of Literary Authority*. Ferris describes the figure of the female reader as a trope at work in the periodical criticism of the same period, where female novel-reading is 'a practice marked by passion, sentiment, and delusion'.[49] Ferris notes the distinction made by the periodicals between this 'Ordinary Novel', the contemporary material of the same corrupt female reading practices as Waverley adopts with regard to his romances, and the 'Proper Novel', the morally edifying fiction written by women such as Burney, Edgeworth, and Austen, a trope of feminine *writing*. The identification of Waverley as an archetypally feminine reader is Duncan's exactly; what is sur-prising is that Ferris, like Duncan, also tends to elide the role of the figure of the female author in Scott's novels. Ferris is indeed

47   Judith Wilt, *Secret Leaves: The Novels of Sir Walter Scott* (Chicago: University of Chicago Press, 1985) 16.

48   Ioan Williams, ed., *Sir Walter Scott on Novelists and Fiction* (London: Routledge and Kegan Paul, 1968) 190.

49   Ina Ferris, *The Achievement of Literary Authority: Gender, History and the Waverley Novels* (Ithaca and London: Cornell University Press, 1991) 35–6.

primarily concerned with the reception of the Waverley Novels;[50] but when she does turn to the interplay of gender and fictionality within Scott's novels, feminine *writing* disappears entirely. The result is the same as in Duncan's study: the role of the gender of the author is effaced, and femininity within the novels is effectively subsumed within the category of romance.

The relation of Scott to the women writers listed then appears very simple. He took their place. Female-authored fiction was moved aside and replaced by Scott's historical fiction as the culture's dominant prose narrative genre.

> [T]he reviews [...] open up a space – higher, deeper, broader than that of women's writing – for the critic and for the male reader and writer of novels. And into this space, answering certain key male anxieties, came the not-so-anonymous Waverley Novels.[51]

Ferris does, however, add in her conclusion:

> In a peculiar way, it was not so much blowsy female romance that threatened the masculinity – and hence literariness – of early nineteenth-century fiction as the contained feminine novel of domestic virtue [...] it was the rational form of the proper novel with its valorization of the space of 'modern civilization' that was placed in definitive opposition to Scott's historical mode.[52]

This study might be seen as developing this hint by Ferris that female writing, rather than female reading, constitutes the defining other of Scott's historical realism; and as demonstrating how this female authorship appears as a trope of authorship in general, including Scott's own. This feminization Scott must then deny by disclaiming interest in his plots themselves: Miss Martha Buskbody's gender is not incidental to her role as supplier of a proper ending for *Old Mortality*, but it turns this role, as Levine notes, into an embarrassment. Duncan is right to suggest that romance plot takes over from the feminine subject to bring the narrative to its proper conclusion, but that feminine subject is herself, to start with, imagined enjoying a potent human agency, and agency which Scott must displace precisely because of its embarrassing gender.

---

50   See ibid. 247.
51   Ibid. 78.
52   Ibid. 252.

To see the Waverley novels thus, as at once the initiating moment of the nineteenth-century novel, and as a space in which a romance plot negotiates the interrelationship of various eighteenth-century discourses, is to problematize McKeon's account of the institution of the novel. For the terms of the dialectic by which that institution develops are now *gendered*. It is here that Smollett takes on a new importance in our revised history of the novel, for he is in many ways Scott's model in using the novel to co-ordinate gendered discourses in this way. If Scott uses the romance plot to legitimate the novel in the new discursive landscape produced by the Enlightenment, Smollett helps us understand precisely what is at stake in that legitimation, because he writes on both sides of the discursive fragmentation that the Enlightenment produces. Some of the strategies which allow *Humphry Clinker* to negotiate that fragmentation were already used by Smollett in response to the pressing political crises of mid-century in *Roderick Random*. One of the things that Scott borrows from Smollett is precisely the gendering of plot-structure and narrative agency in the way that Duncan describes. It is thus not surprising that McKeon, omitting gender as a significant category as he does, also ignores Smollett.

Indeed, by understanding Smollett as a participant in late eighteenth-century romance revival, by positioning him as the link between the mid-century print culture and Scott, this study offers support for Clifford Siskin's suggestion that Richardson and Fielding, far from stabilising the novel as McKeon suggests, were in fact dead ends, whose prominence in accounts like McKeon's eclipses the other developments – the changing status of women's writing above all – which actually drive the development of the novel in the second half of the century: their 'programs' for the novel 'had, in important ways, to be written off before the novel as we know it rose up'.[53] This possibility is nicely if unintentionally expressed by McKeon when he describes the dialectical process that produces the novel as a category as 'a movement that only culminates with Richardson and Fielding'. That 'only', taken in a restricting rather than a temporal sense, threatens to turn this

---

53   Siskin 175.

culmination into a terminus.[54] It is the task of this study, by restoring gender as an operative category at work even in such paradigmatically masculine novelists as Smollett and Scott, to show how they used romance plot to appropriate enlightenment discourse to produce 'the novel as we know it'.

---

54 Looking forward in the century we will find the influence of Richardson everywhere, indeed, but understanding that ubiquity requires attention to gendered conceptions of authorship of the sort that McKeon ignores.

1 Smollett: satire, romance, and feminine agency

What does it mean for Smollett, in the first sentence of the Preface to his first novel, to describe it as a 'satire'? On the one hand, the ensuing contrast with 'romance', in a potted history of European culture that locates *Roderick Random* as a successor to *Don Quixote*, suggests that 'satire' here translates roughly as 'anti-romance', and that satire's concern with the vices and follies of mankind is seen as continuous with the realism of the emerging novel form. Satire and novel share, from this angle, a concern with the historically particular, the imperfect quotidian, and plausibly motivated action, in opposition to romance's conventional plot and celebration of the generically ideal.[1] On the other hand, the 1740s can be seen as a period of sharp decline in the literary centrality of *political* satire as a genre: the resignation of Robert Walpole as Chancellor of the Exchequer (1742) and the deaths of Pope and Swift (1744 and 1745 respectively) usher in a period in which party battle-lines are much less clearly drawn than in a 'golden age of satire' that had lasted since the Restoration and enjoyed its finest hour in the anti-Ministerial campaigns of the 1720s and 1730s. If we define in generic terms the sort of satire that, in Ronald Paulson's term, 'infiltrates' and helps shape the novel, this hardly matters: anti-romance remains a thriving mode in the novel to the end of the century and beyond. Yet, when Smollett first arrived in London as a young man in 1739, his contacts included Sir Andrew Mitchell, a remote relation, and 'an intimate friend of the poet Thomson, and hence in a strong position to introduce his relative to that literary group so loyal to the author of *The Seasons*', a group that included Mallet, who was to be Bolingbroke's

---

1   'Once the romance came under attack, satire infiltrated so many of the long prose forms that any realistic form the novelist turned to for support had satire as an ingredient [...]. The particular conventions in which our two genres, satire and the novel, found their common ground were those of realism.' Ronald Paulson, *Satire and the Novel in Eighteenth-Century England* (New Haven: Yale University Press, 1967) 10–11.

literary executor.[2] The involvement of this group with the ongoing political struggle against the Walpole ministry, including its deployment of literary satire, must have supplied at least part of their conversation with the future novelist. Despite this, discussions of Smollett's satire have either concentrated on the period of his direct involvement in politics, as editor of *The Briton* under the Bute administration; or, like Michael Rosenblum's, have tended to understand its 'conservatism' in the broadest literary terms, as a vision of 'decline and fall, the movement from order and civilization into chaos and barbarism' that Smollett shares with T. S. Eliot as well as Swift.[3] I want to suggest that Smollett's satire in *Roderick Random* adopts a much more specific political position than this: that it is recognisably that of the 'country ideology' deployed in the more explicitly party-political arena. However, the place of satire in this novel is a problematic one, and registers in a variety of ways (I will argue) the rapidly changing literary culture of England in the 1740s. As I am unwilling to make too many sweeping general-isations about the nature of this change, I shall instead draw some parallels between the literary career of Henry St. John, Viscount Bolingbroke, extra-parliamentary leader and chief ideologist of the opposition, and the fate of satire in Smollett's novel.

2   Lewis Mansfield Knapp, *Tobias Smollett: Doctor of Men and Manners* (Princeton: Princeton University Press, 1949) 28.

3   Robin Fabel, 'The Patriotic Briton: Tobias Smollett and English Politics, 1756-1771', *Eighteenth-Century Studies* 8 (1974): 100-14; George Rousseau, 'Smollett and Politics: Originals for the Election Scene in Sir Launcelot Greaves', *English Language Notes* 14 (1976): 32-7; Eric Rothstein, 'Scotophilia and Humphry Clinker: The Politics of Beggary, Bugs and Buttocks', *University of Toronto Quarterly* 52.2 (Fall 1982): 63-78; Robert D. Spector, 'Smollett's Politics and the Briton, 9 October 1762', *Papers on Language and Literature* 26.2 (Spring 1990): 280-4. Michael Rosenblum, 'Smollett as Conservative Satirist', *ELH* 42 (1975) 556-79.

1. Smollett and the country ideology

In the first three decades of the eighteenth century,

> [a] decisive break with the past was taking place in English social history [...] A traditional order was giving way to institutions of a centralized and commercial society, and to an increasingly urban and middle class world [...]. The new depersonalized world seemed to render the individual helpless before forces much larger than himself. These impersonal forces operated the credit mechanism and determined the value or lack of value in the individual's tallies and estates. The individual landowner or small trader seemed no longer capable of controlling his own destiny, but felt himself to be at the mercy of outside and impersonal forces manipulated by men he did not know or trust.[4]

While Isaac Kramnick's account of the opposition mentality has often been criticised for its over-simplifications, he is right to identify *credit* as being at the root of the various anxieties of the country party. The establishment of the National Debt to fund the continental wars of the reigns of William and Anne, of the financial institutions necessary to process that debt, and the tax-burden that fell on landowners in order to pay the interest, all drive the 'decisive shift' in the politics of Britain in these years. Kramnick is also right, no doubt, to restrict these anxieties to smaller landowners and traders: the bulk of the population had presumably always felt at the mercy of outside forces and men they did not know or trust; the baronial elite, on the other hand, had the spare wealth to invest in the Bank of England or the great trading monopolies, and the influence to get family members into the profitable sinecures now available in an increasingly bureaucratic government machine.

However, Kramnick does perhaps exaggerate the extent to which these shared anxieties expressed themselves in a coherent set of opposition values among the gentry. Much recent work has complicated the simple dichotomies of Tory and Whig, Country and Court, that have traditionally structured analyses of this period.[5] As far as the parlia-

---

4   Issac Kramnick, *Bolingbroke and His Circle: The Politics of Nostalgia in the Age of Walpole* (Cambridge MA: Harvard University Press, 1968) 72.

5   See Shelley Burtt, *Virtue Transformed: Political Argument in England, 1688–1740* (Cambridge: Cambridge University Press, 1992); Christine Gerrard, *The Patriot Opposition to Walpole: Politics, Poetry and National Myth* (Oxford: Clarendon

mentary opposition to Robert Walpole's government is concerned, two issues provided the grounds for attack: the maintenance of a standing army, and the use of administrative positions in the gift of the crown to win the favour of MPs and thus guarantee support for the government in the Commons. But as Quentin Skinner has demonstrated, the choice of these issues for parliamentary debate was not arbitrary. The conception of an opposition to the government which was not simply treasonous was a new one, and had to be ideologically justified; it was this opposition ideology that determined on which fronts the government could be justifiably attacked.[6] The writer most important in providing this ideology was Viscount Bolingbroke, principally in his journal, *The Craftsman* (from 1726).

Bolingbroke, himself excluded from his seat in the Lords because of his time in France as Secretary of State to the Pretender, James Stuart, after the accession of George I in 1714, co-ordinated a propaganda campaign against Walpole in an attempt to unite the various factions alienated from government into a coherent political force. To do so, he drew on the republican political theories of both James Harrington and Niccolò Machiavelli in order to explain why not just Walpole's particular policies but his whole mode of government was wrong. The national debt had put huge financial resources in the hands of the crown that allowed them to reward friendly MPs with government jobs; but this amounted to corruption of the constitution, claimed Bolingbroke, because the constitution was designed to balance the power of the crown with an independent legislature. Once that legislature entered the pocket of the ministry, the country would no longer have a mixed government, but a monarchical tyranny. But 'corruption' also names the fate of an enfranchised class that allows itself to become the tool of a tyranny in this way: to put private gain before public duty is to give up the participation in political affairs that Machiavelli calls *virtù*. For Bolingbroke's opposition, accordingly, virtue *is* political agency; the retreat from politics to the private realm *is* corruption.[7]

Press, 1994); Alexander Pettit, *Illusory Consensus: Bolingbroke and the Polemical Response to Walpole, 1730–37* (Newark: University of Delaware Press, 1997).
6 Quentin Skinner, 'The Principles and Practice of Opposition: The Case of Bolingbroke versus Walpole', in Neil McKendrick, ed., *Historical Perspectives: Studies in English Thought and Society* (London: Europa Press, 1974) 93–128.
7 Ibid. 120.

Bolingbroke further argues that the only safeguard against corruption, and the one on which the English constitution in the past relied, was the economic independence of the landowning classes from whom MPs and their electors were drawn. The immediate source of this idea was Harrington's *Oceana* (1656): the Commons are independent of the crown because they own land, and thus do not need the financial rewards the crown can offer in exchange for votes in the House. Behind this lies the notion of a natural political order in which the gentry are the benign day-to-day governors of the country, exerting economic, political, and judicial power as landowners, electors, and Justices of the Peace.[8] A new financial order in which an expanding public credit drives down the real value of incomes from rents, while granting the government huge financial resources with which to reward its friends, will not only, according to Bolingbroke, centralise more and more power in the hands of the ministers of the crown, but reduce politics to the organising of individual self-interest, breaking the emotional bonds a landowner has with his neighbours and those who live on his estates. The long-term product of this type of politics will be a society of atomised individuals, with nothing to unite them except a desire for financial gain. This is in essence the country critique of political modernity behind which Bolingbroke tried both to unite and to legitimise opposition to Walpole.

There are four ways in which *Roderick Random* embodies country ideology. The first, and most obvious, lies in its representation of a commercial Britain in 1739 which is recognisably that of opposition nightmares: in which corrupt authority governs by bribery, reducing almost all relationships to the cash nexus and making economic self-interest society's only organising principle. Most obviously, Roderick's efforts to gain a place as a naval surgeon reveals the extent to which

---

8   The increase in wealth, on the Harringtonian view, 'encouraged freemen to specialise in pursuits which left them no time to be soldiers, judges or participants in government; and the surrender of these functions to salaried experts and servants of the king had opened the way to a professionalised society which was virtually synonymous with corruption.' J.G.A. Pocock, 'Civic Humanism and its Role in Anglo-American Thought', *Politics, Language and Time: Essays on Political Thought and History* (London: Methuen, 1972) 95. That one of the gentry's functions, on this view, was to constitute local militias, legitimated in republican terms the opposition's hostility to standing armies (otherwise based on their enormous cost).

positions in the gift of the administration require to be bought, rather than being distributed according to the qualifications of the applicant; and that bribery has now extended throughout the social hierarchy as its operating principle. After pinning his hopes on Mr Cringer, his MP, he quickly learns

> that there was nothing to be done with a m—b—r of p—m—t without a bribe; that the servant was commonly infected with the master's disease, and expected to be paid for his work, as well as his betters. [9]

This is a lesson that the experiences of Jackson and Thomson, as well as Roderick, confirm, and reaches its comic apotheosis in the aftermath of Roderick's medical examination, when on his way *out* he is 'obliged to give three shillings and six-pence to the beadles, and a shilling to an old woman who swept the hall' (XVII.87–8). But even before they arrive in London, Roderick and Strap have a taste of the corrupt patronage relations of the new order, when in chapter IX they come across a card-sharping curate who was rewarded with this post in exchange for keeping quiet about his former activities as valet-come-pimp to a nobleman who had an interest in the curacy (an exciseman, that most woeful representative of Walpole's regime in country districts, tells this story, and is, according to the innkeeper, just as bad himself: 41–2). More generally, emotional bonds of family and honour have been replaced by financial ones; even in Glasgow, once the money from uncle Bowling dries up, Roderick becomes as a result 'a solitary being, no ways comprehended within the scheme or protection of providence', (although this last word will carry varying significations in the succeeding narrative: VII.25–6).

This detailing of the historical specifics of a corrupt society is indeed novelistic realism put at the service of satire, in the way Paulson suggests provides the common ground of the two genres. The second way in which *Roderick Random* embodies opposition concerns, however, reveals realism in tension with the satirical purposes of the novel: Roderick's status as a member of the gentry.

---

9   Tobias Smollett, *The Adventures of Roderick Random* ed. Paul-Gabriel Boucé (1748; Oxford: Oxford University Press, 1979) chapter XV.73. All citations give chapter and page references to this edition.

The arguments of the opposition against the court are addressed above all to the gentry from which Roderick comes and to which he returns at the end of the novel. This is the group whose income, and relative status position, seem threatened by the new developments in government finance; they are the group with the land that offers them the independence from the executive at the heart of the quasi-Republican ideology of Bolingbroke.[10] But the relevance of Roderick's status as a gentleman in the society in which he finds himself cannot be taken for granted. His relations to others in the first half of the novel at least (with one notable exception) are rather determined by his occupation at any particular time: apprentice apothecary, naval surgeon, soldier and so on. In fact, what Roderick and this novel both confront, without having the vocabulary in which to describe it, is economic *class* as the basis of social hierarchy in a commercial society; that is, a challenge to the older status-structure based on birth and the possession of land.[11] The status-inconsistency that Roderick suffers is produced by a social situation where both hierarchies are in operation.

Much of Roderick's behaviour in the novel makes sense as an acting-out of his status-position in a class context which denies it social legitimacy. His hair-trigger rage at the injustice of others and headlong rush for revenge against them, what he calls 'my own haughty disposition, impatient of affronts' as a child (II.6), and 'pride and resentment, [...] two chief ingredients in my disposition' as an adult (XIX.99), while explicable in generic terms as the responses of a

---

10 'Specifically, Smollett seems obsessed by the absolute lack of what J.G.A. Pocock has reminded us was traditionally associated with civic virtue, "the moral quality which only propertied independence could confer".' John Richetti, *The English Novel in History 1700–1780* (London: Routledge, 1999) 166; quoting Pocock, *Virtue, Commerce, and History* (Cambridge: Cambridge University Press, 1985) 51.

11 I have in mind here the distinction as made by Weber: 'In contrast to the purely economically determined "class situation" we wish to designate as "status situations" every typical component of the life fate of men that is determined by a specific, positive or negative, social estimation of *honor* [...]. Property as such is not always recognized as a status qualification, but in the long run it is, and with extraordinary regularity [...]. But status honor need not necessarily be linked with a "class situation." On the contrary, it normally stands in sharp opposition to the pretensions of sheer property.' Max Weber, *From Max Weber: Essays in Sociology*, ed. H.H. Garth and C. Wright Mills (1948; Oxford: Oxford University Press, 1958) 186–7.

Juvenalian satirist trapped inside a novel, can also be understood as assertions of the gentry right to judge and punish their social inferiors.[12] The disturbing quality of Roderick's revenge on those who cross him is thus an expression of his status-inconsistency: the pettiness and pointlessness of that revenge come from the displacement of a gentry principle of honour from the family context, where local political authority is at stake and the threat of revenge a means of maintaining it, to that of the atomised modern individual; the delight taken in it by the protagonist reveals its function as momentary vindication of an otherwise invisible identity as a member of that status group.

This is to read Roderick's time as a member of the artisanal classes as an ordeal which satirises his society's disregard for the traditional status distinctions which have previously guaranteed social order. In addition, however, one can also read the gentry Roderick's sojourn among the urban poor as acting out, not the difference between the two groups, but what they have in common. For these were the two groups who suffered most from the effects of the financial revolution under William and Anne and were in consequence the most instinctively antiministerial. The high politics of opposition may have required the building of alliances among the enfranchised alone, yet as Christopher Hill notes, the Tory or Jacobite sympathies of the urban, and particularly London, mob made them available for recruitment into

> an uneasy and wholly negative alliance of the two defeated classes of the seventeenth century – the backwoods gentry and the urban poor – against their bourgeois and aristocratic rulers.[13]

The Sacheverell riots in 1710 provide an instance where a Tory mob had an immediate effect on the course of government, but Tory hopes that

---

12   For the generic explanation see Paulson 178.

13   Christopher Hill, *Reformation to Industrial Revolution, 1530–1780*. The Pelican Economic History of Britain vol.2. (Harmondsworth: Penguin, 1969) 214. Similarly, Linda Colley notes: 'A common hatred of the Whig regime encouraged Tory MPs to identify themselves rhetorically with the socially and politically dispossessed'. *In Defiance of Oligarchy: The Tory Party 1714–60* (Cambridge: Cambridge University Press, 1982) 173. I am suggesting that *Roderick Random* deploys just this rhetoric but at the level of *plot*, in the *narrative* linking of the two groups by Roderick's descent from one into the other.

this effectiveness might be repeated proved groundless.[14] Nevertheless, as the work of Nicholas Rogers has shown, politically motivated disorder of this type remained a feature of urban life, and was predominantly, until the 1745 rebellion and its aftermath, Tory or Jacobite in orientation.[15] Crucially for my argument here, the records of those brought to trial (under a Riot Act introduced specifically to counter this threat) reveal the rioters to be drawn predominantly from just that artisanal (and specifically apprentice) class in which Roderick finds himself both in Glasgow and in London.[16]

Once again, then, the generic resources of picaresque realism seem to be put at the service of politically motivated satire. Where this novel undermines its own realism, however, is in its representation (or non-representation) of Roderick's *consciousness* of this status-inconsistency. So little in the world around him confirms his status that Roderick at times seems himself to forget the fact of his birth, and to confuse his status with the outward trappings to which it is reduced by modernity. On his way back from the Cartagena campaign, for example, he writes that 'Being thus provided with money, and all necessaries for the comfort of life, I began to look upon myself as a gentleman of some consequence, and felt my pride dilate apace' (XXXVI.206). One of the ways in which *Roderick Random* frustrates the reader's expectations of a novel is in its refusal to categorise Roderick's status, at any point, as either the truth, to which he sometimes holds fast, and which he sometimes forgets, or an occasional mistake. As he (temporarily) prospers under his London master, M. Lavement, he can observe that he has 'acquir'd the character of a polite journeyman apothecary' (XX.104). A few pages later he implies a further promotion:

---

14   For example the spectre of Sacheverell did not, as Swift had hoped, deter George I from purging his government of Tories on his accession four years later: see Nicholas Rogers, 'Riot and Popular Jacobitism in Early Hanoverian England', in Eveline Cruickshanks, ed., *Ideology and Conspiracy: Aspects of Jacobitism, 1689–1759* (Edinburgh: John Donald, 1982) 75–6.

15   See Rogers, 'Riot' passim; Whigs and Cities: Popular Politics in the Age of Walpole and Pitt (Oxford: Oxford University Press, 1989) passim.

16   Rogers, 'Popular Protest in Early Hanoverian London', *Past and Present* 79 (May 1978): 70–100; see especially 82–86. Rogers's results here centre on the accession and its aftermath, but nothing in his wider survey in *Whigs and Cities* suggests that the social makeup of the mob changed significantly in later decades.

> I now began to look upon myself as a gentleman in reality; learned to dance of a Frenchman whom I had cured of a fashionable distemper; frequented plays during the holidays; became the oracle of an ale-house, where every dispute was referred to my decision; and at length contracted an acquaintance with a young lady, who found means to make a conquest of my heart [...]. (XX.108)

The question raised by such shifts is the nature of the 'reality' *in* which Roderick is a gentleman: is it this collection of outward dispositions, of details adopted at will and available for retrospective dissection by a realistic novel and for conglomeration by Roderick's contemporary consciousness into that status ('I began to look on myself [...]')? Or does it lie rather in Roderick's birth, in something that remains with him throughout the novel, but of which his consciousness as a protagonist is only occasionally aware? As a narrator, Roderick never settles this question for us; unlike Fielding's narrator in *Tom Jones*, Roderick never stands back from his protagonist to reassure us that, in whatever scrapes his picaresque hero might find himself, the gold within of gentle birth guarantees that he can 'in reality' do no wrong: his membership of the gentry is the hidden truth of all Tom's actions, even if he is unconscious of this at the time and it is only revealed to the reader at the end of the novel. So, on the few occasions where the narrator does bring a more informed perspective to bear, we notice the sudden step out of Roderick's own, more limited view: for example, he comments of the lecherous monk with whom he travels towards Paris, 'Libertine as I was, I could not bear to see a man behave so wide of the character he assumed' (XLII.241). *Is* Roderick 'in reality' a libertine? This is the first the reader has heard of it: Roderick as a protagonist is too constantly engaged in asserting himself against the world around him to think of himself in this way, and the narrator does not usually intervene with such judgements. In *Roderick Random*, it is *reality itself* (and not a romance villain like Fielding's Blifil) which lays siege to the hero's knowledge of his own nature; and as long as the narrator remains committed to the historical representation of that reality, Roderick's gentility will tend to slip from the narrator's, as well as the hero's, consciousness.

The only way in which Roderick's status is consistently confirmed in the bulk of the novel is in the perception of him by his servant, Strap. In a modern world of waged labour governed by (self-)'interest', Strap maintains a loyalty towards Roderick from 'a voluntary, disinterested inclination' even in their childhood (V.16); Roderick's gentility means that, when they meet as adults, this loyalty turns into a master-servant relationship without either actually mentioning this (as they set off from Newcastle, we are simply told that Strap is the one carrying the knapsack: VIII.33). This loyalty is entirely one-sided; and yet, like Roderick's perception of his status, not clearly a mistake either. After Roderick's first serious fleecing at the hands of the money-dropper on their arrival in London, Strap hands over to Roderick all his own wealth:

> Strap, who knew my temper, and whose heart bled within him at my distress, after some pause, came to the bed-side, and putting a leathern purse into my hand, burst into tears, crying, 'I know what you think: but I scorn your thoughts. There's all I have in the world, take it, and I'll perhaps get more for you before that be done. If not, I'll beg for you, steal for you, go through the wide world with you, and starve with you, for though I be a poor cobler's son, I am no scout.' I was so touched with the generous passion of this poor creature, that I could not refrain from weeping also, and we mingled our tears together for some time. Upon examining the purse, I found in it two half guineas and half a crown, which I would have returned to him, saying, he knew better than I how to manage it; but he absolutely refused my proposal, and told me, it was more reasonable and decent that he should depend upon me who was a gentleman, than that I should be controuled by him. (XV.72–3)

If the revenge principle exercised in the modern world degenerates into petty vindictiveness, 'reasonable and decent' loyalty between master and servant is displaced into sentiment. This gesture of Strap's is repeated on their return from France, when Strap devotes his new-found resources (the clothes and other paraphernalia he inherited from his last master) to Roderick's (unsuccessful) plan to catch a rich wife. In this second adventure in England, Roderick is quite consciously acting out the role of fine gentleman without an estate to support that role; but the master-servant relation is real enough: Strap is in no way masquerading as his servant. Despite consistently being the more economically prosperous of the two, Strap is still so conscious of the status gap between them that he refuses to sit at the same table as the Randoms after Roderick's reunion with his father. As with Roderick's perception of himself, we are given no indication whether or not Strap is making a mistake in perceiving Roderick in this way.

In generic terms, as Paulson notes, Smollett is making a complicated play with picaresque convention in this regard: the traditional Spanish picaro is the servant, not the master.[17] The reader's difficulties of moral response to Roderick can indeed be explained in the same way. Insofar as Roderick, in his second London sojourn, becomes just another low-life trying to make his way in an amoral universe by pretending to be someone he is not, he is a hero in Picaresque terms, but a villain in terms of Augustan satire.[18] But Strap's loyalty is both at odds with the social reality around him and with the generic world of *either* the picaresque *or* Augustan satire. Rather, the thematizing and valorisation of the master-servant relationship as one at odds with contemporary social reality is itself an expression of broadly Country ideals and thus part of this novel's critique of the new commercial England. For Harrington, and those like Bolingbroke who adapted him, the social relationships which made independent citizenship possible were essentially those of master and servant: it was being a master that made one independent of the crown and thus capable of political agency, while taking money from the crown made one in effect a servant and thus corrupted that agency:

> Harrington's notion of the power which the man who has property exerts over the man who has none does not entail any particular description of the economic relations between the two men, or of the economic process in which they are engaged. All that is necessary to know is that the one is independent and the other dependent on him; the one is master and the other servant [...].
>
> A fairly strong case can be made for holding that this was all that the neo-Harringtonians [among the opposition writers] either found it necessary to envisage or regarded as desirable [...] that is, that their scheme of social preferences was pre-capitalist in the sense that it stopped short at the master-servant household economy and did not envisage a society of investors and wage-laborers.[19]

In this context, Roderick's dependence on Strap for money is the most awful indictment of the society in which they are trapped: such

---

17 Paulson 168.

18 '[T]he typical satiric subject was the man who pretended, appeared, or even believed himself to be a part of society, to be pious or rich, a doctor or a poet, while actually being an interloper from beyond the pale. [...] The villain of Augustan satire became the hero of the new age' (Paulson 5). Again, only an assurance that Roderick's status as a gentleman is *true*, that he is from *within* the pale, prevents him falling from hero to villain in Augustan terms; and we just don't know enough about what is going on inside his head for him to count as a hero of the new age, that is, of the novel as developed by Defoe.

19 J.G.A. Pocock, 'Machiavelli, Harrington and English Political Ideologies in the Eighteenth Century', *Politics, Language and Time* 111, 137.

fundamental status relationships can only survive in this society as their inverse, the dependence of the master on the servant ('it is impossible to express the pangs I felt, when I reflected on the miserable dependance [sic] in which I lived, at the expence of a poor barber's boy' (XVIII.95).[20] On the other hand, Strap's loyalty to Roderick despite this becomes a heroic defence of the old political order in the face of an economic reality that is destroying it. Whatever other humiliations he endures, Roderick refuses to himself become a servant:[21] standing up to Crab, for example, when he treats him like one ('This is fine usage from a servant to a master,—very fine!': VII.28).

So far I have discussed three ways in which the satire of *Roderick Random* is continuous with the concerns of the country ideology of the opposition in the first half of the eighteenth century: in its portrayal of English society as corrupt, in its problematization of Roderick's gentry status in that society, and in the idealisation of the master-servant relationship as an alternative model of social relations. There is one final way in which this novel embodies a country ideology, already alluded to, which is in its final restoration to Roderick of his father and, through his father's buying it back, of the estate that gives him his proper social and political function.

> When we came within half a league of the house, we were met by a prodigious number of poor tenants, men, women and children, who testified their joy by loud acclamations, and accompanied our coach to the gate.—As there is no part of the world, in which the peasants are more attached to their Lords, than in Scotland, we were almost devoured by their affection, in getting out of the coach. [...]
>
> Having welcomed his daughter and me to his house, he [Roderick's father] ordered some bullocks to be killed, and some hogsheads of ale to be brought from the neighbouring village, to regale those honest people, who had not enjoyed such a holiday for many years before. (LXIX.433–4)

---

20 Roderick's (contrastingly futile) dependence on Cringer is another example of this, for the current MP, for all his indifference to Roderick, 'had many a time rode before my grandfather's cloak-bag, in quality of a footman' (XV.74).

21 Except on one quite exceptional occasion: I will argue that his service to Narcissa is purely generic, rather than political or economic, later in this chapter. The only other qualification to this is Roderick's 'eager' embrace of the offer of a post as *maitre d'hotel* at Versailles, of all places: but nothing comes of this (XLII.239). It might be more accurate to say that the *plot* refuses to let Roderick become a servant than that he refuses to himself.

On the restoration of their rightful landlord, suddenly the people are 'honest', and rewarded with the restoration of their own traditional festivities. Now, this country ideal of authentic, disinterested human bonds between landlord and tenant is one that has been gestured at before: Roderick's miserable childhood was marginally mitigated by such loyalty: 'as I strongly resembled by father, who was the darling of the tenants, I wanted nothing which their indigent circumstances could afford', which is, however, not very much (II.5). In general, however, the conservative idyll to which Roderick is delivered by the end of the novel is completely incongruent with the society represented by the novel in between these two quotations. Quite apart from the scene in LXIX, the sheer improbability of Roderick's discovery of his father, living as Don Rodriguez in Brazil, sets the developments of the last three chapters apart from the rest of the novel. This wish-fulfilment ending clearly goes beyond the generic pairing of realism and satire within which I have so far been working, precisely because it is so completely unrelated to the social reality realistically portrayed and satirised in the rest of the novel. Raymond Stephanson observes, citing the numerous occasions on which people or things turn out to be less or worse than they seem, that in this novel

> the dream of the imagination, the psychological need and its projection, or indeed *any* kind of wishful thinking is doomed to a downward curve into an indifferent, discouraging, and unsavoury physical and social reality that is frequently a hell (not a heaven) on earth.[22]

And yet the ending of the novel fulfils just such a dream, just such a need. This question of *form*, of the apparent disjunction between the novel and its ending, has attracted some critical attention over the years. In discussions of the novel informed by the New Criticism and seeking harmony and formal unity among its parts, the abrupt shift from satiric realism to happy ending will be a question that demands an answer.

The least plausible of these argue for some underlying unity at the moral level which this novel clearly does not have at the levels of genre or plot. Roderick could then be shown to undergo a learning process of

---

22 Raymond Stephanson, 'The (Non)Sense of an Ending: Subversive Allusion and Thematic Discontent in *Roderick Random*', *Eighteenth-Century Fiction* 1.2 (Jan. 1989): 104

some sort; or to demonstrate some kind of active virtue which, whatever the state of his mind, could be rewarded by the ending. The problem with the former option, as Stephanson, and Leo Damrosch before him, amply demonstrate, is that Roderick does not really learn *anything* in the course of the story, except more cunning in his *amoral* struggle for survival: in comparison with Bowling, by the middle of the novel, 'I was better acquainted with the selfishness and roguery of mankind; consequently less liable to disappointment and imposition' (XLI.235). Yet even this does not much improve Roderick's chances. He is on guard against the Scottish priest in Boulogne, because of his experience with the money-dropper in London (XLII.236–7), but the priest turns out to be decent enough. The monk he sends Roderick with to Paris *does* steal every penny that Roderick has, but he doesn't see *this* coming. Any sign of *moral* growth is equally hard to find: his love for Narcissa, the one aspect of his final reward that we *can* see coming, does not stop him chasing other women in the meantime. Roderick in fact does very little to *deserve* his final reward, as Damrosch observes.[23] At the moral level, whether that is understood in terms of subjectivity or of agency, there remains a gap between the ending and what has gone before.

Hence in the most self-aware of the new-critical treatments of the novel, Jerry Beasley acknowledges that '[t]he providential manoeuvrings that come at the close of the novel do seem very sudden.' Smollett thus 'violated the novelistic principles of organic unity':

> Presumably [these violations] represent a deliberate feature in the design of his moralised rogue biography. The radical wrenching of the fictional world brought about in these chapters just possibly reflects Smollett's sense of the great distance separating the actual behaviour of mankind from the humanitarian ideals of justice, love and benevolent action that alone can make for social and moral harmony [...][24]

Just how unwilling Beasley is to admit this possibility is revealed by his ultimate insistence that Roderick's final Eden must, retrospectively, turn the rest of his story into a pilgrimage which leads him there, and impose a retrospective moral pattern on the novel; but still,

23 Leopold Damrosch, *God's Plot and Man's Stories: Studies in the Fictional Imagination from Milton to Fielding* (Chicago: University of Chicago Press, 1985) 286.

24 Jerry C. Beasley, *Novels of the 1740s* (Athens: University of Georgia Press, 1982) 121, 123.

It must be said that this moral pattern is often obscured and left awash in the horrid facts of Roderick's experience, which he renders with such violent intensity and furious indignation. The reader [...] may have nearly as hard a time perceiving it as the hero himself.[25]

Quite. We are thus returned to the question of Roderick's perception of himself and of his role as narrator, for the end-point of the plot is also the point from which he tells his tale. As we have seen, the protagonist of this novel is constituted by his instinctive responses to particular situations; but, crucially, there is very little distance between this protagonist and the narrator, the later Roderick, who, if he has learnt anything in the course of his experiences, does not bring that privileged perspective to bear in his narration of that experience, or to generalize moral or spiritual truths from it.[26] It is not only the protagonist Roderick who cannot see a moral pattern unfolding in his life; as a retrospective narrator, from whom one might expect such a perception, he seems just as oblivious.

More useful commentary on the ending of *Roderick Random* comes from those that see the disjunction between thematic content and narrative ending as representing a shift in the literary culture of mid eighteenth-century England: specifically, the rise of sensibility and an interest in the portrayal of individual consciousness for its own sake. As will be clear from what follows, I am much more in sympathy with this general approach, seeing this novel as I do as very much on the borders of two types of literary culture. And the repeated tears of the last quarter of the novel, catalogued in John Warner's essay, are certainly senti-mental, a set of physical reactions to good fortune that displace Roderick's more typical rage against vice.[27] But this is hardly an

---

25 Ibid. 123.

26 In this, *Roderick Random* is significantly different from more conventionally providential first-person narratives such as those of Bunyan or Defoe, and before them Augustine, where the conversion of sinful protagonist into redeemed narrator is the whole point of the plot. Roderick's analysis of his emotions at chapter VI, p.25, writes Richetti, 'leaves it unclear whether he expects readers to see his understanding of that complicated psychological network as part of his experience of the moment or as the result of mature narrative retrospection [...] In effect, Roderick acts and speaks in the same tense' (Richetti, *English Novel* 173).

27 John M. Warner. 'Smollett's Development as a Novelist', *Novel: A Forum on Fiction* 5.2 (Winter 1972): 151.

explanation of the incongruous good fortune over which they are weeping.

Nevertheless, Warner's essay neatly reveals much more of what is at stake in the place of subjectivity in this novel despite the new critical premises it shares with Beasley's. Warner's presupposition that Smollett's aim throughout his career was 'to create a unified art work' turns *Roderick Random* into an effort specifically to reconcile the claims of 'subjectivity' to the material world, via the familiar presupposition that there is something inherently unified about subjectivity.[28] In an effort to find this subjectivity, Warner settles on the relationship between Roderick and Narcissa and decides that this 'symbolises' the subjective: 'Symbolized by this relationship, the subjective note deeply suffuses the novel.'[29] Yet this subjective note does not appear at the level of the narrative itself: it seems we must rather *deduce* it from the fact that the hero is, in the second half of the novel, *nominally* in love, and romantic love is, of course, the paradigm case of subjectivity transcending history and the material world. Starting with this conception of transcendent subjectivity, Warner then searches for that which does indeed transcend history or at least escape it; finds it in Roderick and Narcissa and their happy ending, and decides that this must represent ('symbolize') subjectivity.

> [T]he conclusion of the novel does function as a dream not as the festive dance that ordinarily rounds out the comic rhythm. The world of the subject has become too far divorced from objective reality [...] to be convincing.[30]

This is one way of dealing with the generic jump that is the ending of *Roderick Random*: invent a subject to whose private world that ending belongs or corresponds. But despite the appeal to the love-story element, there seems to be nothing in the novel that corresponds to that subject. Nor should this be too surprising: the historically transcendent subject of art of the type Warner is looking for was, in 1748, a still emerging idea. But a desire to place this novel in this historical context competes in Warner's account with the elevation of the *outcome* of this cultural shift,

---

28   Ibid. 148.
29   Ibid. 151.
30   Ibid. 151.

namely romantic subjectivity, to the realm of trans-historical truth, always already there, somewhere, in the history that produced it.[31]

We are left with the possibility opened up reluctantly by Beasley, that the incongruity of the ending of *Roderick Random* is a 'deliberate feature in the design' reflecting a 'sense of the great distance separating the actual behaviour of mankind from [...] humanitarian ideals'; that the overall form of this novel is significant and not a flaw. But given Smollett's own background, this possibility should not seem so outlandish. An ultimate reward that is not the result of good works or of a consciousness of virtue is fundamental to the Calvinist theology of the Church of Scotland in which Smollett was raised and in which Roderick announces himself bred to the astonished Anglican chaplain of the *Thunder* (XXXIV.192). What Roderick experiences at the end of the novel is the miracle of his own (humanly inexplicable) election from the ranks of the reprobate. The gap between the world the novel describes and the sudden overthrow of its rules by the ending is the gap between the fallen world in which we live and the impenetrable will of Calvin's God.

I have already observed, however, that the restoration to Roderick of his father and his estates clearly functions within the political values of the novel as an image of the restoration of gentry authority, its historical continuity, and of the imagined benevolent patriarchy of the small landowner. Let me draw two conclusions from the discussion so far. What makes Roderick a member of the Elect is neither a consciousness of that election (which as we have seen is only intermittent) nor good deeds (which are pretty thin on the ground), *but simply his gentle birth itself*: *Roderick Random* translates into status-terms this tenet of Calvinist theology.

The name for a providential narrative put at the service of a class position is of course *romance*. The split between the novel and its ending is a generic split between realism and satire on the one hand and romance on the other.[32] It is of course possible, deploying a simple

---

31   Warner's attempt to fit *Roderick Random* into a literary-historical pattern that has romantic poetry as its *telos* is very similar to Michael McKeon's: see Introduction, pp.11–12.

32   This is not an unprecedented move: Paulson notes that Paul Scarron's *Roman Comique* (1651) 'shows that the picaresque structure can be given a semblance of

reading of Northrop Frye, to use this observation to turn the entire novel into a romance, by turning its grimly realistic content into a generic underworld through which our hero must journey before ascending once more to the light. The contrast between novel and ending then becomes an example of 'the polar extremes of romance.'[33] But the sheer contemporaneity of Smollett's satire resists an approach which cancels out its historical embeddedness. The nightmare world into which Roderick is born (there is no balancing green world at the *start* of his journey) is not a generic counter, but a portrayal of a particular society at a particular time. The second conclusion to follow from our discussion so far is that this novel can only imagine a gentry restoration in the miraculous terms offered by religion and its displacement into romance. A world in which the gentry would again enjoy the political agency they (imagine they) once had would be a world beyond this fallen world of grubby particularity, beyond the material world of cause and effect that determines Roderick's actions and his consciousness alike: would be, that is, outside history. The polar extremes that structure this novel are thus not internal to romance, but are rather romance (as a genre) and history. Far from being an anti-romance, *Roderick Random* resorts to romance modes to lift its hero from a historical situation from which there is no escape on its own terms.

---

unity by introducing a romance beginning and (however modified) ending' (Paulson 36).

33   David K. Jeffrey, '*Roderick Random*: The Form and Structure of a Romance', *Revue Belge de Philologie et d'Histoire* 58 (1980) 608. More recently David Blewett, in his introduction to the Penguin edition of the novel, continues to insist both that 'the romance structure imparts to the novel a dream-like atmosphere' and that this reminds us of 'the moral pattern behind the sequence of events in Roderick's life' despite the concrete historicity of the situations evoked; and, again, *what* moral pattern? *Roderick Random* (Harmondsworth: Penguin, 1995) xvii, xviii.

2. Writing in opposition

I now want to argue that this turn itself, this resolution of satire in romance, is itself an outcome of the progress of opposition political discourse in the decades up to 1748. Doing so will, among other things, put some flesh on the bones of the opposition between 'romance' and 'history' that we have seen enacted in this novel in the opposition between plot and discourse, and explain what is at stake politically in those terms. In order to do so, however, we must return to the opposition campaign to examine the status of the writing that was its vehicle. For, without wanting to exaggerate the coherence of Bolingbroke's intellectual resources in *The Craftsman*, the humanist conceptions of civic virtue and political agency to which he appealed carried with them a particular role for the author, and a particular version of the history within which he was an agent.

The role for the author offered by the quasi-republican ideology of the opposition can be summed up as an ideal of *eloquence*. The political writer models himself on the classical orators Demosthenes and Cicero in their denunciation of tyranny and their warnings to the citizens of its rise. This is the pose that Bolingbroke adopts in writing in the years after his first return from France in 1725, when his exclusion from the Lords meant that a live audience of the political elite was no longer available. The promise that such a pose holds out is nevertheless that of political effect: the orator's job is to represent the truth of the state of the *polis* in such a way that his auditors will be moved to act in its defence. The discourse of eloquence assumes its own political agency.

This agency was not simply a matter of being able to force changes in government policy or the removal of ministers, however, but more profoundly in the rhetorical unification of an audience to and for whom the orator claims to speak. Now that historians have picked apart the constituent elements of the opposition to Walpole, one can no longer claim that Bolingbroke is simply speaking *for* a united, coherent constituency, such as the smaller gentry, that existed before he began to write. Rather, his extra-parliamentary campaign *constructs* a constituency in its very address to the enfranchised class. Alexander Pettit in *Illusory Consensus* finds no objective historical reality corresponding to the united opposition party for which Bolingbroke claims to speak, and on this basis dismisses this claim as 'self-serving rhetoric' ('the Bolingbrokeans' appeals to consensus are transparent affective devices, pulse-quickeners without much substance'), as simply disingenuous.[34] But, as Adam Potkay points out, the classical ideal of eloquence which lies behind Bolingbroke's conception of political discourse requires the orator to summon into being in his words a moral community, a uniting set of shared perceptions, that did not exist before he began to speak. He names this act of political *creatio ex nihil* after its most famous classical exemplar: 'The demosthenic moment occurs whenever a moral community bestows the 'palm of oratory' on a speaker for the very reason that he has addressed it with sufficient force to call it, however fleetingly, into being.'[35] Eloquence, and opposition political discourse with it, is not a means of recognising an already existing reality, but a way of acting upon the world, a means of changing that world. Bolingbroke's claim to be speaking for a particular group is simply a way of calling that group into being as a group: however fleeting the effect, or (as I shall argue) however quickly the effect turned into something else, Bolingbroke's eloquence remains an example of discourse as political agency.

Given this role for the writer himself, Bolingbroke's historical narratives in the *Remarks on the History of England* and in *Letters on the Study and Use of History* necessarily include a strong voluntarist element, emphasising the agency of individual statesmen in controlling historical events. The *Remarks* were indeed themselves part of the *Craftsman*'s rhetorical campaign against Walpole, and published there as a series of letters from a fictitious gentry correspondent, Mr Oldcastle. Oldcastle relates the discourses on English history delivered to his circle of friends by an unnamed elderly gentleman. This gentleman draws on Machiavelli's general model of the development of republics, a cycle of decline from an originally just constitution, caused by the private wealth that the very success of that constitution makes possible. Newly wealthy citizens withdraw from active participation in the state into the pleasures of 'luxury'. This model is developed to explain the fall of the Roman Republic, but the tendency of states to

---

34 Pettit 25.
35 Adam Potkay, *The Fate of Eloquence in the Age of Hume* (Ithaca: Cornell University Press, 1994) 33.

follow this pattern is a general truth about human society, and such a universal model turns English history into a storehouse of exempla, each directly relevant to the present political situation, for that situation is always somewhere along the arc described by Machiavelli. Historical agency on this model thus lies with the politician/orator who can draw the comparisons between past and present and warn his fellow citizens of their peril. 'History', Bolingbroke famously writes in the *Letters*, 'is philosophy teaching by examples.'[36] But it can only do so through the orator or writer like Bolingbroke. Historical example is part of the arsenal of the professional orator.

The *Remarks* then use this universal historical model to posit an essentially timeless English political character. English history as narrated by Oldcastle's friend is a struggle between two 'spirits', a spirit of liberty and a spirit of tyranny. Liberty is understood in the Harringtonian sense of independence from government through the possession of land, as described above; tyranny as the power of the crown to erode or destroy this independence. However, the struggle between the two is ongoing at *every* point in English history: although at times the power of the crown over the institutions of the state seems absolute, nevertheless this 'spirit of liberty' survives, an essence of resistance to the court that lives on in and legitimizes the contemporary strand of Bolingbroke's opposition.[37] What is at stake in the present political conflict is just what has always been at stake. Such a view refuses the settlement of 1688–9 any historical uniqueness: the deposition of James was just one more instance, albeit a dramatic one, of the spirit of liberty reasserting itself; the passage of the Bill of Rights did not guarantee the liberty of the citizen for the foreseeable future, but was one more concession wrung by citizens from the crown, which was vulnerable to just the same subversion by the crown as other such

---

36   Lord Bolingbroke, *Historical Writings*, ed. Issac Kramnick (Chicago: University of Chicago Press, 1972) 9.

37   'It [the opposition] is, I think, a revival of the true old English spirit, which prevailed in the days of our fathers, and must always be national, since it has no direction but to the national interest' (Letter 1 of 'Remarks on the History of England' in Bolingbroke, *Historical Writings* 156). This is a long way from Harrington, for whom the possibility of political independence only appears with the breakdown of feudal relationships under Henry VII: see Pocock, *Politics, Language, Time* 130, 135.

concessions, most notably Magna Carta, had been. Humanist history in Bolingbroke's use of it, in other words, legitimated vigilance, even suspicion, towards the activities of the crown *despite* the limitations placed on the crown by the Revolution.[38]

It is the sheer sameness of the issues involved across hundreds of years of English history on Bolingbroke's account that affronts the writers in the government's main vehicle against the *Craftsman*, the *London Journal*. Walpole's defenders deny the relevance of examples from past history to the present day by appealing to a history of ongoing flux, in which the conditions which made an action legitimate in the past are specific to the time of that action; and to a recent point in history, namely 1688, when the nature of English politics itself changed fundamentally, disabling any appeal to earlier precedent as irrelevant to present conditions. Humanist historiography floats particular historical events in an element of sameness, allowing them to be lifted and compared, one with the other: Walpolite historiography roots them in a particular period, and explanation must be by reference to other aspects of that period, not cycles of corruption and restoration which endlessly repeat themselves through all time. And by referring political institutions to wider aspects of the societies in question, the *Journal* comes close to calling for the totalizing social history of the Enlightenment:[39]

> There's hardly a Spot of Ground in *Europe*, where the Inhabitants have not frequently chang'd *their Temper and Genius:* Nor can any Reason be produced, why the *Spirit of a Nation* should be more fix'd in *Point of Government*, than in their Morals, Learning, Religion, their Humour and Conversation, Diet and Complexion; which do all notoriously vary in almost every Age, and may have great Effects on Men's Notions of Government.[40]

Prominent among its arguments for historical difference, for example, is the insistence on the *feudal* nature of medieval society, the tying of inferior to superior by bonds of service, that the opposition neo-Harringtonian position was forced to overlook in its imagining of a

---

38 See Issac Kramnick, *Bolingbroke and His Circle* 177–81 for a summary of the particular issues involved.

39 Enlightenment is indeed the *London Journal*'s own metaphor: '*New England,* or *the present State* of Things caused by the Revolution, as far exceeds the old, as Light does Darkness [...].' *London Journal* no. 575 (August 8, 1730).

40 *London Journal* no. 575 (August 8 1730).

continuously *independent* gentry. All that remains the same through historical change is merely, argues the *Journal*, a 'human nature' unsurprisingly reduced to economic self-interest. Pro-government discourse thus provides one arena for the periodization of history so important to Enlightenment thought in general. The argument over 1688 was thus a struggle not only over the meaning of that particular event, but over the legitimacy of two rival and incommensurable historio-graphic practices.

The historiographic practice argued for by the *London Journal*, indeed, disassociates the activities of the historian from those of the politician. It separates the past, of which the historian can have knowledge, from the present, over which the politician can have control; but the knowledge of the historian does not give him the authority to criticise the actions of the politician. Political agency is no longer a matter of history, of writing, of eloquence, or any other mode of representation: it is rather a matter of meeting or manipulating the economic self-interest of the subject. Burtt cites William Arnall on just this point: given 'human nature', corruption can only be defeated 'not by Declamation, but by over-bidding, and out-buying it. Corruption, like Violence, must be oppos'd by itself.'[41]

This dissociation is a large nail in the coffin in the humanist version of letters within which Bolingbroke works. It undermines the sort of political agency on which their humanist conception of history, and of the role of discourse within history, depend. In the terms of this disenchantment, history and politics become the realm of 'nature', of necessity, as opposed to the space in which the opposition imagines its uncorrupted constitution is called, among other things, *romance*. Contesting Bolingbroke's account of parliamentary independency, the *London Journal* scoffs that "'tis not possible, in the Nature of Things, that the *legislative Power* should be *independent* of the executive [...]. 'Tis in vain to carry Virtue up to a Romance, and fly to *Harrington's Oceana*, and Schemes of Government which never existed but in Men's Heads'. [42] Three months later the *Journal* says Bolingbroke's 'Notions of Liberty and Government are *fictitious and romantic*'; the reversion of the Normans to their ancestral 'Gothic' spirit of liberty on arriving in

---

41   *British Journal* no. 74 (31 May 1729); quoted in Burtt 115.
42   Ibid. no. 558 (April 11, 1730).

England is mocked in similar terms: 'What heroick Tales are here! More idle and romantic than those of *Gargantua!*' [43] Similarly, the effect that the *Craftsman* imagines it is having on government policy is categorised as superstition, as the assumption of magical powers to its own discourse, which can be countered by revealing causal relationships:

> They may, with almost as much Propriety, say, they were *the Cause of the Sun's appearing* after a Fortnight's cloudy weather, because they said 'twould appear again. Don't these Writers know, that all Causes will have their natural Effects, whether they wrote or not; [...] This is the Course of Things [...] [44]

The political agency assumed by humanist discourse is an illusion. The parameters of government are determined by 'the course of things', 'the nature of things': by which the *Journal* names an acquisitive self-interested human nature on the one hand, and the causal relationships of a deterministic history on the other.

Indeed, some critics have suggested that Bolingbroke's later writing is itself a tacit admission of the powerlessness of discourse over history. Unlike the *Remarks*, essays at once satirical and addressed to the wide readership of *The Craftsman*, the *Letters on the Study and Use of History* (written in 1736, but only published posthumously) are addressed to a single opposition figure who Bolingbroke hopes will one day enjoy political power as the writer now knows he never will again:

> [T]he very act of writing the *Letters on History* [...] itself testifies to the frustration and disappointment of a man whom history had passed by. Bolingbroke desperately wanted to be not a philosopher of history or even a student of it but instead the subject of history, a historic figure, the prime minister advising 'the prince', not a writer of epistolary essays on abstruse topics to Lord Cornbury, a political nobody. [45]

The production of the manual of historical examples for use in the training of the prince or statesman is itself a traditional aspect of humanist historiographic practice; yet this narrow intended audience for

---

43 Ibid. no. 570 (July 4, 1730); no. 575 (August 8, 1730).

44 Ibid. no. 640 (October 2, 1731).

45 Joel Weinsheimer, *Eighteenth-Century Hermeneutics: Philosophy of Interpretation from Locke to Burke* (New Haven: Yale University Press, 1993) 73. Bolingbroke had become a liability to the Opposition by this point and had withdrawn from active politics.

the work is also clear in Bolingbroke's proto-enlightenment disinterest in Saxon or medieval history, in contrast to his earlier populist satirical use of it in the *Remarks*. Interestingly, Bolingbroke in this work thus accepts one version of the periodization of history, and indeed of a non-voluntarist 'necessity', demanded by his old Walpolite opponents. The changes that mark the end of one epoch and the beginning of another, he writes, consist not only in conquests or revolutions, but also

> those that are wrought in the same governments and among the same people, slowly and almost imperceptibly, by the necessary effects of time, and flux condition of human affairs [...]. [T]hen is one of those periods formed, at which the chain spoken of is so broken as to have little or no real or visible connection with that which we see continue.[46]

(Note that period here refers to the shift into a new epoch, not the epoch itself.) There is thus no practical political lessons to be drawn from epochs other than our own:

> [A] new system of causes and effects, that subsists in our time, and whereof our conduct is to be a part, arising at the last period, and all that passes in our time being dependent on what has passed since that period [...] we are extremely concerned to be well informed about these passages. To be ignorant about the ages that precede this era would be shameful[...]. But to be learned about them is a ridiculous affectation in any man who means to be useful to the present age.[47]

Although for Bolingbroke the current era begins at the start of the sixteenth century, not in 1688, clearly the prospective statesman no longer needs to bother much with a 'spirit of liberty' which descends to modern Englishmen from the Saxons.[48] However, the enlightenment element in the *Letters* goes further than this periodization in itself to undermine the humanist function of the whole text. For periodization combines with his scepticism to suggest that only once a period is *over*

---

46 Bolingbroke, *Historical Writings* 82.

47 Ibid. 82–3.

48 It is in this acceptance of periodization, as much as in his scepticism towards ancient sources, that I see the Enlightenment element in this work. See Weinsheimer 74: '[I]n his role as a philosopher of history he can be categorised neither as a Renaissance nor an Enlightenment thinker [...] [H]e occupies a liminal position, straddling the crevasse between two distinct historical epochs.'

can we gain true historical understanding of the events within it. Only then can we see those events

> as they followed one another, or as they produced one another, causes or effects, immediate or remote[...]. The events we are witnesses of, in the course of the longest life, appear to us very often original, unprepared, single, and unrelative. [...] [T]hey appear such very often, are called accidents, and looked on as the effects of chance [...]. In ancient history [...] the examples are complete, which are incomplete in the course of experience.[49]

Historical knowledge of previous eras may be a 'ridiculous affectation', but it is knowledge of causes and effects as knowledge of the present cannot be; the price paid for this epistemological superiority is its contemporary political irrelevance. The consequences of this are clear: not only is the historian one alienated from political power, but Bolingbroke's addressee, too, will have no way of applying the historian's wisdom to contemporary events, for the contemporary is just that period over which no real historical knowledge can be had. In the absence of comprehensible causal relationships, the way in which historical examples have their effect in the present is described in supernatural terms: in the case of Roman ancestor-worship, 'The virtue of one generation was transformed, by the magic of example, into several: and a spirit of heroism was maintained through many ages of that commonwealth.'[50]

Bolingbroke's humanist *political* purposes in this text are thus in conflict with the enlightenment *epistomological* lessons that he ultimately draws:

> The very fact that critique is applicable only to a history that is over bespeaks the ideal autonomy of self-consciousness from historical forces. Yet [...] Bolingbroke [also] affirms a notion of history – even past history – as irremediably incomplete, ongoing, and belonging to a perpetually unfinished story. Incomplete history is not an object of consciousness. Rather, consciousness is part of it. Being a participant, consciousness registers history less as an intelligible meaning than as a senseless force which reduces its own autonomy and encroaches on its own power.[51]

---

49 Bolingbroke, *Historical Writings* 18–19. This passage is clearly echoed in opening paragraphs of Hume's 'On the Rise and Progress of the Arts and Sciences' quoted in the Introduction, pp.20–1.
50 Bolingbroke, *Historical Writings* 10.
51 Weinsheimer 101.

In other words, consciousness is split between its knowledge of a past from which it is autonomous and over which it has no power other than that of interpretation, and its immersion in a present history which instead exerts a determining power over consciousness. History is that which we can know, but the price we pay for our knowledge is our powerlessness over it. Bolingbroke has arrived at a conception of history as 'necessity' very close to that of his old enemy the *London Journal*. The effect is to acknowledge the passing of eloquence, including the high appeal to historical example, as a mode of political agency in itself.

Further, the space that the later Bolingbroke finds outside of (enlightenment) historical necessity, the space within which to imagine the possibility of political agency, looks very like what the *London Journal* called 'meer utopian Speculation' and 'romance.' *The Idea of a Patriot King* is addressed to the same small opposition coterie – the 'Patriots' – as the *Letters on History*. The role of the ideal king as set out in this essay is not to reform institutions, but to restore the civic virtue of his subjects by setting them an example: but this is a purely *moral* example. It is not the historical example from which general truths can be drawn and applied to contemporary affairs, the better to understand them. The prince does not act through the understanding to which the orator appeals; rather, his subjects will simply *imitate* him, and the state will be reformed 'of course':

> As soon as corruption ceases to be an expedient of government, and it will cease to be such as soon as a Patriot King is raised to the throne, the panacea is applied; the spirit of the constitution revives of course; and, as fast as it revives, the orders and form of the constitution are restored to their primitive integrity[...] . A Patriot King is the most powerful of all reformers; for he is himself a sort of standing miracle, so rarely seen and so little understood, that the sure effects of his appearance will be admiration and love in every honest breast, confusion and terror to every guilty conscience, but submission and resignation in all. A new people will seem to arise with a new king. Innumerable metamorphoses, like those which the poets feign, will happen in every deed: and, while men are conscious that they are the same individuals, the difference of their sentiments will almost persuade them that they are changed into different beings.[52]

---

52 Bolingbroke, 'The Idea of a Patriot King', *Political Writings* ed. David Armitage (Cambridge: Cambidge University Press, 1997) 251.

The effect of the Patriot King will, that is, be like the effect of the poet on reality, but we are clearly dealing with a quite different sort of poet from Pope or Swift. This is the opposite of art understood as itself a part of political practice: this is political practice imagined as an idealising neo-classical art. The emphasis in *The Idea of a Patriot King* on the appearance and behaviour of the prince as an agent of this change, its understanding of politics as theatre, harks back quite explicitly to the power-as-performance of the Tudor and early Stuart reigns.[53] But I want to suggest that the *Patriot King* itself belongs to another genre: romance. For all its appeal to humanist-republican norms, *The Patriot King* is a fantasy of a returning patriarchal order whose generic roots lie in the wish-fulfilment of religious apocalypse and romance narrative. Any element of satire on the present political order is blunted by the unreality of the counter-order being suggested: the Patriot King is a kind of political Houyhnhnm, an ideal emptied of impact by its sheer irrelevance to any actually existing human world.

At the same time, the sudden appearance of joy among the 'honest', and confusion and terror among the guilty, are of course just the effects we have seen at the return of Roderick's father to the paternal estate. The distance between the orator-politician of earlier opposition writing and the miraculous-poetic agency of the Patriot King; between the particular historical examples of kingship available in the *Remarks* or the *Letters* and the Platonic form of kingship on offer here; this gap, I suggest, is just that between the satire of *Roderick Random* and its romance ending.

In fact, even the *Letters on History* have a hard time stopping what one might call the *aestheticization* of any historiography that holds out the hope of effective political agency. Once true historical knowledge has been shown as irrelevant to the practising statesman, there seems no reason why fables or allegories could not provide him with the kind of exemplary situations he needs to guide his actions. Bolingbroke's *Letters* are close to Aristotle, comments Weinsheimer, in their concern

---

53 '[T]he *Patriot King* becomes the most ludicrous example of Bolingbroke's insistence on the theatrical image of politics over the administrative image. How appropriate, then, that the essay ends by invoking that greatest and most dazzling of all political actors – Elizabeth[...]. [But] [b]y the middle of the eighteenth century [...] the old order could not have been recaptured by humanist methods and aesthetic performances.' Kramnick, *Bolingbroke and His Circle* 168–9.

with the general and the argument that this represents a higher and more philosophical type of knowledge than that of particulars. 'The consequence, however, is that in this respect exemplary history cannot distinguish itself from poetry.'[54] Within this new discursive landscape, the concern of humanist historiography with general truths, and the way they legitimate action by their very applicability to a range of particular circumstances, starts to look more like a feature of an *aesthetic* sphere being separated off from that of active politics. A younger generation of opposition writers, the Patriots, took Bolingbroke's timeless essence of England/Britain some way down this aestheticizing road.

Patriotism is 'the mid-century variant of country ideology';[55] its spokesmen included Cornbury, but also Thomson, George Lyttleton, William Murray and William Pitt. These writers, taking their cue in part from Bolingbroke's *Patriot King*,

> believed that their political cause would be better served by more uplifting and patriotically spirited poetry which would (unlike Pope's) not only attack the degeneracy of the present age but also look forward to a regenerated Britain [...].[56]

For images of that regeneration, as Christine Gerrard points out, the Patriots characteristically looked to British myth and legend in contrast to (for example) Pope's overriding concern with the contemporary. Already in the 1730s 'a striking feature of the Gothic debate' (on the Saxon origin of English identity and liberties) conducted by the Patriots is a suspiciously 'ready translation into poetic and cultural terms.'[57] While the Patriot poets themselves were still committed to achieving an immediate political effect, Patriotism was from the start, suggests Harris, 'an anti-political language' in its insistence on the 'philosophical and moral absolutes' it shared with Bolingbroke's political fantasy.[58] According to Gerrard, it is this aestheticizing movement that the Patriots bequeathed to mid-century poets like Collins, Gray, and the Wartons, who will, in effect, abandon contemporary politics as subject matter

---

54   Ibid. 90.
55   Robert Harris, *A Patriot Press: National Politics and the London Press in the 1740s* (Oxford: Clarendon, 1993) 5.
56   Gerrard 71.
57   Ibid. 104.
58   Harris 48.

altogether. Instead of a Patriot King who could rediscover the theatrical politics of Elizabeth, they will rediscover Spenser; 'Gothic' will increasingly name, not the ancient Saxon liberties evoked in Bolingbroke's *Remarks*, but a style of architecture. One by one, the historiographic recourses of humanist politics are redeployed as style emptied of any practical political meaning. Patriot myth-making thus accepts the Walpolite absoluteness of the difference between past and present, and while it reverses the valuation put on the two periods, the effect is eventually the same: to cut loose the present from the moral precedents of the past.

The 1740s see this withdrawal of poetry from engagement in contemporary politics. They also see opposition politics in general reach their nadir: a combination of a loss of leadership to a coalition ministry in 1744 without any compensating shift in government policy, and the intensification of the Jacobite slur as a result of the '45 rising, left morale at a new low.[59] The two phenomena are not unrelated. It is very hard not to see in the opposition abandonment of satire an underlying acceptance that writing was not in fact going to alter the nature of politics in the new commercial order.[60] It is this political context that seems to me to explain what John Sitter refers to as 'a puzzling but pronounced discontinuity' between the poets of the 1740s and 50s and 'the immediate past' represented by Pope and Swift.[61] Sitter writes of the specifically poetic dimension of this shift:

> For what begins to replace the opposition literary contract is a new agreement with the reader in which poetry will be opposed not to a particular politics but

---

59 See M. M. Goldsmith, 'Faction Detected: Ideological Consequences of Robert Walpole's Decline and Fall', *History* 64 (1979): 1–19, especially 9–12 on Fielding's response to the 'more sceptical, more disillusioned views of politics than had previously prevailed' (9); Colley, *In Defiance of Oligarchy* especially 240–56; and Rogers, *Whigs and Cities*: '[E]ven within London the particular alliance of mercantile and civic interests that gave the Country platform such vitality began to dissolve by 1745' (85).

60 The retreat into national myth of the Patriot opposition that Gerrard describes bears striking similarities to the idealisation of a patriarchal Stuart past, *without* this turning into active Jacobitism, that Pettit identifies and christens the 'Caroline' opposition: powerlessness in the face of the new politics clearly produced similar resorts in the various opposition factions.

61 John Sitter, *Literary Loneliness in Mid-Eighteenth-Century England* (Ithaca: Cornell University Press, 1982) 12.

(ostensibly) to all politics. Such a shift dramatically restricts the province of poetry while at the same time severely limiting the legitimacy of political or economic activity as a theater for any sort of ambition on the part of the intellectual or artist.[62]

Indeed, one can see the whole ideology of the aesthetic in England as emerging from the failure of the opposition to find ways of putting their version of the nation into political practice; restricted instead to writing, that writing must then be granted a status where its political inefficacy *does not matter*, where the irrelevance of the text to the actual running of the country can become a guarantee of its transcendent truth rather than simply a failure of the writing itself. The aesthetic as a category emerges, that is, to compensate opposition writers for their alienation from power, by constructing a version of the world where political power itself is an epiphenomenon of a nationhood whose true legislators are the writers themselves. Recently, Clifford Siskin has suggested something very similar to this in regard to the role of Jacobite symbolic practice in the emergence of the category 'culture' in just the same period. Commenting on Paul Monod's understanding of Jacobitism as a political 'culture' constituted as a 'system of signs', he writes,

> To speak of Jacobitism as a 'cultural phenomenon' [...] is, I would argue, to not quite grasp the historical point: Jacobitism is the occasion for the advent of the phenomenon of culture itself as a constitutive category of modern knowledge[...]. Jacobitism, to put it another way, helped make possible the very mode of analysis which Monod deploys to explain it.[63]

What I am suggesting is that we can look on this as a specific example of a development in the literary politics of opposition more generally (albeit it a particularly good example, given that the crisis experienced by all opposition writers in the 1740s was particularly acute for the Jacobites). With the emergence of a totalizing, historicized, enlightenment notion of culture (of which more in my next chapter), comes a concept of the aesthetic as that which redeems that culture: although not all culture belongs to the realm of the aesthetic, the aesthetic is that area within culture that escapes historical determination. The aesthetic is the place of the timeless, of the valuable, of the essential in human

---

62   Ibid. 108.
63   Siskin 84; Paul Monod, *Jacobitism and the English People 1688-1788* (Cambridge: Cambridge University Press, 1989).

experience; as such, it is that into which the moralised world-view of humanism is displaced and confined within enlightenment discourse. I am not claiming that this category of 'culture' is available to writers in the 1740s, nor am I claiming that the historiography deployed by the government apologists is in any way an important contributor to the conjectural history of the Scottish Enlightenment (although I think a good case could be made for this). Rather, I am arguing that the response of opposition writers to the experience of prolonged alienation from power was to imagine writing as somehow inherently alienated from power; the way they did so was to become increasingly important as more sophisticated theories of historical determination than those deployed by the *London Journal* were developed later in the century. For Kramnick to contrast a Walpolite politics of the manipulation of self-interest with an opposition politics which 'was not simply social and economic, then, but also stylistic and aesthetic' is misleading, insofar as our current use of 'aesthetic' to refer to a sphere outside politics only emerges from the collapse of just this sort of politics.[64]

3. *Roderick Random*, historical determination, and romance

I now want to return to *Roderick Random* to show how both these aspects of the opposition situation, the permanent alienation from power and its compensation in the aesthetic, structure the novel as a whole. In the first section of this chapter, I described Smollett's novel as a satire on contemporary British society rooted in the country ideology of opposition writing under Walpole. Yet Walpole had been out of office for six years by the time *Roderick Random* was published, and the intervening years had seen the final collapse of opposition hopes and the abandonment of the humanist model of the agency of discourse that had underpinned those hopes. The gentry vision of a benign rural landscape of independent patriarchs embodying values unchanged since Arthur, or the Saxons, or somebody, would now become the mythic England, the way in which England imagined itself, a dream-space which did not

---

64   Kramnick, *Bolingbroke and His Circle* 6–7.

demand the overturning of the Hanoverian state and restitution in its place. That state had been produced by an apparently irreversible history; it now became the job of writing, not to participate in that history as a form of political agency, but to imagine a space outside of it in which patriot princes could still work miracles in the name of timeless humanist values. I now want to argue that *Roderick Random* figures this function of writing as *form*, distinct from the historical content of the discourse of the novel itself. But it is a form which neither character nor narrator, immersed in that historical reality as they are, can perceive. That inability to grasp the form of the novel as a whole is, I suggest, itself a particular aspect of the general failure of the protagonist to exert effective agency over the world in which he moves.

In the first half of *Roderick Random,* what is striking in this context is the extent to which Roderick the satirist has in fact no real power over the world around him. The rage that marks him as a Juvenalian satirist is represented as the effect of the world on him, rather than allowing him any effect on it. The word most often used to describe this rage is 'transport': 'I sallied out, in a transport of rage and sorrow [...]' (VI.23); 'I [...] was so much transported with grief, anger, and disdain, that a torrent of blood gushed from my nostrils [...]' (XLIII.243). That is, Roderick is not the agent of this transportation: he is himself transported, by an emotion originating somewhere other than with the 'I' that is being moved, in the determining circumstances of the historical world. Roderick's rage at others' behaviour may serve as an index of its corruption; yet its very unreflective, even physiological, nature means that Roderick is reduced to a determined consequence of that behaviour, an aspect of the material world as surely as those who measure worth in terms of money and appearances. Roderick's actions are an (increasingly predictable) effect of which vice is the cause: Roderick's identity is dissolved in the world around him.

> Roderick inhabits a Lucretian universe of ceaseless change that is at once random and determined: random in that it responds only to the swerving and rebounding of atom against atom in their fall through the void; determined in that every rebound leads to another rebound, and there is thus plenty of causation even though no presiding principle organizes the whole.[65]

---

65   Damrosch 286.

Or, to allude instead to a natural philosopher nearer Smollett's own time, *Roderick Random* represents social interaction as governed by something like Newtonian physics, except without the faith in the ultimate benignity of the great watchmaker in the sky who set the whole thing going. The reduction of social relations to the monetary has reduced the citizen to the material atom.

One of the characteristics of Roderick's childhood is the indifference of those who punish him to his actual responsibility for the things that happen to him:

> [...] every piece of mischief whose author lay unknown, was charged upon me[...]. I was flogged for having narrowly escaped drowning, by the sinking of a ferry-boat in which I was passenger.—Another time for having recovered of a bruise occasioned by a horse and cart running over me.—A third time, for being bit by a baker's dog. (II.6)

Such punishment reverses the law of cause and effect, or at least its moral implications, and attributes agency to Roderick that he could not possibly have exercised; that, indeed, only God, or Nature, can be said to have exercised. Years on, the accusation of treason on board a warship in which both captain and surgeon are Irish Catholics represents a similar misattribution of agency: indeed, his experiences in the navy represent the apotheosis of Roderick's passivity. Roderick, for all his efforts to enlist as a surgeon's mate, finds himself in just such a position by accident after he is press-ganged. Roderick's general experience of helplessness in the face of history indeed culminates on the *Thunder* when he is chained to the deck during an engagement with the French and spattered with the remains of his comrades. The particular horror for Roderick of this passivity lies once again in his isolation from those around him:

> I endeavoured to compose myself as much as possible, by reflecting that I was not a whit more exposed than those who were stationed about me; but when I beheld them employed without intermission, in annoying the foe, and encouraged by the society and behaviour of one another, I could easily perceive a wide difference between their condition and mine. (XXIX.167)

This common purpose is admittedly only visible in the heat of battle: at other times, the *Thunder* is simply a microcosm ruled by the same petty hatreds and rivalries between individuals that structure social encounters on-shore. Roderick can observe and report events on the one hand, and is determined by them on the other, but cannot exert any influence over them. In this, he is simply an example of the modern subject of history, but one that rails against the passive role ascribed to this subject:

> [T]his was the era [1688-1740, roughly] in which political thought became engrossed with the conscious recognition of change in the economic and social foundations of politics and the political personality, so that the *zôon politikon* took on his modern character of participant observer in processes of material and historical change fundamentally affecting his nature [...].[66]

If 'participant observer' describes the relation of the subject to history in modernity, Roderick represents a figure at once submerged and excluded from that modernity: one participating in it, causally determined by it, yet without any ability, even as a retrospective narrator, to observe and understand the general processes of material change that are doing the determining.[67]

I suggest, however, that this failure on Roderick's part to actually have an effect on the world around him, the way in which his rage itself is a reflex produced by the material world against which he rages, figures more specifically the failure of the opposition to Whig oligarchy in the 1730s and 1740s that I earlier described: a failure which might be seen as the moment when this new version of history as 'outside and impersonal forces' becomes naturalised in British political discourse.[68] Indeed, the shifting ground of politics in the 1740s is figured quite directly in the second half of the novel. It is here that we get the only explicit statements of anything resembling party allegiance on the part of Roderick-the-protagonist: 'I looked upon it [England], at this time, as the worst country in the universe for a poor honest man to live in', this time being shortly before the battle of Dettingen in 1743 (XLII.236); and, as Roderick discusses his options in England with Strap, he considers putting his satirical skills at the service of the (post-Walpole) ministry, in order to immediately dismiss this possibility: 'neither would I succeed

---

66   J.G.A. Pocock, *The Machiavellian Moment: Florentine Political Thought and the Atlantic Republican Tradition* (Princeton: Princeton University Press, 1975) 423.
67   See Joel Weinsheimer's comment, cited at p.64 above, that 'being a participant, consciousness registers history less as an intelligible meaning than as a senseless force which reduces its own autonomy and encroaches on its own power', 101.
68   Kramnick, *Bolingbroke and his Circle* 72.

in my endeavours to rise in the state, inasmuch as I could neither flatter nor pimp for courtiers, nor prostitute my pen in defence of a wicked and contemptible administration' (XLIV.254).[69] The account of English liberty with which he regales the Gascon Sergeant sounds very like Bolingbroke's in its emphasis on the continuity of independence in its struggle with the crown:

> those institutions of the English which are branded with the name of rebellion, by the slaves of arbitrary power, were no other than glorious efforts to rescue that independence which was their birthright, from the ravenous claws of usurping ambition. (XLIII.246)

However, this grandstanding of political orientation on Roderick's part prefaces its complex transformation in chapter XLV. The political debate in the ordinary, on Roderick's return to London, includes Medlar, 'a testy old gentleman', a 'trusty patriot, who had never been out of his own country, and drew all his maxims and notions from prejudice and hearsay' (XLV.260), and Medlar's rebuke to the critics of England ends:

> '—Why don't you take up your habitation in your beloved France, where you may rail at England without censure?'—To this the doctor thought proper to make no reply; and an unsocial silence ensued; which I perceiving, took notice, that it was a pity such idle disputes, maintained very often for whim or diversion, should create any misunderstanding among gentlemen of good sense; and proposed to drink down all animosity in another bottle. (XLV.263)

The silence that follows Medlar's suggestion indicates that this thought at least is anathema, and that they are *all* patriots, or even Patriots, at heart. Roderick's appeal to their shared 'good sense' is an appeal outside of politics, an appeal to the separateness of the social from the political that cancels out the frank equation of the two made by the satire of the first half of the novel. At the same time, Roderick's participation in this group hardly makes him a reliable judge of their relative merits: Medlar later reveals that the figures identified as 'the young prince' and 'the ambassador' are in fact an actor and a fiddler from Covent Garden, but when he presses Roderick for his own identity, Roderick resists, because he too, of course, is acting a part here (XLV.265–7).

---

69 Similarly, party political polemic does not figure among the genres in which Melopoyn struggles to make a living (XLII.384–5).

In consequence, *Roderick Random* can be seen to dramatise, not just the country critique of the new Britain, but the practical failure of that critique and its passage from politics into something else. I now want to suggest that the sudden generic jump from satire into romance in the last three chapters repeats within the novel the shift in the relation of writing to politics in the 1740s as a whole, a shift that as we have seen has already been thematized to some extent in the passages quoted above. I ended part one of this chapter by resisting the use of Frye's account of romance to homogenise this text, to turn it into romance and nothing else. I do however wish to appeal to Frye's association of romance with *fiction as such* in this instance, to his idea of wish-fulfilment, a dream of power over the world, as its underlying principle. For despite the apparent absence of any 'presiding principle' which 'organises the whole', despite the inability of Roderick or any other satirist-figure in this novel to exert any kind of agency in their society, despite the fact that *their* actions are determined by that society rather than vice-versa, nevertheless there is an agency at work in the text which guarantees its conclusion.[70] If romance here is an acting out of the will of an incomprehensible god, one that imposes a meaning on human characters *despite*, not because of, what they do or omit to do, that god is of course the author himself. And the agency of the author appears in the generic shift that gives this novel its happy ending. That which is referred to as providence by the characters (throughout the novel, but increasingly towards its end) refers to an agency which only such an author-figure can wield, for all the characters are shown to be similarly powerless in the face of their historical reality.

The responsibility of the author for a space that escapes history, rather than as an agency within that history, is exactly the function granted him or her by the shift in literary culture that we have seen emerging from the failure of the opposition in the 1730s and 40s. In other words, we can now see the relation of romance to the novel, not as a timeless generic possibility rooted in modes of a universal human experience as Frye describes it, but as produced by the changing function of writing in the West in the eighteenth century.

However, the ending itself is not the only sign of this authorial agency. For while the succession of events in this novel may appear

---

70   Damrosch 286 (cited above p.70).

arbitrary, random, as we read them, taken together they form a clear pattern. The location of the action moves from Scotland, to London, to the British navy, to a brief interlude in England (when Roderick first meets Narcissa), to the French army, to London and Bath, then (after the trip to Brazil) back to Scotland. In other words, Roderick's travels form a rough symmetry, with the second half of the novel (military service – English metropolis – Scotland) repeating the first half, but in reverse. Some other aspects of the novel reinforce this symmetry: each of the London sojourns ends with an inset narrative from a character with whom Roderick finds himself confined (Miss Williams, in the garret where they are curing themselves of syphilis, in chapters XXII–XXIII, and Melopoyn, in the Marshalsea debtors prison, in chapters LXII–LXIII); an improbable reunion with Thomson in Jamaica on Roderick's way back from his naval exploits in chapter XXXVI is balanced with an equally improbable reunion with Bowling in Boulogne on his way into the French service in chapter XLI.

If this structure sounds familiar, it is because it is very similar to the much more celebrated symmetry of *Tom Jones*, published a year after *Roderick Random*. Fielding's novel is of course much more precise and profuse in its symmetries. Where Fielding has six books in the country followed by six books on the road followed by six books in London, the periods of Smollett's first novel as I have mapped them out do not correspond closely in length. The sexual temptation and selfish deceit represented in Somerset by Moll Seagrim and Blifil respectively simply reappear in the fashionable guise of Lady Bellaston and Lord Fellamar in London: there is no comparable doubling of characters in Smollett. But in both cases the text makes a pattern which is invisible to the characters but visible to the reader, and which bespeaks an overall authorial control.

It is because the symmetry of its form has this function that the repeated episodes which most fully advertise it have the content that they do. Miss Williams' story and Melopoyn's share a thematics of reading and writing, address in some way or other the issue of the relationship of authors and readers to the text. Miss Williams' is a salutary tale of the terrible moral effects of the wrong sort of reading: she graduates from the freethinking philosophies of Shaftesbury, Tindal, and Hobbes, to an addiction to poetry and romance, which leads her to misrecognise the selfish intentions of a lover. From her sexual fall in this instance it is all, predictably, downhill. Melopoyn's story, on the other hand, is a narrative of frustrated genius: a determination to follow a vocation as an author has landed him in debtor's prison as surely as Williams' reading destined her for prostitution. In both cases, texts do not offer empowerment, but the reverse: female romance reading determines the consciousness of the reader, but the author himself is equally powerless in the marketplace where he must sell his wares. In other words, both tales explore the failure of writing to offer agency, as on the humanist model discourse is meant to do. Yet the tales sit in another relation to each other, as formal counterweights in a pattern which *is*, clearly, the product of authorial control over the text. The author uses these tales, that is, to reveal himself as the possessor of an agency denied to his characters.

I have suggested that the symmetrical structure of *Roderick Random* advertises authorial control in a similar way to the romance ending to which it turns the action. I have also argued that that ending fulfils an ideological function, as a fantasy of gentry restoration in the face of a historical reality that makes such a restoration impossible. It now becomes clear that the symmetry in which the whole novel is folded also participates in this wish-fulfilment. Symmetry in *Roderick Random* does nothing less than run history backwards in order to restore Roderick to his ancestral estate. The implications are twofold: only such a reversal makes this possible: that is, in the world of history, there is no going back; and only an author, only fiction, can make this happen, in the space opened up outside history by art.

At this point a return to the comparison with *Tom Jones* is once more useful. For the politics of the two novels are very similar in their valorisation of the squirearchy. There is nevertheless a formal gulf between them. For one thing, the narrator of *Tom Jones* is conscious of and identified with authorial control over the plot, and frequently comments on the fact to the reader. In *Roderick Random*, authorial agency is never raised to narratorial consciousness. The reader may perceive the pattern that Roderick's life has taken can only be accounted for by some authorial agency, but Roderick as narrator never refers to it. Similarly, and perhaps more crucially, the plethora of detail included in Fielding's novel is all, eventually, revealed as part of the pattern: authorial control is absolute. If we use the term 'historical' to name the particular, the contingent, the arbitrary, then Fielding's novel is not what it calls itself: a history. *Roderick Random*, on the other hand, includes a wealth of historical detail that remains stubbornly irreducible to the form imposed upon it. The vast majority of characters do not share in the special providence enjoyed by Roderick and a few around him, but appear as contingent facts of Roderick's world from which he ricochets. *Roderick Random* dramatises, not authorial agency, but the *gap* between authorial agency and the historical world for which it provides compensation. *Tom Jones* is the work of a novelist who has made his peace with history, with the new England, and is ready to naturalise the Country vision as that England's imaginary version of itself. Smollett, however resigned to the political powerlessness of the novelist, still wants to draw attention to the fact that such a vision is only imaginary. From this angle, *Roderick Random* appears as the demystification *in advance* of Fielding's project in *Tom Jones*.[71]

Earlier, I referred to the gap between the novel and its ending as the gap between realism or satire and romance, and refused to reduce the whole novel to a romance (at some generalised formal level) because to do so would be to erase the historical particularity of the society represented and the ideology informing that representation. But now it seems that the novel as a whole has a symmetrical structure which cannot be assimilated to Smollett's realistic/satiric enterprise, and of which the ending now appears to be simply the end point. Does it make sense to refer to this entire *form* as an exercise in romance? On the face of it, clearly not. Symmetry is not a property one associates with romance as a genre: Gawain's journey back from his encounter with the Green Knight is *not* like his journey out in reverse, for example; romance quests just aren't like that. At yet, in a most peculiar way, romance remains implicated in the symmetry of both *Roderick Random* and *Tom Jones*: and that is, in the appearance of romance *discourse* at the centre point of the symmetry, 'the keystone of the arch in the

---

71 Hence while I concur in John Richetti's identification, in an earlier essay, of Smollett's 'disaffection from the conservative ideology that governs Fielding's narrative practice in the special political context of mid-century Britain', I am arguing that the symmetry which Richetti misses grounds this disaffection in another type of conservatism, one more profound, and more profoundly pessimistic, than Fielding's. 'The Old Order and the New Novel of the Mid-Eighteenth Century: Narrative Authority in Fielding and Smollett', *Eighteenth-Century Fiction* 2.3 (April 1990): 183–196; 196.

mathematical centre of the novel', in both cases.[72] And in both cases, that romance discourse is gendered feminine.

In *Tom Jones*, the plot hinges on the scenes at the inn at Upton: this is the material centre-point of the book, before which Sophia is chasing Tom, and after which Tom will chase Sophia, and round which the incidents noted above are arranged. The most important action at Upton is (what will seem in brief retrospect, at least) Tom's moral nadir, when he sleeps with a woman, Mrs Waters, believed to be his mother; it is in this action that Tom's good-natured spontaneity allows him to break society's most fundamental taboo. I say in this 'action': part of the point of Tom's encounter with Mrs Waters is that she is positioned by the text as the agent in this scene, as the seducer and not the seducee. And her agency in this regard is figured in the language of romance, invoked by the narrator from the Graces:

'First, from two lovely blue eyes, whose bright orbs flashed lightning at their discharge, flew forth two painted ogles. But happily for our heroe, hit only a vast piece of beef which he was then conveying into his plate, and harmless spent their force. The fair warrior perceived their miscarriage, and immediately from her fair bosom drew forth a deadly sigh. A sigh, which none could have heard unmoved, and which was sufficient at once to have swept off a dozen beaus [...].'[73]

This kind of language is usually assimilated by critics into a generalised 'mock-heroic' discourse with which Fielding ironizes the quotidian reality he represents. However, it is noticeable that the most extended exercises in mock-heroic are deployed in this novel to describe instances of female initiative and action: for example, the 'Battle sung by the Muse in the Homerican Stile' fought by Molly Seagrim against assorted village girls in book IV chapter 8. And at Upton, it seems that female *sexual* initiative can only be represented in such ironic terms. However, the passage quoted above is quite distinct from the mock-Homeric language deployed elsewhere in the novel: heroines (in so far as there are any) in classical epic do not routinely reach for metaphorical

---

72 Martin C. Battestin, *The Providence of Wit: Aspects of Form in Augustan Literature and the Arts* (1974; Charlotteville: University Press of Virginia, 1989) 149.

73 Henry Fielding, *Tom Jones*, ed. R.P.C. Mutter (1749; Harmondsworth: Penguin, 1966) book IX, ch.5, p.455.

weapons in pursuit of a love-object. Rather, Fielding is here appropriating the language of romance, in the specific form most popular in his time and with which he would have been most familiar: seventeenth-century French prose romance and those English writers who drew on them, such as Aphra Behn, Delarivier Manley, and Eliza Haywood.[74] Nor is the relation of this discourse to its subject the same as in the case of the battle of the churchyard in book IV: for the mock-Homerics deployed there, the chapter-heading warns us, 'none but the classical Reader can taste', and such readers Molly and her friends clearly are not.[75] In contrast, amatory fiction of this type is *exactly* the kind of fiction that Mrs Waters is likely to read: and rather than being simply an exercise in narratorial irony, romance discourse here *could* be read as representing Mrs Waters' own subjectivity, as providing the terms in which she understands her own sexual agency in the seduction of Tom.[76] Reading the passage thus assimilates Mrs Waters to the figure of the female romance reader, morally corrupted by the wrong reading, that was a subject of ongoing concern at mid-century and whom we have already seen embodied in Smollett's Miss Williams. (The danger of such romances, it seems from both instances, is that they give women ways of imagining themselves *as agents*, which is both threatening for a patriarchal society, and potentially disastrous for the women themselves, as that society will simply not recognise that agency in point of law.)

In *Roderick Random* the centre-point of the novel's symmetry is a much more marked and extended deployment of romance topoi. Roderick's sojourn with Narcissa at her home is set apart from the picaresque text on either side of it by the sheer fortuitousness of the events that land Roderick there and remove him again (he is, quite literally, washed up there after the wreck of his ship, and the episode ends when he is equally abruptly kidnapped by smugglers from the same

---

74 'Despite the diversity in the different forms of "romance" available to the late seventeenth century, it appears that the French heroic romance was the hegemonic form [...] [which] set the generic norm for romance in general in France and Britain[...]. [T]he vital links that the heroic romance established between a gender (femininity) and a genre (the romance) [...] provided the aesthetic basis on which Behn, Manley, and Haywood were to enter the prose fiction market.' Ros Ballaster, *Seductive Forms: Women's Amatory Fiction from 1684 to 1740* (Oxford: Clarendon, 1992) 42–3.

75 Ibid. 172.

76 Special thanks to Abby Shovlin for suggesting this.

beach); and by its bracketing conversations between Roderick and Mrs Sagely, an old woman suspected of witchcraft by the locals. This generic helper-figure not only offers him advice on both occasions, but having heard his story, does not weep sentimental tears for his sufferings but 'drew a happy presage of my future life, from my past sufferings' (XXXVIII.213): in other words, at the very point in the novel from which it will run backwards to its happy ending, Roderick encounters a woman who knows that this is going to happen, the only such foresight in evidence in the whole text. It is she who advises Roderick to leave the country in their last conversation (before, typically, the choice is made for him); and it is she who advises that he approach the big house in the guise of a servant and conceal his gentle birth, 'for it was a maxim among most people of condition, that no gentleman in distress ought to be admitted into a family, as a domestick' in case he gets ideas above his present station (XXXVIII.216).

Roderick thus becomes a manservant in the household of Narcissa and her aunt, the only occasion in the novel when he takes on this role. However, the discourse of this episode empties his service of the political significance which we saw imbued in the master-servant relationship as represented elsewhere in the novel. For having fallen in love with Narcissa,

> I led a pretty easy and comfortable life, drinking daily intoxicating draughts of love from the charms of Narcissa, which brightened on my contemplation, every day, more and more.—Inglorious as my station was, I became blind to my own unworthiness, and even conceived hopes of one day enjoying this amiable creature [...]. (XXXIX.222)

The key word here is 'unworthiness': from the immediate context, Roderick seems to have in mind his 'inglorious' position as servant in Narcissa's household. Yet the word also carries with it its connotation of the unworthiness of the courtly lover for his beloved, and Roderick's service here is not at odds with his gentlemanly status precisely because Narcissa's presence translates it into these romance terms. Similarly, in the following chapter, Roderick finds the cook and the dairymaid have fallen in love with him, '[w]hile my thoughts aspired to a sphere so far above me' (XL.227): once again, any possible reference to a status-sphere here is subsumed within a romance rhetoric in which the beloved belongs in the ideal *metaphysical* sphere constructed in the poetry he has been writing for Narcissa.

In other words, Roderick here lives out the romance trope of the lover as servant, a trope that translates the love-relationship into status terms.[77] The three chapters at the centre of the novel belong to a different genre to those which fold around it: belong, that is, to romance. As well as forming the fulcrum of the symmetrical form that the novel will eventually turn out to have, these chapters, in their deployment of the tropes of romance, offer a promise of some ultimate form, of some end to Roderick's narrative, by reminding the reader that the heteroglot novel can jump from one genre to another if it pleases. And by making that promise through the invocation of this matriarchal idyll, form, closure, is gendered feminine. The form of *Roderick Random* in this way makes visible '"the feminine" as the organizing agent in culture' which Ballaster finds valorised in Scudéry's heroic romances.[78]

One other way in which the world of these chapters inverts the rules that operate outside is worth observing: it is only here that Roderick's education and literary skills are of any use to him, only here that these things matter. He is able to win Narcissa's attention by translating a passage in Tasso which had perplexed both Narcissa and her aunt (XL.223). Indeed, Narcissa's aunt is a crucial figure in this regard, a warning of the dangers and limitations not of female romance reading,

---

77 The most famous example of a romance lover disguised as the beloved's servant is I suppose Arcite in Chaucer's *Knight's Tale*: more relevant here is perhaps the mockery that this trope undergoes in Charlotte Lennox's anti-romance, *The Female Quixote*. Arabella, another female romance reader, decides that the new gardener simply *must* be a disguised gentleman in love with her: 'Having discerned so many Marks of a Birth far from being mean, she easily passed from an Opinion that he was a Gentleman, to a Belief that he was something more; [...] she remained, in a little time, perfectly convinced that he was some Person of Quality, who, disguised in the Habit of a Gardener, had introduced himself into her Father's Service, in order to have an Opportunity of declaring a Passion to her, which must certainly be very great, since it had forced him to assume an Appearance so unworthy of his noble Extraction.' Charlotte Lennox, *The Female Quixote, or, The Adventures of Arabella* (1752; Oxford: Oxford University Press, 1989) book I, ch.vii, p.22.

78 Ballaster 45. Summing up masculine objections to such romances from the likes of Pepys, Ballaster observes that '[T]he romance's corruption of history lay in its insistence on placing the heroine at its centre' (47). What works as a metaphor for Ballaster, *Roderick Random* turns into material reality; but the effect is not the *corruption* of history complained of by Pepys, but its aesthetic transcendence.

per se, as of female aspirations to learning and authorship. The aunt is in some ways a figure of the new literary culture emerging at mid-century in which women would play an important part: hence her fascination with the gothic ('her disposition was gloomy, and her imagination delighted with objects of horror') and the association of her authorship with a madness which seems to consist in sympathetic powers of identification gone too far: 'sometimes fancying herself an animal, sometimes a piece of furniture' (XXXIX.221). But she is ignorant, notes Roderick, of Latin and Greek; and Roderick's education puts him in a position of superiority in this regard, as well as his ability to translate more fluently from Italian. The vindication of Roderick's education here, that is, depends on the invocation of a feminized aesthetic sphere, and its simultaneous subordination to the restoration of the hero. Within that aesthetic sphere, Roderick's masculine education offers him a gender superiority that mirrors and replaces the status superiority that modernity has rendered meaningless.[79]

Given the location of this episode in the dead centre of the novel, from which it will move towards closure, and Mrs Sagely's role as prophetess of that closure, it is also worth noting that Narcissa's aunt, although a poet, can never actually complete the poems and plays that she begins ('which, as whim inspired, she had begun, without constancy or capacity to bring to any degree of composition': XXXIX.221). The world of the woman writer may appear here as a sign for closure, as a promise of ultimate form, but it is a closure and form that she cannot herself provide. Her significance lies rather in the generic autonomy of the world over which she presides from the historical world that surrounds it. It is this autonomy, this transcendence of the historical and its subordination to the rules of art, that the novel wishes to claim among its various generic resources; the novel thus turns the female writer and her world into the symbol of an authorship that is not her own.

I have up till now been proceeding on the assumption that the transcendence of the historical that romance claims can be taken at face value, as if as a genre it was innocent of already-inscribed political

---

79 In this way, Roderick's education fulfils the role of the aristocratic aura that in for example Aphra Behn shines through any disguise to confirm gentility as independent of the trappings of status, as a reality transcendent of contingent social fact. Indeed, his becoming a servant in this generic sense thus *confirms* his status position as only his relationship with Strap does elsewhere.

values. Yet as my earlier definition of romance as providential narrative put at the service of a class position implies, this is not the case. As my earlier mention of Behn, Manley, and Haywood as Fielding's immediate exemplars of romance writing might have reminded us, 'romance' in the first half of the eighteenth century was already gendered feminine, and was, further, a vehicle for various kinds of conservative critique of political modernity: Behn's Stuart panegyrics in the 1680s, for example, or Manley's use of scandal narrative as Tory satire in the first decade of the century.[80] I have discussed in this chapter two types of opposition writing, the humanist satire of the *Craftsman* campaign, and the Patriot myth-making that took its place. I have suggested that (male) opposition writers working within the sphere of public politics and party polemic shifted from one mode of writing to the other in response to their ongoing and apparently permanent alienation from power. But of course another literate group in society were suffering an ongoing and apparently permanent alienation from power: women.[81] The mid-century Patriot turn away from engagement with the historically particular and towards myth might be seen as a male repetition of a move already made by female conservative writers in their deployment of romance. In so far as *Roderick Random* acts out that turn, it represents it as an occupation

---

80   Ballaster quite explicitly replaces the aristocracy/bourgeoisie opposition, that governs most accounts of the Rise of the Novel since Ian Watt, with the party - political one of Whig and Tory, for her account of female romance-writing *before* the domestic ideology becomes hegemonic at mid-century and banishes women writers from such public concerns. John Richetti similarly observes that Manley's portrayal of aristocratic life in *The New Atalantis* (1709) is similar to Behn's 'except that Manley's [corrupt, Whig] grandees are placed quite deliberately within this ideological opposition that Pocock evokes', that is, between court and country: Richetti, *English Novel* 31. With regard to Manley, one might note that the other example of feminine authorship in *Roderick Random*, alongside the sentimental/gothic type represented by Narcissa's aunt, is precisely the scandal-monger working in the same punitive-satiric field as Roderick: his revenge on Odonnell is complete when his love-letters 'fell into the hands of a certain female author, famous for the scandal she has published; who, after having embellished them with some ornaments of her own invention, gave them to the town in print' (XX.107).

81   Ballaster argues convincingly that the sexual agency that amatory fiction allowed the woman reader to imagine was a displacement of that political agency denied them as women and their male Tory compatriots alike: hence 'it is tempting to suggest that the battle for control over sexual representation acts as an analogy for women's search for political "representation" or agency' (Ballaster 40).

of territory made available for opposition purposes by woman writers since the Restoration.

Indeed, there is much in Richetti's recent discussion of female-authored amatory fiction that is strangely reminiscent of *Roderick Random*, although, in his discussion of Smollett's novel in the same volume, Richetti himself does not make the connection.

> Amatory fiction in England would seem to have served precisely as an escapist distraction from mundane existence, and the extravagant intensities that this fiction habitually represents must have been, in practice, the compensatory opposite of an actuality that we can all recognise [...][82]

The move that *Roderick Random* makes in respect to such fiction would then appear as a repositioning of extravagant emotional intensities as a *response* to an actuality that we can in fact only recognise if we are familiar with the country party's representation of England under the Whigs. Once alert to the possibility that Roderick's satiric rage is a masculine version of an emotional powerlessness experienced by romance heroines, the following description of the feminine (Tory) subjectivity besieged by the rational self-interest of her (Whig) manipulators at the heart of the fictions of Behn and Manley is even more striking:

> [T]heir [the Duke and his Countess, in *The New Atalantis*] acquisitive and accumulative self-seeking is placed for scandalous shock-value next to the intensely spontaneous and malleable subjectivity of the innocent Charlot, whose lack of agency and passive capitulation in the face of her awakened sexual desire enact [...] a generalized and repeatable personality type [...]. Charlot is an object of psycho-sexual experimentation who reacts to external stimuli; in her helpless innocence she is a subject without agency and lacking a position relative to others from which she can negotiate or maneuver.[83]

While Roderick is just the opposite of innocent or malleable, nevertheless this reduction of the atomised subject to a set of physiological responses over which they have no control seems to me at the root of Smollett's conception of his hero, and one deployed to similar ideological purpose to Manley's heroine.

---

82   Richetti, *English Novel* 21.
83   Ibid. 36.

However, the encounter with Narcissa scarcely grants Roderick any more positive agency in the succeeding half of the novel than he had in the first. In Bath, for example, the impulse moving Roderick tends to be the appearance of Narcissa ('I am transported with desire', LVII.351; 'I [...] expressed myself with such transport and agitation, that my mistress, fearing I would commit some extravagance, rung the bell for her maid [...]' LVII.353) rather than his more usual rage at fortune ('At length my transport subsided, I became melancholy, and wept insensibly', LVIII.357), but the vocabulary is the same. However, another key word does decisively shift its meaning when it becomes attached to Narcissa:

> I grew mad with admiration! [...] She was startled at my ravings, reasoned down my transports, and by irresistible eloquence soothed my soul into a state of tranquil felicity; but lest I might suffer a relapse, industriously promoted other subjects to entertain my imagination. (LVI.346)

'Eloquence', as we have seen, is the name of that opposition discursive practice that at once summons the citizenry into being as a group and gives them a voice which can have an effect in the historical world. In keeping with its general revision and cancellation of the political, the second half of *Roderick Random* deploys this term to name instead the delusional, the manipulative, and the vulgar, in accordance with the critique of eloquence being made in the name of 'politeness' discussed by Adam Potkay in *The Fate of Eloquence in the Age of Hume*. Hence in chapter XLV, and in pretty quick succession, 'eloquence' is used by Roderick to try to seduce a young lady at the theatre ('I repeated my entreaty with all the eloquence and compliment I was master of', XLV.258); by the young lady when Roderick abandons her, realising that she is a prostitute ('Upon which she held forth against me with an eloquence peculiar to herself', 259: the familiar association of eloquence with what Strap calls 'Billingsgate' a page later); and the self-celebrating oratory of an incompetent general who owed his promotion to interest but whom the administration (in the face of Roderick's avowed opinion of it as 'wicked and contemptible') have rightly pensioned off ('the subject of war was introduced, on which the general declaimed with great eloquence, recounting many of his own exploits by way of illustration', 263).[84]

In the mouth of Narcissa, however, eloquence becomes a healing balm, able to calm Roderick from love-crazed mania into a state of tranquil felicity: into one capable of making polite enquiries about her aunt; indeed, into *politeness per se*, a mode of discourse at odds with Smollett's novel as a whole. Narcissa's eloquence is now this novel's moral agency, a replacement for the moral agency of satire (a mode within eloquence in its neo-classical opposition sense) which, as exerted by Roderick, was never really a mode of agency at all, and has in any case slipped into the background with the death of politics in the second half of this novel.[85] As such, Narcissa's speech takes on the task of civilising the uncouth gentry male so spectacularly achieved by the letters of Pamela Andrews: Narcissa's feminine moral agency is that of the emerging culture of sensibility in which Richardson was playing so large a part. We have seen Narcissa associated with the agency of the author by her formal position in the centre of the novel; when she appears within the satirised world that is Roderick's more usual habitat in chapters LV–LX, she has within that world an agency of her own. Just as this novel displaces its political critique into the wish-fulfilment of romance under the sign of the feminine, so even particular aspects of that critique, such as its understanding of 'eloquence' as a type of agency, are reapportioned to a feminized private sphere in a form emptied of public political significance. 'Eloquence' now names an essentially private mode of agency to be exercised by women in the reform of individual men.

One can see the shift in the relation of writing to politics mapped out by Sitter and Gerard as at once a problematic and an enabling one for the novel as a genre: for while poetry makes increasing claims to

---

84 Potkay comments that by midcentury, 'the high Ciceronian eloquence traditionally associated with the nobility comes to be seen not as a token of superiority but as a sign of vulgarity', and this is exactly the case here (Potkay 95).

85 Klein notes how in Shaftesbury's version of polite 'interpersonal interaction', 'the eloquence of senators was transformed into an all-embracing medium for society'; Potkay suggests that Hume's own doctrine of sympathy is derived from the descriptions of the orator's effect on his audience in classical handbooks of rhetoric, but displaced into private intercourse. It is exactly this transformation that is thematized at this point in *Roderick Random* (Klein, *Culture of Politeness* 198; Potkay 46).

historical transcendence, the novel must continue its claim to some kind of historicity. Its problem is to co-ordinate this historicity with an appeal to the extra-historical that will legitimate it as an art-form, as a participant in the emerging aesthetic sphere. But it is able to do this precisely because the novel was, from the start, a space in which different genres and codes and dialects can be brought together in the same literary space. Its very heteroglossia allows the novel to negotiate between history and transcendent values by translating them into generic terms. It is thus that we can place *Roderick Random* in its historical moment: not as another example of the mid-century abandonment of politics that Sitter describes, nor as a defiant continuation by other means of opposition writing, but as a space where satire and romance, the historical and the transcendent, powerlessness and agency, are juxtaposed and their respective territories mapped out, as legitimating elements of the novel. In other words, the split in literary culture that occurs in the 1740s and 1750s provides not just this novel's historical context but its content as well.

However, as we have seen, the genres which this novel co-ordinates come already *gendered* as masculine or feminine. The extra-historical sphere of romance through which the novel can claim its aesthetic status is associated both with the power of authorship to rearrange reality and with the feminine. It is not too much of an exaggeration to say that authorship itself now appears to the male novelist (perhaps the male writer generally), now that he is stripped of his public political role as satirist/historian, as a *feminine* agency: feminine, that is, precisely in its separation from the public sphere of politics and history. This is certainly a perception that Smollett shares with Scott, in the next decisive renegotiation of the gender and genre relations of the male-authored novel, in the 1810s and 1820s.

4. *Humphry Clinker*, gender, and the discourse of society

Between 1748 and 1814, however, the discursive landscape within which the novel is located alters dramatically with the emergence of a new discourse of history and society which we have already seen lurking in simple form in pro-Ministry writing in the 1730s and 1740s. Before turning to Scott, who most influentially appropriates this discourse for the novel, it is worth examining Smollett's own response to this shift in a novel published in the year of Scott's birth, *Humphry Clinker*.

This novel, Smollett's last, repeats the move away from satire staged in his first. The satirist figure is now a middle-aged man, but his response to vice remains a spontaneously physical one. As this response takes the form of gnawing illness, rather than explosive rage (Bramble comments, 'I find my spirits and my health affect each other recip-rocally—that is to say, every thing that discomposes my mind, produces a correspondent disorder in my body', London, June 14; 154), Bramble is even more conspicuously helpless than Roderick in the face of the viciousness of the society around him. However, his membership of the gentry unquestionable, and accompanied by a family group over which he enjoys (not unchallenged) patriarchal authority, Matthew Bramble has leisure, unlike Roderick, to anatomise social evils of which he is not otherwise the victim. For nearly half the novel, Matthew Bramble haunts the public spaces of a metropolitan England now ablaze with the conspicuous consumption made possible by Britain's mid-century imperial successes, and 'where he picks up continual food for ridicule and satire' (Jery, Bath, April 24; 33). The target of his satire is just this increase in 'luxury', so feared in the civic humanist tradition for its ability to disengage individuals from their public duties; and the breakdown of distinction between the social classes that this allows.

> All these absurdities arise from the general tide of luxury, which hath overspread the nation, and swept all away, even the very dregs of the people. Every upstart of fortune, harnessed in the trappings of the mode, presents himself at Bath, as the very focus of observation—Clerks and factors from the East Indies, loaded with the spoil of plundered provinces; planters, negro-drivers, and hucksters, from our American plantations, enriched they know not how; agents, commissaries, and contractors, who have fattened, in two successive wars, on the blood of the nation; usurers, brokers, and jobbers of every kind; men of low birth, and no breeding,

have found themselves suddenly translated into a state of affluence, unknown to former ages; and no wonder that their brains should be intoxicated with pride, vanity and presumption [...]. [A]ll of them hurry here to Bath, because here, without any further qualification, they can mingle with the princes and nobles of the land.

[...][T]his will ever be the case, till the streams that swell this irresistible torrent of folly and extravagance, shall either be exhausted, or turned into other channels [...].[86]

Bramble finds, in Bath, the great image of this breakdown of class distinction are the waters of the spa itself. Just as social collapse makes Bramble physically ill, so the supposedly healing waters are in fact a medium for the physical breakdown of the boundaries between individuals, which are broken down, circulated, and reingested in the pump-room.

[W]e know not what sores may be running into the water while we are bathing, and what sort of matter we may thus imbibe [...].

I can't help suspecting, that there is, or may be, some regurgitation from the bath into the cistern of the pump. In that case, what a delicate beveridge is every day quaffed by the drinkers; medicated with the sweat and dirt, and dandriff; and the abominable discharges of various kinds, from twenty different diseased bodies, parboiling in the kettle below [...]. (Matt Bramble, Bath, April 28; 46)

The waters at Bath are an image of that 'tide' or 'stream' of luxury that Matt Bramble sees among its people: the problem of disintegrating class distinctions is translated into a problem of disintegrating bodies.

A little earlier, they meet a doctor who argues scientifically that this process is actually good for you, and that

he himself (the doctor) when he happened to be low-spirited, or fatigued with business, found immediate relief and uncommon satisfaction from hanging over the stale contents of a close-stool, while his servant stirred it about under his nose [...]. In short, he used many learned arguments to persuade his audience out of their senses; and from stench made a transition to filth, which he affirmed was also a mistaken idea, in as much as objects so called, were no other than certain modifications of matter, consisting in the same principles that enter into the composition of all created essences, whatever they may be [...]. (Jery, Bristol, April 18; 18)

---

86   Tobias Smollett, *The Expedition of Humphry Clinker*, ed. Lewis M. Knapp (1771; Oxford: Oxford University Press, 1966): Bramble, Bath, April 23; 36–7. All citations are of this edition and give writer, location and date of letter as well as page numbers.

This is Smollett's satire at its most Swiftian; the corruption of the senses is an index of the corruption of society as a whole, and modernity, here in the guise of natural science, is seen as engaged in the denial of the physical and the instinctual and the reversal of natural processes altogether. The Bath doctor here is a direct descendent of the scientist whom Gulliver meets at the Royal Society of Lagado:

> His employment from his first coming into the Academy was an operation to reduce human excrement to its original food, by separating the several parts, removing the tincture which it receives from the gall, making the odour exhale, and scumming off the saliva. He had a weekly allowance from the Society of a vessel filled with human ordure, about the bigness of a Bristol barrel.[87]

In *Gulliver's Travels* this functions as a satire on science: but in *Humphry Clinker*, as we have seen, this reversal has become institutionalised at the heart of social life, as well as medical practice, in the spas of Bath.

However, my interest here is less in Smollett's satiric strategies themselves (lacking as they do the party-political edge that remained sharp in *Roderick Random*) as with the fate of satire as a mode in the overall scheme of the novel. For here, as in *Roderick Random*, the centre of the novel is occupied by a move away from the scene of satire and into a generically different world. The place occupied by Roderick's service in Narcissa's household in the earlier novel is here occupied by Scotland itself. If Roderick there found himself in a world where all the usual rules of insult and revenge had been suspended, Bramble too undergoes nothing less than a miracle cure on crossing England's northern border. Within 24 hours of arriving in Edinburgh, we find him writing this: 'I now begin to feel the good effects of exercise—I eat like a farmer, sleep from mid-night till eight in the morning without interruption, and enjoy a constant tide of spirits, equally distant from inanition and excess [...]' (Bramble, Edinburgh, July 18; 219). Why does this happen?

One answer returns us to the specifics of Smollett's political situation, this time in the 1760s. Smollett had spent a large part of that

---

87   Jonathan Swift, *Gulliver's Travels* (1726; Harmonsworth: Penguin, 1967) book III, ch. v, p.224.

decade defending the Bute adminstration – the first British ministry to be headed by a Scot – from the attacks of John Wilkes, who did not scruple to fill the pages of the *North Briton* with anti-Scottish prejudice, at a time when English memories of invasion by a mostly Highland Jacobite army were still pretty fresh. On publication, *Humphry Clinker* was immediately identified as an attempt to 'vindicate the Scots', in Horace Walpole's words. It does this in part by representing Scotland, and particularly Edinburgh, as a pre-capitalist idyll of unquestioned social hierarchy and stability, one which allows the social mingling of the Leith races, including the formal saturnalia of the cawdies' banquet, without any sense that this is eroding the differentiation of status-groups (described by Jery, August 8; 226–7). There is, however, another, generic answer, which accounts for the particular shift in discourse of Bramble's and Jery's letters on entering Scotland. The most immediately striking symptom of this shift returns us, I'm afraid, to ordure. We saw how attitudes to human waste in Bath functioned as an index of the corruption of that society. But in Edinburgh, that most famously shitty city, we get none of this. The undifferentiated crush of humanity in Edinburgh is not condemned, and the custom of emptying chamber-pots into the street at night he classes as

—A practice to which I can by no means be reconciled; for notwithstanding all the care that is taken by their scavengers to remove this nuisance every morning by break of day, enough still remains to offend the eyes, as well as other organs of those whom use has not hardened against all delicacy of sensation.

The inhabitants seem insensible to these impressions, and are apt to imagine the disgust that we avow is little better than affectation; but they ought to have some compassion for strangers, who have not been used to this kind of sufferance [...]. (Bramble, Edinburgh, July 18; 218)

Attitudes to excrement are no longer evidence of corrupt senses or intellectual decay: they are to be understood as part of a set of customs, specific to the society in which Bramble finds himself. He is no longer the satirist, with a personal, moral (even *physical*) stake in the society around him: he has become instead a detached *sociological* observer. This is the role he continues to fulfil for the remainder of his stay in Scotland, and it is one that his nephew also adopts. Bramble describes the distinct nature of Scottish Law, education, and religion; Jery describes Highland society in the aftermath of the '45; and Bramble continues with thoughts on northern agriculture and the rise of Glasgow as a commercial centre, on improvement, industry, and colonisation. We are given a mass of sociological and economic information on Scottish society, conceived of as a whole, whose various classes and activities have to be understood in their mutual interrelation.

It is in a letter from the Highlands that the sources of this new perspective become clear. Clan life, Bramble writes, is organised

> on something prior to the *feudal system*, about which the writers of this age have made such a pother, as if it was a new discovery, like the *Copernican system*. Every peculiarity of policy, custom, and even temperament, is affectedly traced to this origin [...]. The connection between the clans and their chiefs is, without all doubt, *patriarchal.* (Bramble, Sept 6; 254–5)

At first this seems like a rejection of the periodized history, and specifically the totalizing claims of stadial history which traces 'policy, custom, and even temperament' to forms of economic organisation. But Bramble, it turns out, is in fact only rejecting the specific stage to which Highland social organisation is attributed, and proceeds to attribute it to another period, *within* the terms of Scottish Enlightenment historiography. It is in this novel, after all, that Bramble famously describes Edinburgh as 'a hot-bed of genius' and in which he meets Hume, Robertson, Smith and Ferguson, among others (Bramble, August 8; 233). Bramble and Jery adopt the discourse of speculative history to describe the country in which it is being developed, and in the case of the Highlands, the society whose difference from commercial lowland Scotland provided some of the impetus for that development.

In other words, once the Bramble party move to Scotland, the discourse of Swiftian satire is replaced by the discourse of Hume's 'human science' in this novel's representation of society. The improvement in Bramble's health comes about not simply because Scotland has not yet been corrupted by luxury. In addition, the shift from satire to social science results in the suspension of those moral categories deployed in the representation of society by Bramble in England; his health, previously tied to those categories, improves as a consequence. The novel shifts, that is, from a humanist version of history, where the historically specific is analysed in terms of a recurring moral problem (the luxury consequent on imperial conquest), to an Enlightenment account of History, in which historically specific societies are categorised in economic and sociological rather than moral terms. The suspension of the moral categories of satire is also the suspension of the body's direct implication in the society around it; Bramble's subjectivity becomes that of the detached observer, an almost disembodied observer, that constructs that society as an object of knowledge, not of moral judgement. Bramble thus regains his health: but it should be noted that he does *not* gain any more agency over the society around him than he did in England. To be a detached observer of a society is to accept, as a grounding epistemological principle of your science, that powerlessness over your object that was forced on the satirist by contingent political developments.

So far I have restricted my discussion of *Humphry Clinker* to its male correspondents. But before I examine the female voices in this novel, I want to look at the role of gender in the discourse of the men; for the place of women is one of the aspects of Edinburgh society commented upon by Bramble. The sanitary arrangements (or lack of them) that characterise Edinburgh in Bramble's letters are not simply a matter of the organisation of public space, as they are in Bath, but rather of the differentiation between public space and a sanitised, private space that comes under feminine government. Of tenement apartments in the Old Town, Bramble observes,

[T]he stair being common to them all, is generally left in a very filthy condition; a man must tread with great circumspection to get safe housed with unpolluted shoes—Nothing can form a stronger contrast, than the difference betwixt the outside and the inside of the door; for the good-women of this metropolis are remarkably nice in the ornaments and propriety of their apartments, as if they were resolved to transfer the imputation from the individual to the public. (Bramble, Edinburgh, July 18; 217–8)

John P. Zomchick observes that in Bath, filth found its way back through the human body: here, the individual finds his way through the filth. We have seen how, in Scotland, the masculine body is emptied out of its own implication in the public world around it and has become instead simply the site from which a knowledgeable gaze can be cast on that public world; the feminine equivalent of this process is a strict demarcation between the public world, a space of potential contamination, and the domestic space from which contamination has been expelled. But while these two shifts are equivalent, they remain different, and their consequence is a reinforcement of gender distinction in the organisation of social space.[88] A man can keep his distance from a degraded public world by turning it into an object of knowledge even while remaining within it; a woman, on the other hand, must be removed altogether into the private space of the home. Hence the comparatively few letters sent from Scotland by the women writers in this novel. However, note also that this demarcation between the private and public accords women an effective moral agency within the former that the men do not enjoy in the latter. Women can clean up the house, it seems, where Bramble, for all his rage, could do nothing about the filth infecting the public spaces of Bath.

It is this sharp distinction between a masculine public sphere and a feminine private one that mediates the various solutions that the novel offers to the problems that remain outstanding when the Bramble party return south. Most obviously, it allows Bramble to consolidate his power over the family and its domestic economy in Wales, as his sister Tabitha's energies are diverted into their proper course by her courtship and marriage of Lismahago. But more fundamentally, it allows for the problems of luxury and the consequent collapse of status distinctions that so afflicts Bramble to be recast in terms of a family narrative, and thus as the sort of problem that can be solved by the plot of a novel. The last volume of the novel does this most clearly in two ways: through the figure of Humphry Clinker himself, and in the restoration of the Baynard estate. I will take these in turn.

One of the ways in which Tabitha's authority within the family group is satirised as unnatural is through the confusion between the human and the animal that ensues. On the journey to London on which the Bramble party first encounter Clinker, Tabitha, left in charge of seating arrangements on the coach, gives her lap-dog Chowder a place of its own opposite the squire himself. 'I could scarce refrain from laughing when I looked into the vehicle, and saw that animal sitting opposite to my uncle, like any other passenger. The squire, ashamed of his situation, blushed to the eyes [...]' comments Jery (London, May 24; 79). Such a confusion is of course a conventional element in the rhetoric of satire,

---

88 '[T]he corruption [of Edinburgh] is dissociated from the people, who are paragons of order within their own private spheres. Society is parcelled into orderly households [...].' John P. Zomchick, 'Social Class, Character and Narrative Strategy in *Humphry Clinker*', *Eighteenth-Century Life* 10 (1986): 179.

with the fourth book of *Gulliver's Travels* once again providing an example. The confusion becomes crucial to the plot on this journey, for it is Clowder's snap at Bramble's manservant, and the ensuing row, that leaves that position vacant; but Tabitha objects to Clinker filling this place, on account of his poverty and nakedness: she calls him a 'mangy hound' (Jery, London, May 24; 85) and demands his dismissal, and it is this demand that prompts Bramble's demand that Chowder be abandoned instead. This does the trick: Tabitha meekly gives up the dog in London, and Humphry Clinker stays on as Bramble's man-servant. The restitution of the animal/human hierarchy is dependent on the restitution of masculine authority over female members of the family: the gender hierarchy is as natural, the implication is, as that between species.

The struggle over Chowder and Clinker is, however, also important for the novel in what it does to the *class* hierarchy within the family group. For Tabitha is not the only one to assimilate servants to animals: for all the fun he has at Tabitha's expense, Jery has to be restrained by his uncle from giving the servant who insults her 'a good horse-whipping for his insolence' (Jery, London, May 24; 80). And most disturbing of all is Clinker's classification of himself in this regard. Clinker himself later offers an unexpected challenge to Bramble's authority over the family, when he appears to seduce the women-folk into Methodism. Bramble, implicitly paralleling his own position as head of the family with that of the King as head of the national church, objects to this: 'What you imagine to be the new light of grace [...] I take to be a deceitful vapour, glimmering through a crack in your upper story—In a word, Mr Clinker, I will have no light in my family but what pays the king's taxes, unless it be the light of reason, which you don't pretend to follow' (Jery, London, June 10; 138). For as well as being another threat to his domestic authority, this is also, obviously, an inversion of the class hierarchy that says that the gentry should be able to dictate the religion of their servants and not vice-versa. But this displaced political struggle between establishment and dissent is resolved by its safe discharge into the domestic: all three women, it turns out, are only attending chapel in the course of various matrimonial schemes (Win Jenkins in pursuit of Clinker himself, Lydia as part of a match-making scheme on the part of Lady Griskin, Tabitha in the delusion that she might win the target of this scheme, Mr Barton, for herself). Once this is revealed as the source of their interest in Methodism, Clinker is left free to practise his religion as much as he likes.

What is interesting to us here are the terms in which Clinker, in the meantime, submits:

> I'm bound to love and obey your honour—It becometh not such a poor ignorant fellow as me, to hold dispute with gentlemen of rank and learning—As for the matter of knowledge, I am no more than a beast in comparison of your honour; therefore I submit; and, with God's grace, I will follow you to the world's end [...].
> (Jery, London, June 10; 139)

We are faced here with exactly the same problem as in the case of Strap in *Roderick Random*: Clinker is just *too* devoted a servant, and, as with Strap, there is no indication in most of the text whether this is some kind of mistake or not, and certainly no hint that Clinker is being ironic when he says this. Bramble, like Roderick, gives this loyalty his full approval; yet, especially given the prevailing attitude to the relative rights of servants and animals exhibited by Tabitha and Jery, Clinker's equation of *himself* with an animal here remains profoundly disturbing. The (unsatisfying) solution offered by *Roderick Random* is to restore hero and servant alike to a pre-capitalist idyll distant enough from reality for Strap's loyalty not to seem out of place. The equally unsatisfying, but significantly different, solution offered by *Humphry Clinker* is to transform Clinker, not into a feudal retainer, but into a blood-relation. The function filled in the earlier novel by a fantasy restoration of pre-modern emotional bonds between master and servant is here taken over by sentimental bonds within the private family. For Clinker is, of course, Bramble's natural son. This is the explanation the novel offers for his otherwise degrading subjection to Bramble: he is not degrading himself before a master, but submitting to the natural authority of a father.

The consequences of this discovery on Bramble's perception of himself are enormous. The real threat to Bramble's authority remains, throughout the novel, feminine sexuality: the women's drive for marriage and children, most obviously in the case of Tabitha, but also in Lydia's illicit affair with 'Wilson' in Gloucester which sends them off on this journey in the first place. Indeed, the very existence of Lydia and Jery, the children of Bramble's other, deceased, sister, is a consequence of this unreasonable feminine fertility: Bramble grumbles on the very first page of the novel, 'As if I had not plagues enough of my own, those children of my sister are left me for a perpetual source of vexation—what business have people to get children to plague their neighbours?' (Bramble, Gloucester, April 2; 5). Aileen Douglas notes that 'Bramble's reading of his body [...] depends upon, and defines itself against, negative versions of female physicality.'[89] The bodies of the women are in fact consistently defined in terms of their ability to procreate. Bramble's is at first a register for the social ills around him, and then pretty much vanishes altogether in Scotland. But now Bramble's body is revealed in a third guise: as itself fertile, as itself the source of a child who has, through the parish's obligation to care for it, plagued his neighbours. The explanation of Clinker's loyalty in terms of an idealized patriarchal bond between father and son has the paradoxical effect of eroding the distinction between Bramble's body and those of the women on which he had been so insistent. Displacing the social problem of master-servant relations into the family appears here to be a feminizing move.[90]

The second case in which social or political problems are solved by being displaced into the family is that of Bramble's old friend, Baynard, whom he visits at his country home on the way back to Wales. The place is on the point of bankruptcy, and the reason is the wife that Baynard married, for her money, after he had frittered away his own inheritance.

> Baynard had flattered himself [...] that she would chearfully enter into his views, which were wholly turned to domestic happiness[...]. This, however, was a visionary scheme, which he never was able to realize. His wife was as ignorant as a new-born babe of everything that related to the conduct of a family; and she had no

---

89 Aileen Douglas, *Uneasy Sensations: Smollett and the Body* (Chicago: University of Chicago Press, 1995) 163.

90 Douglas notes that Bramble is already feminized by his hypochondria, a condition that early-modern medicine understood as the male equivalent of hysteria (176-8). One could argue that Bramble's role as theorist of the social world in Scotland is put in tension with privacy by the letter form itself; epistolary form, argues Elizabeth Heckenhorn Cook, 'puts into play the tension between the private individual, identified with a specifically gendered, classed body that necessarily commits it to specific forms of self-interest, and the public person, divested of self-interest, discursively constituted, and functionally disembodied. This is the citizen-critic who is the proper subject of the Republic of Letters.' *Epistolary Bodies: Gender and Genre in the Eighteenth-Century Republic of Letters* (Stanford: Stanford University Press, 1996) 8.

idea of a country-life [...]. [H]er ruling passion was vanity, not that species which arises from self-conceit of superior accomplishments, but that which is of a bastard and idiot nature, excited by shew and ostentation [...]. (Bramble, Sept. 30; 286–7)

His wife's money came from an uncle in the East India trade; in this, and in her passion for 'show and ostentation', Mrs Baynard acts out the role of the nouveau-riche mob at Bath and London, spending their money on the house, on furniture, new gardens, carriages, liveried servants and so on, all for the purpose of outward display. The consequence is the same as that observed by Bramble earlier: the breakdown of distinctions between status-groups. He discovers that Baynard

had two neighbours who, like himself, were driven by their wives at full speed, in the high road to bankruptcy and ruin [...]. The views of the ladies were exactly the same. They vied in grandeur, that is, in ostentation, with the wife of Sir Charles Chickwell, who had four times their fortune; and she again piqued herself upon making an equal figure with a neighbouring peeress, whose revenue trebled her own[...]. [O]ne large fortune, and three moderate estates, in a fair way of being burst by the inflation of female vanity [...]

[...] I believe it will be found upon enquiry, that nineteen out of twenty, who are ruined by extravagance, fall a sacrifice to the ridiculous pride and vanity of silly women [...]. (Bramble, Sept. 30; 293–4)

The barriers being eroded here are between the gentry and the aristocracy rather than between the gentry and the bourgeoisie, but the cause, the luxury produced by the influx of wealth from the empire, is the same. There are two conspicuous differences. Firstly, luxury, ostentation, is now described as a specifically *feminine* vice, whereas in Bath, it was '*men* of low birth, and no breeding' (36, my italics: see above, pp.88–9), the heads of families, who were held responsible. Secondly, where in Bath Bramble was complaining about the breakdown of a fairly abstract (if Tory-inflected) notion of proper social hierarchy, here in the country we are offered a concrete alternative, a realisable ideal with which the moral decay of these families can be contrasted: 'domestic happiness' and 'the conduct of a family.'

The opposition being deployed here is just that which Nancy Armstrong has identified as grounding what she calls the domestic ideology developed in the course of the century in conduct books for women:

> As the conduct books represent them, such activities [idle aristocratic amusements] always aimed at putting the body on display, a carry-over from the Renaissance display of aristocratic power. For a woman to display herself in such a manner was the same as saying that she was supposed to be valued for her body and its adornments, not for the virtues she might possess as a woman and wife.[91]

The problem with Mrs Baynard and her friends is that they engage in precisely the sort of public display that Armstrong describes, to the detriment of the private, interior space of the home. This is an exact inversion of the feminine economy that Bramble discovered in Edinburgh, where the public world, the street and the shared stairwell, were disregarded, but domestic spaces were spotless, under the management of the good-*women* of Edinburgh. *Humphry Clinker's* answer to the corruption of social spaces by imperial wealth, that is, is the marking off of a private space for which women are responsible, one made immune from that corruption by the domestic virtues of the women in charge. There is a shift in the site of moral argument from the crowded public spaces of the Bramble party's first sojourn in England to the private space of the gentry *or* middle-class home in the closing chapters (the distinction is one of the things made irrelevant by this shift, precisely in so far as the domestic ideology develops as the ground of a new hegemonic class alliance between the land-owning and trading classes in the second half of the eighteenth century). And this shift, transferring moral authority from a failing public culture into the hands of women who will then use it to rescue their men-folk and families from that corrupt public world, repeats exactly the transfer of 'eloquence' in *Roderick Random* from coffee-house, opera-house, and street, where it was a means of exerting power over others to selfish ends, into the mouth of Narcissa, where it is used to reform Roderick.

Smollett, of course, appeals to this feminine domestic authority only in order to immediately transfer it into the hands of men: for in place of the complex plot developments of a novel by Burney or Austen of the type analysed by Armstrong, Smollett simply kills off Mrs Baynard, allowing Bramble to rally her widower's (male) friends to rescue his by now deeply indebted estate. The novel ends by restoring a patriarchal idyll both on the Baynard estate and on Bramble's own, both firmly

---

91 Nancy Armstrong, *Desire and Domestic Fiction* (Oxford: Clarendon Press, 1987) 75.

under masculine control. The appearance of the spendthrift fashionable lady as figure in the latter part of the novel certainly casts Tabitha in a new and contrastingly sympathetic light, but she is not granted authority over the Bramble household on their return for all that. *Humphry Clinker* invokes feminine domestic authority only the more firmly to enclose it within the overall authority of a restored patriarchy.

However, in examining the plot developments that allow Smollett to address social problems within family circumstances, that is Baynard's estate and Bramble's paternity of Humphry Clinker, we have seen that both involve the feminization of Bramble in one way or another. Bramble is able to exert power of any kind only by abandoning the male-gendered public world of history (whether humanist or enlightenment) and entering a domestic sphere that we have seen to be gendered feminine. The family, in fact, takes on the role that romance occupied in *Roderick Random:* it is the space outside history in which patriarchalism and social hierarchy can be recovered from their erosion outside. This might seem an incidental point, since it does not significantly qualify the authority that Bramble is left with at the end of the novel; were it not for the fact that the space of the family, used in this way as the site of moral agency, is not also the site of the female-authored domestic *novel*. For the very domestic ideology that we have seen is invoked here had also legitimated the woman-authored novel as an aesthetic form: where the woman novelists to which *Roderick Random* glanced, Behn, Manley and Haywood (at least in her earlier career) were figures of the public world and increasingly seen to be morally corrupt as a result, a new generation of women novelists had arisen since 1748 who were able to adopt quasi-public careers as writers precisely because their writing was devoted to propagation of *private* virtue.[92] Jery observes this development when he

---

92 'The redefinition of womanhood included a reappraisal of women's proper authority, and women were now seen as having a legitimate authority within the private sphere: including domestic life, emotions, romance and the young girl's moral welfare. When the private sphere became the central concern of a literary genre, women's authority extended to that too.' Jane Spencer, *The Rise of the Woman Novelist: From Aphra Behn to Jane Austen* (Oxford: Basil Blackwell, 1986) 21. This feminine authority in literature accompanied the withdrawal of literature from its active involvement in party politics that we examined in *Roderick Random*: 'this feminization of literature defined literature as a special category supposedly outside the political arena' (Spencer xi).

meets a group of writers at the house of one Mr S, a representation of Smollett himself. One struggling hack there

> had made shift to live many years by writing novels, at the rate of five pounds a volume; but that branch of business is now engrossed by female authors, who publish merely for the propagation of virtue, with so much ease and spirit, and delicacy, and knowledge of the human heart, and all the serene tranquility of high life, that the reader is not only inchanted by their genius, but reformed by their morality. (Jery, London, June 10; 127–8)

Jery is noticing here the rise to cultural prominence of the female author which accompanied the rise of the domestic ideology. I want to end my discussion of *Humphry Clinker* by suggesting that just this type of feminine authority appears here in the letters of Lydia Melford.

On the face of it, Lydia seems of all the women the most obedient to Bramble's rule, earning the love and devotion of both her uncle and brother on the journey, and not expressing her sexual desire in the disruptive ways of her aunt Tabitha (in the way she dresses) or Win Jenkins (in the accidental but deeply revealing double-entendres of her semi-literate writing). Instead, she distances herself from these two:

> My dear Willis, I am truly ashamed of my own sex—We complain of advantages which the men take of our youth, inexperience, insensibility, and all that; but I have seen enough to believe, that our sex in general make it their business to ensnare the other [...]. In point of constancy, they certainly have nothing to reproach the male part of creation [...]. (Lydia, Glasgow, Sept. 7; 259)

For much of the novel, it would be easy to see Lydia as an extra-dutiful daughter (or at least niece) equivalent to Clinker's hyper-obedient son. This is the line taken by Aileen Douglas, for whom, in contrast to the 'raging force of female sexuality' represented by Tabitha and Win, Lydia 'can be accommodated within the patriarchal economy because [...] she will never articulate her own desires.'[93]

However, it is Lydia's sexual desire that sends the whole party on its gallivant in the first place, as a means of removing her from the Gloucester milieu where she is conducting an affair with the travelling player, Wilson. Alongside the recovery of the long-lost son, the element that *Humphry Clinker* most obviously borrows from romance is the

---

93   Douglas 170, 171.

outcome of this affair: for of course Wilson turns out to be in fact the eminently eligible George Dennison, and Lydia's falling in love with him becomes retrospectively a recognition of that aura of gentility that shines through the conventional disguise and reveals him to her from the start as 'not what he appears to be' (Lydia, Clifton, April 6; 9). What I want to point out here is that Lydia *never* in fact abandons her devotion to Wilson under the pressure exerted on her by the men of the family. In the first letter of the novel, Bramble describes his anger at what has happened at Gloucester and their flight to Bristol: this letter is dated April 2. Our first letters from Lydia include the two following passages:

> —I am still persuaded that he [Wilson] is not what he appears to be: but time will discover—mean while I will endeavour to forget a connexion, which is so displeasing to my family [...]—My uncle, who was so dreadfully passionate in the beginning, has been moved by my tears and distress; and is now all tenderness and compassion; and my brother is reconciled to me on my promise to break off all correspondence with that unfortunate youth [...]. (Lydia, Clifton, April 6; 9–10)

> —O my dear Letty! what shall I say about poor Mr Wilson? I have promised to break off all correspondence, and if possible, to forget him: but alas! I begin to perceive that will not be in my power[...]. I beseech him not to write to me, nor attempt to see me for some time; for considering the resentment and passionate temper of my brother Jery, such an attempt might be attended with consequences which would make us all miserable for life— (Lydia, to her friend Letty Willis, Clifton, April 6; 10–11)

There are some striking differences in the accounts that Letty writes to her old schoolmistress and to her friend and confidant. In the first instance, she will try to forget Wilson; in the second case, she has already given up trying to forget him, which suggests that she hasn't tried very hard; in the first case she mentions her promise to break off her correspondence with him, but in the second case she is quite explicit that this is only a temporary measure, adopted not because her male mentors have told her to, but because of the danger of lethal violence from her brother if she maintains contact with Wilson. Lydia constructs different versions of her situation in order to maintain different types of relationships with different correspondents: rather than simply reporting reality, as Bramble's and Jery's letters do, Lydia's letters are her mode of agency. Compare this to Bramble description of Lydia's behaviour:

[...]but, she's deficient in spirit, and so susceptible—and so tender forsooth!—truly, she has got a languishing eye, and reads romances.

[...] Thinking it was high time to remove her from such a dangerous connexion, I carried her off the very next day to Bristol; but the poor creature was so frightened and fluttered, by our threats and expostulations, that she fell sick the fourth day after our arrival at Clifton, and continued so ill for a whole week, that her life was despaired of [...]. You cannot imagine what I have suffered, partly from the indiscretion of this poor child, but much more from the fear of losing her entirely. This air is intolerably cold, and the place quite solitary [...]. (Bramble, Clifton, April 17; 12, 14)

Bramble plans to set out for Bristol on the morning of the third; four days from their arrival is the seventh, the day after Lydia writes her two letters. But those letters do *not* sound like they were written on the point of emotional and physical breakdown. Rather, the ease with which Bramble turns himself into the sufferer in this crisis suggests that he is rather projecting his own 'deficiency in spirit' onto his niece, perhaps as a way of dealing with his guilt at the bullying tactics, the 'threats and expostulations', which he has inflicted on her. These threats and expostulations never work: Lydia never gives up her attachment to Wilson, even during their prolonged separation.

Of course, Lydia sometimes describes herself in similar terms to those used here by Bramble: 'I am such a faint-hearted timorous creature!' she whimpers at one point (Oct 4; 309). But to take this self-categorisation at face value, as Douglas does, is to miss the extent to which Lydia knowingly adopts the rhetoric of Richardsonian sentiment: these are exactly the terms in which Pamela or Clarissa describe themselves, and open to the same observation, that the rhetoric of powerlessness is in fact an expression of a profound will-to-power; that the correspondence in which the feminine subject describes herself in this way is in fact a means whereby she defends her own subject position against the assaults of the powerful males around her. The Richardsonian mode is useful to Lydia because the correspondence between two young women as represented in *Clarissa* and *Sir Charles Grandison* allow the heroine to create for herself, in their writing, an identity over and against the one being imposed on her by the men around her. Douglas takes Lydia's comment to Letty Willis, 'You know my heart, and will excuse its weakness' (Bath, April 26; 41) as a refusal by Lydia to express herself at all, as if she had no story to tell in the first place;[94] but on the contrary, in its evocation of a heart trans-parent to the female correspondent as it is not to others, and of the shared morality that is the result, this comment sums up the way in which the textual relationship between the two young women allows them to construct their own version of reality, a definition of themselves independent of the definitions forced on them by their patriarchs.[95] The epistolarity of Lydia's writing, that is, while it allows Smollett to (occasionally) slot it in alongside that of her uncle and brother, is of an entirely different generic order; where the male writing participates variously in satire and the epistolary travel narrative in vogue in the eighteenth century and which Smollett had himself written, Lydia's writing is that of a type of *novel*.[96]

This generic status of Lydia's writing is something outside of Bramble's conceptual scheme. When he tells Lewis that she 'reads romances' as another piece of evidence for her girlish vulnerability, he is misunderstanding the possibilities of genre in 1771, for romance plots had by now been appropriated by women novelists, as by Richardson, in novels that assumed a degree of feminine moral autonomy. When Lydia is finally reunited with Wilson/Dennison, Bramble tells us that she

> blushed, and trembled, and faultered—'To be sure, sir, (she said) it is a very surprising circumstance—a great—a providential—I really know not what to say—but I beg you will think I have said what's agreeable.' (Bramble, Oct. 11; 330)

Douglas reads as self-abnegation on Lydia's part what is clearly a joke, a clever discursive move by Lydia in the odd situation of finding her private discursive world brought suddenly into harmony with the world of power outside her; finding herself, that is, the heroine of a romance. When the conventions of fiction are abruptly realised in your own life, it

---

94 Ibid. 171.

95 One could pull any number of examples of similar moments from *Clarissa*: 'I shall think I have reason to be highly displeased with you, if, when you write to me, you endeavour to keep from me any secret of your heart' (Anna to Clarissa, letter 37); 'But of this I assure you, that whatever interpretation my words were capable of, I *intended not* any reserve to you. I wrote my heart, at the time—' (Clarissa to Anna, letter 38). Samuel Richardson, *Clarissa; or The History of a Young Lady* (1747–8; Harmondsworth: Penguin, 1985) 174, 176. I will comment further on feminine epistolarity in the following chapter.

96 And, it seems, of a predominantly female-authored novel, the example of Richardson notwithstanding: see Spencer 4 and 33, note.

seems reasonable to refer your auditors to the conventions that they already know, just as Letty Willis could be relied on to know the contents of Lydia's heart. Lydia's joke, in other words, is on the conventionality of the situation in which they all find themselves at this point in the plot; on the conventionality, indeed, of that plot itself. This is the more striking given Lydia's hesitant reference to 'providence' here: for her first letter to Letty, quoted from above, continues, '—let us trust to time and the chapter of accidents; or rather to that Providence which will not fail, sooner or later, to reward those that walk in the paths of honour and virtue'(Clifton, April 6; 11). Lydia's model of Providence owes less to the Old Testament and more to those romances that Bramble tells us that she reads; and as in *Roderick Random*, what the sudden providence of the romance plot signals is authorship itself:

> [...] in three weeks or a month, if no unforeseen accident intervenes, your friend Lydia Melford, will have changed her name and condition—I say, if *no accident intervenes*, because such a torrent of success makes me tremble!—I wish there may not be something treacherous in this sudden reconciliation of fortune—I have no merit—I have no title to such felicity! (Lydia, Oct. 14; 335)

Such passages make another joke out of the conventionality of such an outcome: no accident intervenes, indeed, because there are no accidents in the romance plot. At moments like these, Lydia can be seen as herself a critic of the conventionality of her own story.[97]

Further, it is important here, as in her admission of timorousness, not to take Lydia's claims of undeservingness at face value. Roderick Random, after all, is genuinely undeserving of the happy ending which his author gives him; but Lydia has in fact in her own correspondence acted out just that domestic ideology which the novel as a whole comes to affirm. For Lydia's virtue is established not by her obedience to her uncle, but by her self-definition in opposition to the fashionable world to which Mrs Baynard submits, and ultimate rejection of this world. Lydia's story, after all, is of a young provincial woman (a 'country hoyden' as she calls herself: May 31; 94) who goes to the great metropolis; who enjoys (unlike her uncle) its pleasure gardens,

---

97   These last two letters from Lydia, a pair to Letty and then Mrs Jermyn, even gesture at the sort of symmetry we found in *Roderick Random*, as they repeat and reverse the order of the first two.

assemblies and routs; is brought under the questionable guidance of 'a person of fashion' as she calls Lady Griskin (94); but who is also able to reject the fashionable world for that of true feeling:

> I wish my head may not grow giddy in the midst of all this gallantry and dissipation; though, as yet, I can safely declare, I could gladly give up all these tumultuous pleasures, for country solitude, and a happy retreat with those we love; among whom, my dear Willis will always possess the first place in the breast of her ever affectionate
> Lydia Melford (London: May 31; 94–5)

> Nature never intended me for the busy world—I long for repose and solitude, where I can enjoy that disinterested friendship which is not to be found among crouds, and indulge those pleasing reveries that shun the hurry and tumult of fashionable society—Unexperienced as I am in the commerce of life, I have seen enough to give me a disgust to the generality of those who carry it on. (Lydia, Oct. 4; 308)

Lydia learns this from her own experience, not from the instruction of her uncle or brother: that is, Lydia is just that autonomous feminine moral subject that Nancy Armstrong describes as becoming the paradigm case of moral subjectivity in the eighteenth-century novel. It is thus that Lydia takes her place within this novel as a figure for the sort of female authorship which Jery discovers is establishing a moral hegemony over the novel form itself, for Lydia is herself an embodiment of the domestic virtue that the Baynard case can only establish by giving power to men. I have already argued that a Richardsonian epistolarity is useful to Lydia; I further, more tentatively, want to suggest that this rhetoric was useful to Smollett, as a metonym for female authorship in general, and, specifically, that of the domestic novel. In including this, rival type of novel within his own, Smollett acknowledges the moral authority that domestic fiction now enjoyed, since it is the type of domestic virtue that Lydia comes to embody in her letters which provides *Humphry Clinker* as a whole with its closure: the private sphere which Smollett's novel ends up legitimating as the site of morality is one that comes under feminine authority.

In this chapter, I hope I have demonstrated the extent to which Smollett begins and ends his career as a novelist engaging with the work of female predecessors and contemporaries, and appropriates feminine modes of writing, either romance or the domestic epistolary novel, as a space within his texts where successful moral agency can be imagined.

The need to imagine such agency comes, in *Roderick Random*, from the general retreat from the idea of writing as itself a form of agency within the public, masculine world of party politics, consequent on the changing nature of politics itself in the modern state. In *Humphry Clinker*, it comes from a broader shifting of discursive boundaries consequent on the parallel rise of the human sciences and the domestic novel, the one naturalising a historical world of impersonal forces that had before been felt to be the product of a degenerate moment in the life of the nation, the other preserving moral agency within a feminized domestic sphere. In both novels, we see the male-authored novel developing not autonomously, but in a state of continuing dialogue with its female-authored predecessors and contemporaries. Indeed, one of the remarkable things about *Humphry Clinker* is the extent to which it appears to *anticipate* later developments in the novel. Lydia's story itself is strikingly similar to that of another, later, heroine of the 1770s: Frances Burney's Evelina Anville. In retrospect, the anxieties Jery discovers among London hacks about the feminine (re)appropriation of the novel seem premature, since it is in the last three decades of the eighteenth century that the women-authored novel finds a new respectability in the hands of Burney, Charlotte Smith and others. It is the achievement of these writers and those that followed them that forms the background for my discussion of Scott in the following chapters. For Smollett's use of the novel to negotiate the boundaries between sociology and domestic virtue, between knowledge and ethics, is just the move that Scott repeats nearly half a century later in his effort to re-masculinize the novel form itself.

2 Enlightenment, agency, and romance in Scott's *Guy Mannering*

In this chapter I wish to develop my argument, begun with my discussion of *Humphry Clinker*, that the male-authored novel only appropriates enlightenment models of social organisation and historical development by also appropriating the discourse of female-authored fiction to signify a space outwith the social and the historical as thus constructed; a space which was also necessarily the novel's own, if it was to claim any kind of privileged aesthetic status over and against the texts of science. In particular, I want to argue that the sophisticated co-ordination of these discursive spheres achieved in Scott's second novel, *Guy Mannering* of 1815, not only uses the epistolary mode of domestic fiction in just this way, but that the feminine agency thus evoked cannot be reduced to the magical or primitive agency associated with romance narrative. In doing so, I am arguing against the equation of romance with narrative form made by Northrop Frye and Frederic Jameson and discussed in my introduction.[1] For as we shall see, the subsumption of agency by plot, while fulfilling a compensatory or redemptive function in the face of history as described by Jameson and Frye, also involves an effacement of another sort of agency within the novel; involves, that is, the silencing of a discourse which represents a genuine resistance, however compromised or limited, to a discourse of historical determination. I will, however, channel my argument with Jameson and Frye through a debate with Ian Duncan, who in *Modern Romance* provides a usefully extended and detailed reading of *Guy Mannering* from a broadly Jamesonian position. As in Jameson, romance form is here *opposed* to history as the promise of the possibility of the human subject's realisation in the material world: Scott's novels 'pose the status of their discourse [...] upon a radical tension between the record of historical experience and the conventional forms, derived from the miscellaneous tradition of romance, which make that experience

---

1   See above, pp.27–9.

coherent to the needs of the imagination.'[2] At the same time, however, Duncan suggests that romance form *mediates* between history and human desire: 'Romance reproduces itself as the figure of mediation and synthesis [...] between fatal historical fact and extravagant spiritual possibility.'[3] Now this is a problem: for if the realm of imaginative freedom from the historical world is already *embodied* in romance, then romance appears to mediate between historical determination and ... *itself*. This, because despite following Jameson's inversion of Frye's critical priorities (romance here is always historically located and politically effective), Duncan uncritically assumes Frye's version of romance as at once a particular type of plot structure and also the principle of absolute agency. So while Duncan shows that romance plot in Radcliffe subsumes and replaces any individual agency within that plot as that which guarantees a happy ending, Duncan himself subsumes any agency at work in a novel as always already an instance of romance.

I suspect that the rhetoric of mediation crops up in Duncan's argument as the trace of another version of romance that I shall be developing here: as occupying a third space which is neither that of agency nor of historical knowledge, but of the aesthetic. This is the position hinted at in Michael McKeon's brief but suggestive comments on the return of conservative ideology to romance form for its expression in the later eighteenth century and the coincidence of this with the rise of the idea of an aesthetic sphere autonomous from both politics and the demands of overt didacticism. It is only within this sphere that realism of Scott's kind can emerge: 'Realism [...] validates literary creation for not being history but history-like, "true" to the external reality that still makes a difference, but also sufficiently apart from it (hence "probable" and "universal") to be true to itself as well.'[4] In this chapter I want to argue against McKeon that, rather than the aesthetic being that reality to which this novel is accountable, the boundaries of art and reality are clearly demarcated here, and coincide with the distinction between plot and discourse; and, against Duncan, that agency is figured in *Guy Mannering* as distinct from romance, if not quite independently of romance. Only by thus understanding romance

2   Duncan 109.
3   Ibid. 15.
4   McKeon 120.

plot as authorised by this newly autonomous aesthetic sphere, and thus fulfilling a third function independent of both knowledge and ethics (McKeon's 'truth' and 'virtue'), can we see just what sort of mediatory or synthetic work romance plot has to do in this novel. Romance revives as a third, mediating term, certainly, but that which it mediates is no less than the separation of cognitive and ethical discourses which is the mark of modernity itself.

1. Ideology and science

The romance plot of *Guy Mannering* stages a Tory-nostalgic ideology of feudal continuity in the face of economic and social upheaval – in the face, that is, of modernity. The Bertrams of Ellengowan, the Dumfries-shire family on whose fate the action hangs, represent a gentry in decline since a violent medieval heyday, but in the period of the novel their decline is accelerated by an unscrupulous bourgeois, the lawyer Gilbert Glossin. Glossin eventually gains control of old Bertram's affairs and forces a sale of the estate at which his is the only offer. It is also Glossin who arranges for Bertram to be made a Justice of the Peace, in which capacity Bertram himself becomes the agent of economic rationalisation, cracking down on previously connived-at smugglers, poachers, and itinerants. The damage to the social fabric is mourned in the organic imagery of Burkean conservatism:

> Even an admitted nuisance, of ancient standing, should not be abated without some caution[...]. The 'long-remembered beggar', who for twenty years had made his regular round within the neighbourhood, received rather as an humble friend than as an object of charity, was sent to the neighbouring workhouse. The decrepid dame, who travelled round the parish upon a hand-barrow, circulating from house to house like a bad shilling, which every one is in haste to pass upon his neighbour; [...] even she shared the same disastrous fate[...].
>
> These things did not pass without notice and censure. We are not made of wood or stone, and the things which connect themselves with our hearts and habits cannot, like bark or lichen, be rent away without our missing them. The farmer's dame lacked her usual share of intelligence, perhaps also the self-applause which she had felt while distributing the *awmous* (alms,) in the shape of a *gowpen* (handful) of oatmeal, to the mendicant who brought the news. The cottage felt

inconvenience from interruption of the paltry trade carried on by the itinerant dealers [...]. (I.vi.93–5)[5]

The same emphasis on the function of even the lowest social classes in generating a social and economic 'neighbourhood' occurs in the novel's lengthy discussion of the gypsies. They are not only makers and menders of petty household goods, but also carriers of the traditional superstitious lore of the area. One of the forms of occasional service they give the landowner in return for toleration is the legitimation of his family's continued authority in terms of this lore: the older women 'blessed the bridal bed of the laird when he married, and the cradle of the heir when born' (I.vii.105). We first meet Meg Merrilies, matriarch of those long-established on Bertram's land, when she arrives at Ellengowan to perform just this latter function. And from then on she looks out for little Harry Bertram in his many infant escapades, even after her family has begun to suffer by the suppression of smuggling: 'Upon these occasions he was generally brought back by Meg Merrilies, who, though she could not be prevailed upon to enter the Place of Ellengowan after her nephew had been given up to the press-gang, did not apparently extend her resentment to the child' (I.viii.113). However, this personal loyalty to the old family does not save her tribe. When the five-year-old Harry disappears, Meg falls under suspicion, and her whole clan is driven onto the road shortly after.

Young Bertram has in fact been kidnapped by the surviving partisans of free trade, and is raised in ignorance of his gentle origins as Vanbeest Brown, a merchant in the Netherlands, before ending up as a volunteer with the British army in India. After twenty-two years and several adventures, the romance plot of *Guy Mannering* returns him to his paternal lands: he is recognized, confronts his abductor face to face, the *arriviste* Glossin is driven out, and the Bertram family re-established on its ancient grounds. But in order to do so, the plot returns him to the attention of Meg: she is the one who recognises him, who legitimates his identity and leads him home, just as she did when he was a child. Meg's traditional knowledge not only legitimates traditional social hierarchy and produces it as an aspect of an organic society; it is also an agent of the restoration of that hierarchy and that society, through its function in

---

5   References to *Guy Mannering* give volume, chapter and page numbers for the first edition (Edinburgh: Archibald Constable and Co., 1815).

a romance plot. A conservative organicist political ideology is reaf-firmed by a narrative form that is itself conservative in its recuperation of an original social unity and organicist in presenting a member of the lowest social caste as the agent whereby this restoration can take place. A traditional knowledge does the work of recognition within a plot which will reassert traditional social forms. *Guy Mannering*, thus described, seems to be founded in just that 'analogical structure of questions of truth and virtue' which grounds the explanatory and problem-solving power of the novel as a genre for McKeon.[6]

The culmination of Meg's intervention in the plot is her return with Brown back to the wood at Warroch point, from which he was kidnapped as a child and where his companion, Frank Kennedy the gauger, was murdered. Meg's action here is however the second attempt to explain what happened on that day. The first is conducted by the lawyer Pleydell in volume I chapter x (he is not identified by name as being the investigating Sheriff here until volume II chapter xvi). It is positivistic: discrete instances of the material world, including a subject reduced by murder to an instance of the material world, are interpreted as the effects of posited material causes. The narration follows the investigation's point of view:

> [...] a deep cut in the head, which, in the opinion of a skilful surgeon, *must have been* inflicted by a broad-sword. [...] [T]he folds [of his neckerchief] were also compressed, *as if* it had been used as a means of grappling the deceased [...]. It *seemed* plain, from the appearance of the bed [of rock], that the mere weight of one man [...] *could not have* destroyed its bias [...]. (I.x.152–3, 155: my italics)

and so on. The investigation as a whole proceeds back in the same way from Kennedy's corpse to the place where he was thrown from the cliff to the place where he was ambushed. But little in the way of conclusions can be drawn: no-one is convicted of Kennedy's murder, and the boy is not found. The reader, too, is left none the wiser, for the narrator gives us no privileged information about the events of that day.

And indeed never does. To be told what happened, the reader has to wait until volume III chapter xiv. Meg's journey takes the opposite geographical course to Pleydell's: it retraces the route of the boy's abduction, moving through the wood to the cliff, and ends when Bertram

---

6   McKeon 22.

descends to confront his kidnapper, Hatteraick, in the cave at the bottom. But Meg insists that 'We maun go the precise track' (III.xiv.279) because she is taking the opposite route to Pleydell in another sense as well. This is not a drawing of deductions from a collection of facts, but a concrete act of remembering, of reliving a traumatic event from the past, both on the part of Meg, and of the young man that she guides.

> Bertram's brow, when he had looked round the spot, became gloomy and embarrassed. Meg, after uttering to herself, 'This is the very spot,' looked at him with a ghastly side-glance,—'D'ye mind it?'
> 'Yes!' answered Bertram, 'imperfectly I do.' (III.xiv.280)

It is clear that empirical facts, determined through the identification of cause and effect relationships, are not Meg's concern here. Even the fact of Bertram's true identity is not at issue here, for she has been convinced of that all along. Rather, this retracing of the primal event is a way of *undoing* that event and of *giving* Bertram that social identity. The discovery of causality at work in the world is thus contrasted with the ability of subjects to act as causes themselves, to freely intervene in the world around them in order to realise a set of social values.

Just as Meg's intervention here puts into practice a whole cognitive regime, that of traditional knowledge, so the empiricism of Pleydell is an instance of another, that the text thus sets in opposition to Meg's: that of enlightenment science. By naming this cognitive regime 'science' all I wish to evoke is the very wide eighteenth-century use of this term to name any empirical enquiry, but especially that study of human societies discussed in my introduction.[7] Pleydell is, in fact, one of a group of male

---

7   I have borrowed this opposition between scientific knowledge and traditional knowledge from Lyotard's *The Postmodern Condition* because the emphasis placed there on the role of narrative in traditional knowledge offers a clue for understanding the relation of Meg's knowledge to the romance narrative structure that it serves and thus the role of that structure in the text as a whole. '[T]he speech acts relevant to this form of knowledge are performed not only by the speaker, but also by the listener, as well as by the third party referred to. [...] [A] narrative tradition is also the tradition of the criteria defining a threefold competence – 'know-how', 'knowing how to speak', and 'knowing how to hear' – through which a community's relation to itself and its environment is played out. What is transmitted through these narratives is the set of pragmatic rules that constitutes the social bond' (21). This function of traditional knowledge is exactly what we have seen fulfilled by Meg: she does not repeat a fact to a passive hearer, but makes him

characters who together thematize this broad 'Science of Man' in *Guy Mannering*. The young Mannering himself, who we first meet on a walking tour at the time of Harry Bertram's birth, is not merely an idle traveller but one 'curious to investigate the manners of the country' in which he finds himself (I.v.81); his very name announces the centrality of this enlightenment interest in social forms to the novel. He collects folk-songs, making his own verse-paraphrase of one of Meg's (I.iv.64–5). He is the curious observer of a society from which he is himself detached, the unseen spectator of Foucault's classical *episteme*: 'While Mannering was gazing round the ruins, he heard from the interior of an apartment on the left hand the voice of the gypsy he had seen on the preceding evening. He soon found an aperture, through which he could observe her without being himself visible [...]' (I.iv.63). Meg and her culture become the objects of Mannering's enlightenment gaze.[8] Mannering's friends exhibit the same enlightenment interests: Mervyn prefaces a letter with a dissertation on the right to defend one's property in civil society (I.xvi.253–6), and Pleydell, now practising at the Edinburgh bar, is able to introduce Mannering to all the illuminati of the Athens of the North on his visit there. The empiricism of Pleydell's investigation in chapter x, while it might seem only incidentally linked to these rather grander perspectives, in fact picks out just that which distinguishes this nascent human science from the traditional knowledge of someone like Meg: namely, a particular concern with tracing chains of cause and effect (see Introduction). Pleydell's very profession puts him in that class who, along with the moderate clergy, were the driving force behind speculative endeavour in eighteenth-century Scotland, and he indeed explicitly opposes Meg's mode of action to that of the law: 'The devil take the bedlamite old woman [...] will she not let things take

---

tell the story himself by re-enacting and remembering it. In doing so, she (re)constitutes the social bond, turning the wandering, atomised Vanbeest Brown into the socially-constituted Henry Bertram, Laird of Ellengowan, as the merely denotative function of Pleydell's speech (or Mannering's or Mervyn's) never could.

8   '[N]atural history [...] exists as a task only in so far as things and language happen to be separate. It must therefore reduce this distance between them so as to bring language as close as possible to the observing gaze. Natural history is nothing more than the nomination of the visible'; and for Foucault, natural history is the paradigm example of the classical *episteme* (Foucault 132).

their course, *prout de lege,* but must always be putting in her oar in her own way?' (III.xiv.271).[9]

So far we have examined two contrasting cognitive regimes as they are thematized in the actions of Meg and Pleydell. Within the story, it is Meg's traditional knowledge that is shown to be efficacious in preserving community, the latter understood in Burkean organic terms: the scientific approach of the gentlemen of the novel proves unable to restore the rightful heir. Given my characterisation of their human science above, and indeed its role in *Humphry Clinker,* one can already see why this might be. For a scientific discourse of society is by definition a value-free discourse of society: to understand social relations in terms of cause and effect is necessarily to suspend any moral judgement on those relations, and thus any grounds for intervening on behalf of one set of relations or another. My argument thus seems to have much in common with Ian Duncan's when he comments that Pleydell is limited to 'retrospective, rationalizing and explanatory' activity as opposed to Meg's 'performative word of mouth'.[10] However, his prior allocation of all agency, of agency per se, to the realm of romance means that Pleydell and his friends as well as Meg can be subsumed by the romance plot as 'two groups of helpers or donors', and this narratological equivalence allows Duncan to efface the incommensurability of the cognitive regimes they represent.[11] This in turn

---

9   For the centrality of Scottish Law, lawyers, and the legal system to the culture of the Scottish Enlightenment, see Anand C. Chitnis, *The Scottish Enlightenment: a Social History* (London: Croom Helm, 1976) chapter 4; Neil MacCormick, 'Law and Enlightenment' in R.H. Campbell and Andrew Skinner, eds., *The Origins and Nature of the Scottish Enlightenment* (Edinburgh: John Donald, 1982) 150–166; and Peter Stein, 'Law and Society in Scottish Thought' in Rosalind Mitchison and Nicholas Phillipson, eds., *Scotland in the Age of Improvement* (Edinburgh: Edinburgh University Press, 1970) 148–168. Chitnis describes lawyers as 'like a hub of a wheel in the eighteenth century, with spokes going out to touch most areas of élite activity' (75). Their effects on theoretical history came 'through the concern that legal and non-legal intellectuals had for the Law as a social discipline [...]. [For example,] Adam Ferguson was one of the intellectuals who saw that law, in its intimate connection with property, would necessarily be an instrument in the hands of the wealthy and powerful. As their composition changed so too might the Law' (85–6).
10   Duncan 130, 131.
11   Ibid. 117.

116

allows Meg unproblematically to replace Pleydell and Mannering and fulfil their purposes.

Enlightenment science is not so easily subsumed by the romance plot as this suggests (and given the problematic status of narrative for enlightenment thought identified by Lyotard, it would be surprising if this were otherwise). This is clear if we turn our attention from the plot, from *récit*, to the discourse of this novel. For it is the scientific discourse of these men, and not Meg's, that constitutes the bulk of the narrative discourse itself. At times, indeed, it is hard to distinguish narratorial judgement from that of Mannering; for example, the statement that

> It is disgusting also, to see the scenes of domestic society and seclusion thrown open to the gaze of the curious and the vulgar; to hear their coarse speculations and jests upon the fashions and furniture to which they are unaccustomed,—a frolicksome humour much cherished by the whiskey which in Scotland is always put in circulation on such occasions. (I.xiii.213)

might seem to be the narrator's opinion as well as the hero's, (especially given the general knowledge of Scottish life exemplified in the last sentence that seems to imply a more general acquaintance with Scottish manners than Mannering could have at this point in the story). Until, that is, we return to it aware that Brown's estimation of Mannering as 'an oppressive aristocratic man' made just before (I.xii.203) is borne out in the opinions of others. Then it seems less a report on the nature of the scene, than an admission of the limitations of Mannering's point of view. The interpenetration of the classes, the multiplicity of voices that so offends Mannering, is a principal feature of Scott's text itself, as it is of all the Waverley Novels. As in *Humphry Clinker,* the conservative politics of the novel's principal narrator are undercut by the relativizing of his perspective by alternative points of view: by the discursive enactment in the text itself of the social heterogeneity of which he complains. Indeed, Matthew Bramble is the obvious precedent for Scott's embittered middle-aged hero with a hidden sentimental side who discovers a resolution of his personal unhappiness in Scotland.

Similarly, in thematic terms, Scott's novel itself deploys the wide-ranging anthropological curiosity of its gentlemen heroes. In my first quote above, for example, the account of the social effects of Bertram's innovations includes attention to the traditional custom of giving *awmous* (alms) in the shape of a *gowpen* (handful) of oatmeal to

117

beggars, giving us both the local terms, and a translation for the benefit of the educated metropolitan reader. This translation is the same in kind as Mannering's tidy paraphrase of Meg's song, and it is indeed this paraphrase, and not any putative original, that the novel gives us. But the narrative discourse of *Guy Mannering*, more explicitly than any of the novel's characters, deploys a general schema of enlightenment stadial history within which the socially particular that is the object of their attention can be placed. In the narrator's ironic disparagement of the Bertrams' feudal past ('They had made war, raised rebellions, been defeated, beheaded, and hanged, as became a family of importance, for many centuries', I.ii.17) the irony is at once at the expense of the Bertrams, and at the expense of a previous and unenlightened age: this *was* the behaviour that became a feudal overlord, as defined by his place in a feudal economic order. The Scottish Enlightenment grand narrative of a stadial history informs the novel's understanding of the decline of the Bertram family under the new commercial dispensation.

This has two consequences for the novel. In the Introduction and in the previous chapter we saw how the rise of an enlightenment discourse of society problematizes the status of human agency in general. Hence, to class the enlightenment gentlemen of the novel as agents alongside Meg, as Duncan does, is to efface a defining powerlessness produced by their inhabiting this type of discourse. I shall return to the question of agency shortly. In the meantime we must note that this historical perspective is one restricted to these gentlemen: it is not shared with the folk whose culture it explains. The second effect of both translation and socio-historic context is the production of this society as an object of knowledge, and of the reader as an enlightened subject who stands outside of a society which is, however, entirely transparent to him; a situation we have already seen figured in Mannering's peering at Meg through a hole in a wall. This scientific objectivity is clearly at odds with the Burkean conservatism that seems to be *Guy Mannering's* governing ideology: while the romance *récit* recounts the restoration of an organic social whole, the enlightenment discourse enacts its society's fragmentation into the knowers and the known.[12] This contradiction is

---

12   In Lyotard's terms, 'Even in the case of the human sciences, where it is an aspect of human conduct, the referent is in principle external to the partners engaged in scientific dialectics' (26).

especially marked if, like Duncan, you see this organic community as in itself a romance trope, a Shakespearean 'green world': it is clearly also, at the same time, a particular historical society represented in proto-anthropological terms. The 'absorption' of history into romance at the level of plot is contested by the absorption of Meg, figuring romance, into the discourse of history.

2. Plot and discourse

This split between plot and discourse becomes even more pronounced when we examine the omissions of the latter in mediating the former. Until Bertram comes under Meg's control, he functions as the young Mannering functioned, as a wandering viewpoint allowing the reader an objective-seeming portrait of an alien culture, in this case the society of Dandie Dinmont's Liddesdale (in volume II chapters ii–v). In other words, he is a function of the novel's cognitive discourse. After his first encounter with Meg, his function is very different: it is his own identity that is in question, an identity which, when discovered, will make him a member of society rather than its external observer. In volume II chapter vii, Meg systematically strips Bertram of his old identity in preparation for his accession to his new one. He is forced to give up the portmanteau with all his identifying documents, leaving him 'unprovided with means of establishing his own character and credit' (II.vii.115). In return, he is given a purse full of stolen gold; this exchange placing him outside the law, as soon his shooting of Hazlewood will do even more dramatically. His adoptive father is dying of the bullet-wound inflicted by Mannering during the smugglers' attack on his new residence, Woodbourne: his new father-figure has killed the old one, for his ordeal, deprived of a father and outside the law, will only end when he is rescued from prison, at Meg's instigation, and brought to his future father-in-law, Mannering, at Woodbourne.

It is however in the circumstances of Bertram's initial encounter with Meg that the comparison with the younger Mannering is most clearly made. He finds her in a ruined tower, at night, when he is lost, by following the light from 'a long narrow slit or loop-hole, such as are usually to be found in old castles. Impelled by curiosity to reconnoitre the interior of this strange place before he entered, Brown gazed in at this aperture [...]' (II.vi.85). Here we have a quite exact repetition of Mannering's position in volume I chapter iv that we identified it as a synecdoche for his detached cognition of events.[13] Bertram is reduced to observing events through a small opening in a wall or partition; once more that of a ruined castle, once more the protagonist is on the outside looking in, and once more it is Meg who is the object of interest. This makes two differences between the scenes all the more striking. In the first scene Meg is telling a new-born child's fortune as she sings: and the new-born child is of course Bertram. In the second scene she is watching over a dying man, and then, again singing, preparing the body for the grave: the deceased turns out to have been Bertram's pirate foster-father in Holland. In both cases, Bertram's own identity is just what is at stake in the scene that is observed. Hence, where Mannering can retreat from the scene, maintaining his position of detached cognitive subject, Brown is taken within the chamber by Meg and under her control.

For Mannering's original retreat from Meg's sooth-saying is more than a physical one. Meg is of course not the only character to predict the crises in little Harry Bertram's life at the start of the novel: the subtitle of *Guy Mannering* is *The Astrologer*. The kidnapping and the Indian trauma (the duel between Mannering and Brown, the subsequent capture of Brown and the death of Mannering's wife) are the first and the third of the crises that Mannering himself predicted for Harry Bertram at his birth in volume I chapter iv; the second is an attempt at ten years old to escape his Dutch foster-home by crossing the North Sea in a skiff. In the early chapters fortune-telling appears, not only as traditional knowledge, but as an art Mannering learnt at Oxford from the last of its high-culture practitioners. They first meet in the parlour at Ellangowan on the night of Bertram's birth, and it is the only occasion on which Meg is silenced by another, when she hears Mannering half-seriously defending astrology to Sampson, and is 'overpowered by a jargon more mysterious than her own' (I.iii.44). I say half-seriously:

---

13   The image of the hero or heroine reduced to observing the world through a small opening in a wall or partition has already occurred in Scott's fiction as a figure for powerless at the hands of the plot, in II.xiv.216 (xxxvii.180) of *Waverley*, where Edward peers through a hole in his sick-bed partition at old Janet, and with her Rose looking after him.

shortly after, going outside to see the stars for the purposes of his horoscope, '[...] Mannering, while gazing upon these brilliant bodies, was half inclined to believe in the influence ascribed to them by superstition over human events' (I.iii.48). The narrator goes on to quote from Coleridge's translation of Schiller's *Wallenstein* to make a general opposition of astrology, superstition, folk-culture and romantic love (Mannering's for his wife-to-be Sophia, in this case) on the one hand, and the 'faith of reason', the Enlightenment, on the other. So while the Latin astrological terminology with which Mannering beats Dominie Sampson into submission a few pages earlier seems alien to Meg, the very fact that she is impressed by it suggests that it has something in common with her own practices. Both, in fact, are discourses placed beyond the bounds of enlightenment science.

The contrast between Mannering and Meg is rather that the latter remains true to her beliefs, where Mannering abandons his for the 'faith of reason'. He 'mentally relinquished his art, and resolved, neither in jest nor earnest, ever again to practise judicial astrology' and resolves to tell Bertram, in another judgement at once Mannering's and the narrator's, of 'the futility of the rules of art on which he had proceeded' (I.iv.58). If Bertram's story is a staging of Burkean conservatism, Mannering's story is in this respect a staging of enlightenment, and not merely the story of an enlightenment man. It is just after this abjuration that Mannering comes across Meg, telling the child's fortune in her own way. Mannering refuses the performative demands placed on him by his knowledge and becomes once more the interested but uninvolved collector of other people's performances. His reaction is not to approach Meg to find out if her predictions tally with his, but only to watch and listen to her song.

The congruence of Mannering's and the narrator's point of view implicit in the latter's producing Mannering's paraphrase of this song rather than the original has already been noted. The narrator in fact disowns Mannering's prediction outright: 'It will be readily believed, that, in mentioning this circumstance, we lay no weight whatever upon the pretended information thus conveyed' (I.iv.55). He continues with a paragraph of psychological explanations for the apparent coincidence between the two horoscopes before turning to Mannering's own reaction. But the narrator denies the prediction in another way. I observed earlier that the kidnapping is never described by the third-person narrator. It is not the only crucial event of the story that we are not given in the general narration. The escape attempt across the North Sea is only explained in the speech of the pirate Hatteraick to Glossin (II.xiii.219–20). The events in India are all given us only in Mannering's confession to Mervyn in volume I chapter xii, without comment from the narrator, and in occasional references in the speech of the other characters. Having described the background to these events, namely Sophia Mannering's encouragement of the romance between Julia and Brown, the narrator concludes, 'The scenes which followed have been partly detailed in Mannering's letter to Mr Mervyn; and to expand what is there stated into further explanations would be to abuse the patience of our readers' (I.xviii.281). As is often the case in Scott, the chronic impatience of the reader is used as an excuse for an exclusion made on entirely other grounds. Clearly, if the omniscient narrator described these accidents, he would have to admit outright that astrology, in this case, had actually and remarkably succeeded in predicting the future; and clearly, this is something that the narrator cannot do within his enlightenment denotative discourse.

The persistence of this failure on the part of the narrative discourse to narrate the events of the plot, of this gap between what we know has happened and that in which the narrator is prepared to invest his epistemic authority, means that history, *pace* Duncan, is never simply subsumed under or replaced by romance. The tension between romance plot-structure and the cognitive or realistic function of the discourse remains to the end, and is one whose roots in late-enlightenment culture we discussed in the introduction. In fact, to say that Mannering simply abandons astrology in the way in which the narrator does is not quite the whole truth. Instead, he hedges: while mentally relinquishing his art, he also gives the horoscope to Bertram's father, with the proviso that it should not be opened until the first predicted crisis was past and its general content already proved untrue (with the unstated implication that if it did prove true, it would already be impossible to act on, as is the case in the event). In this hedging reaction we find Scott's own position. For Mannering's *partial* abjuration of his astrology is also Scott's, or at least advertised as Scott's in the 1829 Introduction to the novel. There Scott tells us that he changed his plan for *Guy Mannering* shortly after beginning it, and decided to down-play the astrological element that is central to the oral narrative on which it was based.

It appeared, on mature consideration, that Astrology, though its influence was once received and admitted by Bacon himself, does not now retain influence over the general mind sufficient even to constitute the mainspring of a romance [...] In changing his plan, however, which was done in the course of printing, the early sheets retained the vestiges of the original tenor of the story, although they now hang upon it as an unnecessary and unnatural incumbrance. The cause of such vestiges occurring is now explained, and apologised for. [14]

His embarrassment at the astrological motif was evidently not enough to make him abandon the coincidence of Bertram's three crises with Mannering's predictions in I.iv, however; the plot continues to assert that which the narrator cannot acknowledge. It is *Scott,* as implied author, rather than the narrator, who hedges as Mannering does, by at once omitting the success of the predictions from the enlightenment discourse of his general narrator, while still building that success into the plot of his novel. The supernatural coincidences discovered by Mannering and Meg in this way come to figure authorial control of the plot in general. But this is a control that the narrator, committed as he is to an Enlightenment understanding of discourse as that which narrates *after* the fact that over which it has no control, cannot acknowledge. We thus have a similar situation here as in *Roderick Random,* whose narrator also could not perceive the pattern into which his own life had in fact fallen.

We can now see in this suppression of plot an enlightenment embarrassment with narrative in the first place. And this is an embarrassment that Duncan, committed as he is to the subsumption of *all* narrative agency under romance, misses. [15] There remains a split

---

14   Sir Walter Scott, *Guy Mannering,* Border Edition ed. Andrew Lang (1892) vol. III, xxxvi.

15   Mannering himself is *not* a figure within the text for this agency, but for its self-contradictory denial. I make this point because Duncan seems at times to give Mannering a degree of effective authority over the plot to balance Meg's: 'This division of the powers of the patron [between the 'rational-modern' Mannering and the 'natural-magical' Meg] is crucial: it raises the question of narrative authority, and thus of the status of 'romance', to thematic consciousness' (118). But at other points he recognises that the 'symbolic paternity' of Mannering's prediction 'is above all textual, in that it exposes a system already written, of which oneself, and the very act of paternity or authorship by which one enters the system, is an effect, a figure, rather than the cause or origin' (130), in which case it is hard to see Mannering as a figure for narrative authority at all. He evades this contradiction

between the denotative discourse of the narrator and this purposiveness at work in the story he is ostensibly telling, even while that purposiveness works to assert a reconciliation of social forces within the story. Is this fracture, between the scientific knowledge of this novel's discourse and the social/ideological function of its narrative structure, absolute? Lyotard indeed comments that the two cognitive regimes seem, in principle, entirely incommensurable: it is impossible, he writes, 'to judge the existence or validity of narrative knowledge on the basis of scientific knowledge and vice versa.'[16] However, scientific knowledge does not exist in a vacuum: it must explain and justify itself to the society which produces it, and to do this, it inevitably turns itself into narrative. So that, by the late eighteenth century, 'Narrative knowledge makes a resurgence in the West as a way of legitimating the new authorities' of the various scientific disciplines.[17] What Lyotard has in mind here are the grand narratives of progress, emerging from the Enlightenment, of political emancipation or Hegelian intellectual unification: but it is striking that it is the same period, the second half of the eighteenth century, that also sees the revival of romance as a narrative form. Could it make sense to say that romance form in *Guy Mannering* functions to legitimate what seems at first to be its opposite, scientific knowledge? If so, we will have shown romance to be a magic more powerful than even Frye proposes, capable of not only appropriating but justifying that to which it seemed to be radically opposed.[18]

---

with a pun: 'In a striking parental allegory that reaches far across Scott's work and much of nineteenth-century fiction, Mannering conceives the romance plot while Meg Merrilies actually bears and delivers it' (125–6). Mannering certainly conceives of (that is, imagines) the course of the plot as a series of crises at the start of the novel: but he is far from seminal in bringing those crises and their resolution about (except unintentionally and unknowingly, that is, as a character in the plot rather than its author).

16 Lyotard 26.
17 Lyotard 30.
18 This possibility relates to Clifford Siskin's recent argument that 'English Literature', of which romance revival could be seen as a central and legitimating part, emerged as the core of a 'national culture' in the late eighteenth century to displace the enlightenment cosmopolitanism of 'Scottish Philosophy' as that unifying centre which co-ordinated the increasingly fragmented and institutionalised disciplines of the sciences and brought them to bear on the common human experience. But Siskin does not explore the changing and contra-

3. Richardson, Burney, and the autonomy of feminine discourse

In order to answer this question we must look again at the discourse of *Guy Mannering*, because the objective voice of the enlightened narrator is not the only narrative voice that makes up this text. We have already seen two rival cognitive regimes within its story, those of Meg and Pleydell; but the discourse of the novel is itself fragmented, and scientific discourse opposed, not by traditional knowledge in some form, but by the epistolary voice of a young woman, Mannering's daughter Julia.[19]

I have already noted that Matthew Bramble is an obvious precedent for Guy Mannering himself. But the most striking borrowing by *Guy Mannering* from *Humphry Clinker* lies in its use of a very similar heroine to write very similar letters which interrupt the male, enlightenment discourse that constitutes the bulk of the text. It is worthwhile to pause and note just how similar the stories of Lydia Melford and Julia Mannering are. Both write to a school-friend from whom they have been separated by their father or uncle (Lydia to Laetitia Willis, Julia to Matilda Marchmont). Both are in love with young men, apparently penniless performers, but in fact heirs to large estates (Brown first approaches Julia at her guardian Arthur Mervyn's house in a boat, playing the flageolet, from the inn across the lake, 'the resort', Mervyn writes to Mannering, 'of walking gentlemen of all descriptions, poets, players, painters, musicians [...]' [I.xvi.263]); the alienation of both

---

dictory place afforded the ethical in either of these versions of (essentially) cognitive enterprise, which is my concern here.

19 My move at this point, countering enlightenment science with the discursive heterogeneity of the text in which it is embedded, glances back at Hume's enclosure of scientific rhetoric within the needs of a polite readership (we shall see that the relation between author and reader is just what is thematized in Julia Mannering's letters). But my not placing the sublime Meg as the other of science at the level of discourse also exemplifies Siskin's point when he writes, 'Scientificity's valorization of "objectivity" [...] has its humanistic counterpart not in "subjectivity" (they constitute a self-validating binary), but in the heteroglossia of novelism' (*Work of Writing* 189). Insofar as Meg embodies the visionary pose of romantic poetry, Siskin's comment seems to me a useful counter to McKeon's understanding of the novel as this period as grounded in this opposition of the subjective and the objective.

young men has been exacerbated by a duel or the prospect of a duel with one of the young lady's relatives (Bramble arrives just as Jery and 'Wilson' are priming their pistols; Mannering has actually shot and wounded 'Brown'); both are moved from their established residence to be with their father-figures (Julia to Scotland, Lydia all round the country) and away from these presumptuous lovers; and the boys in both then follow their beloveds on their travels.

O my dear Letty! what shall I say about poor Mr Wilson? I have promised to break off all correspondence, and if possible, to forget him: but alas! I begin to perceive that will not be in my power. (*H.C.* April 6; p.10)

I wish he may forget me, for the sake of his own peace; and yet if he should, he must be a barbarous—But it is impossible—poor Wilson cannot be false or inconstant: I beseech him not to write to me, nor attempt to see me for some time [...]. (*H.C.* April 6; p.11)

I am vexed, that neither you nor I have received any further information of a certain person—Sure it cannot be wilful neglect!—O my dear Willis! I begin to be visited by strange fancies, and to have some melancholy doubts; which, however, it would be ungenerous to harbour without further inquiry. (*H.C.* May 6; p.58)

I have used every argument to convince him that this secret intercourse is dangerous to us both—I even pressed him to pursue his views of fortune without farther regard to me [...]. (*G.M.* I.xviii.282)

I must own, I think that by this this time the gentleman might have given me some intimation what he was doing. Our intercourse may be an imprudent one, but it is not very complimentary to me, that Mr Vanbeest Brown should be the first to discover that, and to break off in consequence [...]. Yet I have so good an opinion of poor Brown, that I cannot but think there is something extraordinary in his silence. (*G.M.* II.viii.124–5)

Despite these remarkable similarities, the role of Julia's correspondence in *Guy Mannering* remains a problem in a way that Lydia's in *Humphry Clinker* is not: for where the latter's inclusion is *allowed* by the epistolary form of Smollett's novel, the former *introduces* epistolary form to a novel that is otherwise narrated in Scott's usual omniscient third person mode. What this suggests is that epistolary form in itself carries some meaning in the context of Scott's novel. We must now look at how that meaning is generated by the history of the novel in the 45 years between *Humphry Clinker* and *Guy Mannering*, precisely those

126

years when the novel came to be dominated by female-authored domestic fiction. Before I go on to examine in greater depth the way in which Scott's novel uses similar resources, I want to spend some time examining the way in which the most influential of those women novelists, Frances Burney, developed Richardson's legacy.

I have already suggested that Lydia's letters in *Humphry Clinker* draw on the correspondence between two young women as represented in Richardson's *Clarissa* and *Sir Charles Grandison* to allow the heroine to create for herself, in her writing, an identity over and against the one being imposed on her by her menfolk. Clarissa Harlowe is able to maintain her moral autonomy only because her correspondence with another young unmarried woman offers her an alternative set of assumptions and priorities to those of her family. While Clarissa and Anna frequently disagree over the precise meaning of a word or an event, it is within a correspondence that assumes those values that they negotiate what that meaning is. They construct their own identities, their own reality, by each defining and redefining the other in a continuing dialogue. For example, Anna replies to Clarissa's description of the Harlowes' favoured suitor for her, Mr Solmes, with a redescription of her own in even harsher terms. Anna's mother tells her to tone it down somewhat:

> But excuse me, my good mamma! I would not have the character lost upon any consideration, since my vein ran freely into it; and I never wrote to please myself but I pleased you. A very good reason why—we have but one mind between us— only, that sometimes you are a little too grave, methinks; I, no doubt, a little too flippant in your opinion.[20]

This interchangeability of their respective subjectivities does not mean that they invariably make the same judgements, but rather that the judgements that they do make, including their perceptions of themselves, take shape in reply to the judgements and perceptions of the other. Their subjectivities are not independent entities but are constituted in dialogue with the other. And the terms on which that dialogue is conducted are always open to revision as Clarissa's relationship with her family is not. She replies to Anna's criticisms of the Harlowes in the letter quoted above:

20　*Clarissa* letter 27, p.131.

Then you have so very strong a manner of expression where you take a distaste, that when passion has subsided and I come by reflection to see by *your* severity what I have given occasion for I cannot help condemning myself. Let me then, as matters arise, make my complaints to you; but be it your part to soothe and soften my angry passions by such advice as nobody better knows how to give: and this the rather, as you know what an influence your advice has upon me.[21]

The meaning of Clarissa's words only becomes apparent in Anna's reply to them, and Clarissa's sense of her moral self is thus dependent on Anna's reply too. Clarissa's letters are shaped by her anticipation of how Anna is likely to read them, and this anticipation is revised in the light of the letters that Anna actually writes, so that the reality that is reported in their letters is the result of an intersubjective dialogue. It is only when Lovelace begins intercepting and forging these letters that this mutual definition on the part of the young women is dangerously weakened:

> Clarissa tells her own story, describing excellence in action, but it is Anna as correspondent who prompts the description and encourages it. As the women's correspondence becomes attenuated, Clarissa's story grows less clear, falling into allegory and incoherence. She needs the image of herself in Anna's writing to continue her own recreation. Divorced from this image, the conflict overwhelms, for it is in this correspondence alone that her female autonomy is respected. Separated from Anna's prose and her own self-creating response, the woman is raped into a daughter and wife.[22]

Richardson was not the first to write an epistolary novel around a female-female correspondence, and several critics have drawn (albeit brief) attention to his debt to earlier women writers to balance the wide acknowledgement of his influence on later ones.[23]

---

21 *Clarissa* letter 28, p.134.
22 Janet Todd, *Women's Friendship in Literature* (New York: Columbia University Press, 1980) 47.
23 Margaret Ann Doody, for example, mentions Elizabeth Rowe's *Letters Moral and Entertaining* (1731?), where 'the correspondence between the grave Emilia and her friend, the light-hearted Leticia, foreshadows Richardson's use of Anna Howe and Charlotte Grandison as confidantes of Clarissa and Harriet.' *A Natural Passion: A Study of the Novels of Samuel Richardson* (Oxford: Clarendon Press, 1974) 23. But Doody locates the originals for such pairings much more firmly in Restoration and contemporary comedy (287 and *passim*). Of the novelty of *Clarissa*, Doody writes, '[...] the ironic conception of the tragedy demanded some innovation in epistolary technique. For instance, the position of the heroine's female confidante had already

Richardson himself was following a long tradition of epistolary fiction, much of it written by women, and his achievement owed much to cultural definitions of feminine writing and to the traditions established by women writers [...]. [Women writers were influenced by Richardson's novels, especially *Sir Charles Grandison*] but they were not thereby cut off from the women's tradition before them, which continued to exercise its influence both directly, and indirectly through Richardson. Richardson's importance for women novelists was not so much that he provided them with a model to imitate, as that he helped to create the climate in which they would be accepted.[24]

That acceptance was conditional, however, and one of the conditions was that female novelists should not follow the example set by Richardson's epistolary novel in conspicuously deploying an auto-nomous feminine discourse. It is on this, purely negative influence of Richardson's on the domestic novel, that I am interested here, and the early novels of Frances Burney, *Evelina* and *Cecilia*, will provide my examples. For given the form of the epistolary novel as Richardson had developed it, it is significant that the great majority of Evelina Anville's letters in Burney's first novel are addressed not to a young female confidante but to an ageing father-figure, the Rev. Mr Villars. Burney in *Evelina* rejects the autonomous feminine correspondence made available by Richardson as a basis for her heroine's self-understanding.

Indeed, as Jane Spencer points out, *Evelina* belongs in a tradition of novels by women about the reformation by a lover-mentor of a thought-less young lady who makes a series of blunders on her first entry into society but ends up in happy marriage to her moral guardian. This is a tradition that pre-dates Richardson and on which he drew.[25] *Evelina*

---

been established in novels, both those told in letters and those told in the first person. In most epistolary amatory novels, however, in which writing to the moment is of importance, the correspondence is between the hero and the heroine' (Doody 129–30).

24 Spencer 89. Similarly, Doody notes that all three of Richardson's novels were 'not an innovation but a development, by an artistic genius, of a minor tradition established by the writers of love stories told in the feminine voice' (Doody 24).

25 Spencer comments of Burney and Austen, 'Their pictures of the minutiae of domestic life drew on *Sir Charles Grandison*, their ironic narrative voice on Fielding's novels. However, in the development of this key character-type – the mistaken heroine who reforms – they were following a tradition begun by women and almost exclusive to them. [...] Richardson [...] created mistaken but reform-

develops this 'reformed coquet' tradition by splitting the functions of mentor and lover between two men, Villars and Lord Orville. At the same time she establishes their moral equivalence in Evelina's comparisons of the two in her letters. Mr Villars is for most of the novel the heroine's moral touchstone: 'Unable as I am to act for myself, or to judge what conduct I ought to pursue, how grateful do I feel myself, that I have such a guide and director to counsel and instruct me as yourself!'[26] Villars's advice can never be more than general, isolated as he is from the social whirl of London and the fashionable resorts in which Evelina's dilemmas arise, and tells her on her second visit to London that she now 'must learn not only to *judge* but to *act* for yourself';[27] but Lord Orville comes forward to take his place instead. On her return to Villars's house after her second London trip she draws an explicit comparison between the two men:

> Never do I wish to be again separated from him [...] Once, indeed, I thought there existed another,—who, when *time had wintered o'er his locks*, would have shone forth among his fellow-creatures, with the same brightness of worth which dignifies my honoured Mr Villars [...][28]

This other is of course Lord Orville, and the temporary alienation from him which prompts the letter last quoted is one of the central complications of *Evelina*'s plot. When Evelina takes the bold step of writing to Lord Orville to apologize for the behaviour of her vulgar relatives, the Branghtons, the letter is intercepted (we discover much later in the novel, in volume III, letter xvi) by the rakish Sir Clement Willoughby, whose shockingly forward reply is in Orville's name. This is enough to shatter her image of Orville as a moral paragon.

This alienation from Orville has interesting effects on the novel's epistolary structure. I have written that *Evelina* returns to the pupil-mentor mode of epistolary narration, rejecting the sentimental female correspondence of *Clarissa* or *Sir Charles Grandison*. This is in general true, but at this point in the text, where its heroine has been tricked into

---

worthy female characters in Anna Howe and Charlotte Grandison, but he did not make them the focus of his plots' (Spencer 141).

26   Frances Burney, *Evelina, or the History of a Young Lady's Entrance into the World* (1778; Oxford: Oxford University Press, 1968) volume II, letter vi, p.160.

27   Ibid. II.viii.164.

28   Ibid. II.xxviii.260–1.

unjustified disillusionment with her destined husband, Evelina turns to a female confidante, Maria Mirvan. Maria is a light-hearted foil to her serious friend rather as Anna Howe is to Clarissa, although we can only infer this from Evelina's letters as none of Maria's are included. The different terms on which the two correspondences are maintained can be gathered from two letters written on consecutive days on Evelina's second arrival in London. To Mr Villars she writes of Mme Duval's plan to take her to Paris: 'I started at this intimation, which very much surprised me. But I am very glad she has discovered her intention, as I shall be carefully upon my guard not to venture from town with her.'[29] Her letters to Villars, that is, describe her attempts to put his prudential principles into practice. Her letter to Maria has other pre-occupations:

> Tell me, my dear Maria, do you never re-trace in your memory the time we past here when together? to mine, it recurs for ever! And yet, I think I rather recollect a dream, or some visionary fancy, than a reality.—That I should ever have been known to Lord Orville,—that I should have spoken to—have danced with him,— seems now a romantic illusion: and that elegant politeness, that flattering attention, that high-bred delicacy, which so much distinguished him above all other men, and which struck us with such admiration, I now re-trace the remembrance of, rather as belonging to an object of ideal perfection, formed by my own imagination, than to a being of the same race and nature as those with whom I at present converse.[30]

Where her letters to Villars are concerned with the rights and wrongs of social intercourse, her letter to Maria re-describes what really happened in terms of illusion, of imagination, of fiction. Events are reconstructed as dream, a realm beyond questions of truth and falsehood, let alone right and wrong. This is the only letter to Maria that is included in the discourse of the novel until the crisis of Orville's reply, although in the story the correspondence is maintained in the intervening days. Its inclusion is necessary because, it seems, Evelina is unwilling to discuss what has obviously been an erotic attraction to Orville in letters to her mentor, when the truth of such an attraction can be teased out in her letters to Maria just as Anna teases out the truth of Clarissa's feelings for Lovelace: 'I must own myself somewhat distressed how to answer your raillery: yet believe me, my dear Maria, your suggestions are those of *fancy*, not of *truth*. I am unconscious of the weakness you suspect

---

29   Ibid. II.ix.166.
30   Ibid. II.x.172.

[...].'[31] Hence it is first to Maria that she describes her disillusion with Orville: 'my first determination was to confine my chagrin totally to my own bosom; but your friendly enquiries have drawn it from me [...].'[32] Eventually she confesses to Villars, and she can once again be completely open with *both* her correspondents: 'To you, *and* to Mr Villars, I vow an unremitting confidence' (my emphasis).[33] This promise closes letter xxix in volume II; letter xxx is her first from Bristol, and she promises to maintain the correspondence, but it is the last letter to Maria that the reader is given. In volume III, the only letters needed to tell Evelina's story are those to the paternal Villars.

This should not come as a surprise. Even in her letters to Maria, Burney is careful to signal that this friendship is no substitute for Evelina's self-defining relationships with the two father-figures in her life. Falling between these relationships because of the forged letter, she loses grip on a moral identity that her correspondence with Maria cannot provide. Discussing her mixed feelings on being asked home by Villars from London, she writes, 'I believe you would hardly have known me; —indeed, I hardly know myself.' But she continues: 'Perhaps had I first seen *you*, in your kind and sympathizing bosom I might have ventured to have reposed every secret of my soul; and then—but let me pursue my journal.'[34] 'And then—' – what? The way in which Evelina breaks off here is a taste of what is to come at the end of this letter, where her discourse fragments and contradicts itself.

> O Miss Mirvan, to be so beloved of the best of men,—should I not be happy?— Should I have one wish save that of meriting his goodness?—Yet think me not ungrateful; indeed I am not, although the internal sadness of my mind unfits me, at present, for enjoying as I ought the bounties of providence.
>
> I cannot journalise; cannot arrange my ideas into any order.
>
> How little situation has to do with happiness! I had flattered myself that, when restored to Berry Hill, I should be restored to tranquility: far otherwise have I found it, for never yet had tranquility and Evelina so little intercourse.

---

31   Ibid. II.xxviii.259.
32   Ibid. II.xxvii.258.
33   Ibid. II.xxix.268. Indeed, Orville at times is described by Evelina as a substitute for Maria as well as for Villars: 'As a sister I loved him,—I could have entrusted him with every thought of my heart, had he deigned to wish my confidence; so steady did I think his honour, so *feminine* his delicacy, and so amiable his nature!' Ibid. II.xxviii.261.
34   Ibid. II.xxvi.254.

I blush for what I have written. Can you, Maria, forgive my gravity? but I restrain it so much and so painfully in the presence of Mr Villars, that I know not how to deny myself the consolation of indulging it to you.

Adieu, my dear Miss Mirvan.

Yet one thing I must add; do not let the seriousness of this letter deceive you; do not impute to a wrong cause the melancholy I confess, by supposing that the heart of your friend mourns a too great susceptibility; no, indeed! believe me it never was. never can be, more assuredly her own than at this moment.[35]

Her disappointment in Orville threatens her correspondence with Maria, as well as with Villars, although in a different way. Their relationship does not generate moral identities autonomous from the laws of men: in this letter Evelina tries to write in a state of mental alienation from *any* male mentor, Orville *or* Villars, and the attempt breaks down. The possibility of an autonomous feminine moral identity is hinted at (it is what should follow Evelina's 'and then—') but ultimately rejected.[36]

Ultimately rejected, but not simply rejected, however. For if Evelina behaved entirely with the prudence advocated by Villars, it is hard to see how she could ever find a husband at all. The letter of Evelina's in which Orville declares his desire to take Villars's place, a declaration which makes her 'the happiest of human beings' (volume III, letter v), is replied to by Villars with the demand that she leave Orville's company and return home. To convince her of the necessity of this, he re-

---

35   Ibid. II.xxvi.255.

36   Julia Epstein comments, '[T]here is a second novel here, over which *Evelina* rests like a palimpsest: the novel that Evelina's letters and conversations with a peer, another young woman, would comprise'; Julia Epstein, *The Iron Pen: Frances Burney and the Politics of Women's Writing* (Bristol: Bristol Classical Press, 1989) 102. The function of the letters to Maria, according to Epstein, are to demonstate by way of contrast the limitations of the letters to Villars, prompting the reader to examine the ways in which Evelina edits her experience to manipulate her mentor therein. But this hardly explains why the letters to Maria should appear and disappear when they do. Burney suggests that Evelina *could* maintain an identity independent from her mentors, yes, but also suggests that such an autonomy would be morally and psychically dangerous for her. Epstein misses the extent to which the effort that Evelina puts into her letters to Villars is less to shape his reactions and maintain his approval as to shape and maintain her own identity in her relationship to him as her mentor: a relationship whose moral priority over others *Evelina* does nothing to question. It suggests an alternative novel only in order to reject it.

describes her story up to that point, repeating her own phrases back to her in a new discursive context:

> Your first meeting with Lord Orville was decisive [...] Young, animated, entirely off your guard, and thoughtless of consequences, *imagination* took the reins, and *reason*, slow-paced, though sure-footed, was unequal to a race with so eccentric and flighty a companion. How flighty was my Evelina's progress through those regions of fancy and passion whither her new guide conducted her!—She saw Lord Orville at a ball,—and he was *the most amiable of men!*—She met him again at another,—and *he had every virtue under Heaven!*
>
> [...] [Y]our new comrade [imagination] had not patience to wait any trial; her glowing pencil, dipt in the vivid colours of her creative ideas, painted to you, at the moment of your first acquaintance, all the excellencies, all the good and rare qualities, which a great length of time, and intimacy, could alone really have discovered.[37]

Evelina delays, and her reward is marriage to Orville. What is more, the novel leaves us in no doubt that Orville really does have 'every virtue under Heaven': Evelina's early judgements are proved correct. Villars's prudence and morality do not allow for the leap of faith, of sympathetic imagination, that is necessary for partnership in companionate marriage. Evelina's experience of desire for Orville goes beyond anything that Villars is competent to judge.

What is striking about the passage quoted above, however, is the way in which it re-deploys as derogatory terms the vocabulary in which Evelina had described her adventures in her letters, not to Villars, but to Maria. The world of 'fancy', of 'imagination', of reality recast as illusion, was constructed in the novel's feminine correspondence, however briefly presented, not in its ethical-educational one. Villars unwittingly identifies for us a condition for the success of Evelina's love-affair with Orville: namely, that she be capable of responding to events as an imaginative being as well as a moral agent. And that capacity is fostered and displayed in her relationship with Maria, not with him. While Burney refuses to allow Evelina a sense of right and wrong autonomous from her father-figures, then, she makes an autonomous feminine creativity, a capacity on the part of women to invent their own alternative reality, essential to the happy outcome of her plot. But this necessity is quietly implied, where the ethical

---

37   *Evelina* III.vi.308–9.

dependence of the heroine on her mentor is asserted on almost every page.

Before considering why this should be so, it is worth examining Burney's next novel, which abandons epistolary form and yet repeats many of *Evelina*'s concerns within its third-person narrative. Cecilia Beverley too takes her leave of a male guardian to brave the perils of London society, and he too provides a moral touchstone by re-describing her experience for her, opening up meanings in past events which she was not aware of at the time.[38] However, unlike Mr Villars's, Mr Monckton's advice is not disinterested, and Burney is enabled by her use of an omniscient narrator to warn the reader right from the start that '[...] to faculties the most skilful of investigating the character of every other', Monckton added 'a dissimulation the most profound in concealing his own.'[39] Cecilia turns to him at her departure:

> '[...] I hope, sir, you will honour me with your counsel and admonitions with respect to my future conduct, whenever you have the goodness to let me see you.'
> This was precisely his wish. He begged, in return, that she would treat him with confidence, and then suffered the chaise to drive off.[40]

We know Monckton's wish as Cecilia does not, and it is to marry her. But Monckton has already married an old dowager for her wealth, under the mistaken impression that she had not long to live, and so he endeavours to keep Cecilia single until his wife dies. Monckton tries to use his position of mentor to frustrate Evelina's relatonship with his younger rival Delvile. Cecilia, traumatised with doubt at the thought of elopement, wonders where she can '"find a friend, who, in this critical moment will instruct me how to act!"', and Delvile tells her to look in her own bosom.[41] But instead Cecilia chooses Monckton as that 'male confident who might be entrusted with their project', with disastrous results.[42] Cecilia's problem is in part the loss of a *female* confidante to

---

38   For examples of such redescriptions, see Frances Burney, *Cecilia, or Memoirs of an Heiress* (1782; Oxford: Oxford University Press, 1988) book II, chapter vii, p.164; III.iii.197; IV.iii.254; V.vii.369–70; V.xiii.435–6.
39   Ibid. I.i.7. It is perhaps, as Julia Epstein suggests, an exaggeration to describe Villars as totally disinterested in his advice to Evelina: see Epstein 104–5.
40   *Evelina* I.ii.19.
41   Ibid. VII.vi.572.
42   Ibid. VII.vi.574.

whom she could talk or write. The heroine's identity remains tied up with her father-figures in both novels: a solution to her crisis lies in reconciliation to the patriarchs. Cecilia's madness finally ends her trials by shaming Delvile's father into recognition of her as his daughter.

Cecilia nevertheless includes some of that feminine creativity that we saw implied in Evelina's letters to Maria. It does so in the shape of Lady Honoria Pemberton, with whom Cecilia talks during a stay at Delvile Castle. It is a melancholy place that Lady Honoria hates:

> 'Even if by chance one has the good fortune to hear any intelligence, Mrs Delvile will hardly let it be repeated, for fear that it should happen to be untrue, as if that could possibly signify! I am sure I had as lieve the things were false as not, for they tell as well one way as the other, if she would but have patience to hear them.'[43]

She goes on to repeat the most ludicrous gossip concerning Cecilia and young Delvile, including that he meant to marry her sister Euphrasia, and that he meant to marry Cecilia, gossip at which Cecilia learns to laugh:

> 'For shame, Lady Honoria!' said Cecilia, again changing colour, 'I am sure this must be your own fancy,—invention,—'
>
> 'No, I assure you; I heard it at several places [...] others said you had promised your hand to Sir Robert Floyer, and repented when you heard of his mortgages, and he gave it out every where that he would fight any man that pretended to you; and then again some said that you were all the time privately married to Mr Arnott, but did not dare own it, because he was so afraid of fighting with Sir Robert.'
>
> 'O Lady Honoria!' cried Cecilia, half laughing, 'what wild inventions are these! and all I hope, your own?'
>
> 'No, indeed, they were current over the whole town. But don't take any notice of what I told you about Euphrasia, for perhaps, it may never happen.'
>
> 'Perhaps', said Cecilia, reviving by believing it all fiction, 'it has never been in agitation?'[44]

As in *Evelina*, the female voice gives a privileged place to invention, to *fancy*, in mediating male-female relations. The question of truth and falsity is simply suspended, and she speaks from the pure pleasure of story-telling. Lady Honoria's speech, in short, is *fiction*.

---

43   Ibid. VI.iv.466.
44   Ibid. VI.iv.467–8.

Now, Lady Honoria is ostensibly part of that world of cruel vacuity that Cecilia must learn to reject: she is, like Lady Griskin in *Humphry Clinker*, a woman of fashion, whom Mrs Delvile accuses of 'a saucy indifference whom she pleases or hurts, that borders upon what in a woman is of all things the most odious, a daring defiance of the world and its opinions.'[45] The first part of this accusation would clearly carry weight with Cecilia, who shows sensitivity in all things. But Cecilia is nearly paralysed with concern for 'the world and its opinions', when marriage to Delvile, which alone can make her happy, requires and lacks some of Lady Honoria's defiance. Lady Honoria does not indeed make a decisive intervention in that action, but her attitude to the Delviles is one that the text as a whole supports. *Cecilia* does not advocate the abject submission of the single woman to her father-figures. Katherine Sobba Green notes how young Delvile's father, forced into acknowledging Cecilia's personal worth, 'suffers a substantial loss of power when he receives Cecilia into his London house'.[46] Dr Lyster, the Delvile's physician, who is in many ways the male confidant that Cecilia should have had but did not, assures her that her ordeal has resulted not from her own actions but from patriarchal 'pride and prejudice'. 'Further, with Cecilia sitting primly beside her, Lady Honoria, Delvile's irrepressible niece, sabotages and disrupts her uncle's solemnity with various attacks against male prerogative.'[47]

Here is one of those attacks:

'[...] [O]ne's fathers, and uncles, and these sort of people, always make connexions for one, and not a creature thinks of our principles, till they find them out by our conduct: and nobody can possibly do that till we are married, for they give us no power beforehand. The men know nothing of us in the world while we are single, but how we can dance a minuet, or play a lesson upon the harpsichord.' [48]

---

45   Ibid. VI.viii.498
46   Katherine Sobba Green, *The Courtship Novel 1740–1820: A Feminized Genre* (Lexington: University Press of Kentucky, 1991) 89.
47   Ibid. 89. Epstein too recognizes the example of autonomy that Lady Honoria represents for Cecilia, but the slight importance she affords Monckton means that she does not place that example in the context of the heroine's relation to her mentor as I do here. See Epstein 167.
48   *Cecilia* X.x.934–5.

Lady Honoria can only speak thus freely against mentors because she is not a major figure in the text. That the heroine, or the heroine's best friend, in a Burney novel should be thus outspoken is unthinkable. As in *Evelina*, the autonomous female voice is marginalized at the same time as it articulates the core concerns of the novel. It is as if Burney were anxious about a feminine creativity independent of male mentors, as it appears in female-female correspondence or in gossip, in a way that Richardson was not. Why should this be?

Let us continue our comparison of *Evelina* and *Cecilia* in this regard. *Evelina* implies limitations in Villars's advice to his ward by contrasting it with the discourse shared by her and her female friend. In *Cecilia* the mentor-figure is not limited in terms of his experience: he knows everything about the unmarried Cecilia, a dangerous exception to Lady Honoria's rule. His advice is instead downright duplicitous, and as readers we can appreciate this because the omniscient narrator tells us. So when Monckton re-describes some of Cecilia's experiences to her, we already have the narrator's version of events to contrast with his self-interested one. In other words, Monckton and the narrator rival each other as omniscient interpreters of Cecilia's story. The challenge to patriarchy's right to distinguish truth and falsehood, right and wrong, comes not only from a character within the novel (Lady Honoria) or from an autonomous feminine discourse within the novel (Evelina and Maria) but from the narrative discourse itself.

And this is because *the narrative itself is an autonomous feminine discourse*. Burney's anxiety about the feminine creativity of Evelina or of Lady Honoria is an anxiety about the moral status of *her own* feminine creativity, a fear of openly advocating within her novels the creative autonomy from men that her novel-writing, by a woman and for a largely female readership, in fact gives her. This is an anxiety from which Richardson, as a man, never suffered. *Evelina* and *Cecilia*, despite their abandonment of Richardson's female-female correspondence as a narrative technique, are themselves pieces of female-female communication.[49] Indeed, these novels' narrative strategies are built around

---

49 Burney of course expressed great anxiety about the indecorum of coming into the public eye as a woman, writing famously to one of her own father figures, Samuel Crisp, soon after the success of *Evelina*, 'I would a thousand Times rather forfeit my character as a *Writer*, than risk ridicule or censure as a *Female*. I have never set my Heart on Fame, and therefore would not if I *could* purchase it at the expense of

the need to deny that autonomy even while they exemplify it: they abandon Richardson's technique *because* they are pieces of female-female communication. Women authors earlier in the century had been seen as committing something close to prostitution in their indecent entrance upon the public stage, and women as a mass market for escapist fiction as a corrupting influence on the publishing trade.[50] One of the ways that later women novelists gained acceptance and respectability was by absorbing into their work the content of the conduct books, thus presenting themselves in part as useful guides to the behaviour considered proper for young ladies. Novels like Burney's were written for a female readership, and they were ostensibly written to improve. The portrayal of female friendship in such novels could be put to the same moral end:

> Outside the text, sentimental friendship becomes a means of befriending the female reader; through her relationship with her friend, the heroine can display her exemplary state, and under the mask of sentiment, stand as a model for other young ladies who may unwisely yearn to stray.[51]

Novelists like Burney, in other words, won their literary authority at the price of preaching a conditional acceptance of patriarchal norms. Women were free to practice fiction, but only if female fictionalizing was warned against in the process. The rise of the feminine novel in the second half of the century was made possible 'by purging it of its disreputable associations with female sexuality and the subversive power of female "wit", or artifice'.[52] The anxiety about the relation of feminine discourse to a patriarchal Truth that we see at work in novels like *Evelina* and *Cecilia*, is the consequence of this paradoxical

---

all my own ideas of propriety.' Lars E. Troide and Stewart J. Cooke, eds., *The Early Journals and Letters of Fanny Burney* Vol. III (Oxford: Clarendon Press, 1994) Letter 72 (c.7 Jan, 1779) 212.

50　Although one should note that the idea of a huge and voracious female readership for the novel seems itself to have been produced by the sort of male fears that Jery hears in London (the size of the readership for women's fiction seems to have been exaggerated: see Ballaster chapter 2), nevertheless such fears structured the context in which Burney was writing.

51　Todd 3.

52　Ballaster 3.

progress.[53] The autonomy from a male-governed society seen in female-female correspondence, or in female-female dialogue, could suggest that the woman novelist and her readers were generating the same sort of autonomy, their own alternative reality, between themselves. To avoid such a scandalous implication, such correspondence, such dialogue, was bracketed, avoided, or omitted altogether. Yet women continued to write, and women to read their writing, until the novel could be claimed by them as a genre of their own. When Scott comes to image this autonomous feminine creativity, he does so in the correspondence or dialogue of two young ladies, like Clarissa and Anna, like Evelina and Maria.

4. The freedom of Julia Mannering

Once in Scotland, Julia Mannering has a present candidate for the position of confidant in the shape of Lucy Bertram, but chooses instead to maintain her correspondence with Matilda Marchmont.

> Is it possible for me to forget that you are the chosen of my heart, in whose faithful bosom I have deposited every feeling which your poor Julia dares to acknowledge to herself? And you do me equal injustice in upbraiding me with exchanging your friendship for that of Lucy Bertram. I assure you she has not the materials I must seek for in a bosom confidante[...].
> [...] She is, to be sure, a very pretty, a very sensible, a very affectionate girl, and I think there are few persons to whose consolatory friendship I could have recourse more freely in what are called the *real evils* of life. But then these so seldom come in one's way, and one wants a friend who will sympathize with distresses of sentiment, as well as with actual misfortune. (II.viii.119–20)

However, the implication of Julia's words here, that the 'distresses of sentiment' are somehow not '*real*' or 'actual' evils or misfortunes, is not an implication that we find in the writing of Lydia Melford, or, for that

---

53 This anxiety is thus the manifestation at the level of content of what Jane Spencer calls Burney's 'internalization of feminine diffidence'. In general, Spencer writes, 'As women writers' talents were more generally acknowledged they began to claim less for themselves' (Spencer 95).

matter, of Richardson's heroines. It is a doubt about the factuality of what is written or spoken between women that we have already seen in the early novels of Frances Burney. Julia's letters to Matilda share with Burney's novels an awareness of the fictional nature of the world that they create. This fictionality is understood, as in Burney, as offering the potential for moral autonomy form their male mentors.

Mannering has always been a distant parent to Julia, but the events in India have driven them even further apart. As in *Evelina*, the heroine cannot (to begin with) bring herself to tell her paternal guardian her feelings for her young lover. As in *Evelina*, the contrast with the terms on which female friendship is maintained is obvious. 'My father, constantly engaged in military duty, I saw but at rare intervals, and was taught to look up to him with more awe than confidence' (I.xvii.268); 'I have this instant received your letter—your most welcome letter!—Thanks, my dearest friend, for your sympathy and your counsels—I can only repay them with unbounded confidence' (I.xviii.284). Julia's alienation from her father is an extreme case of a general distance between her and her mentors. Her father's friend Mervyn doesn't understand her either: 'I hold that the gentleman has good taste for the female outside, and do not expect he should comprehend my sentiments farther' (I.xvii.273). So taken for granted is this linguistic autonomy of Julia's from their plans that her expressions of submission to her mentors are understood not as reporting her state of mind (which it is presumed is *not* submissive) but as placing herself in a role which will make life easier under their rule. 'Miss Mannering acquiesced with a passiveness which is no part of her character, and which, to tell you the plain truth, is a feature about the business which I like least of all' writes Mervyn (I.xvi.261). Mannering is similarly suspicious: 'O, there is a little too much of this universal spirit of submission; an excellent disposition in action, but your constantly repeating the jargon of it puts me in mind of the eternal salams of our black dependants in the East' (I.xviii.293). As in *Clarissa*, as in *Humphry Clinker*, the young woman's professed powerlessness is understood as an expression of a feminine will-to-power.

Her relationship with Matilda, on the other hand, is mediated by their shared status of fiction-readers. Julia is herself a reader of novels, and she tends to interpret events around her in terms of their potential as elements of a romance plot: for example, Lucy Bertram's star-crossed love for young Hazlewood 'has a great deal of complicated and romantic interest' (II.viii.126). However, 'romance' has a complex relationship to the novel as those terms are used by Julia. In the first extract, Julia contrasts the novel, as read by young ladies of Matilda's class, with the oral narratives that she has heard recited in India: 'You will call this romantic—but consider I was born in the land of talisman and spell, and my childhood lulled by tales which you can only enjoy through the gauzy frippery of a French translation [...] No wonder that European fiction sounds cold and meagre, after the wonderful effects which I have seen the romances of the East produce upon the hearers' (I.xvii.267–8). Romance here clearly belongs with the traditional knowledge and performative utterances of Meg, *as opposed to* the novel. Then again, a few pages later, she writes, referring to the Lake District, 'If India be the land of magic, this, my dearest Matilda, is the country of romance' (I.xvii.271): romance here seems at once distinct from, yet analogous to, the 'magic' of traditional knowledge; and, relocated to the picturesque Lake District, a domestication of that knowledge. 'Romance' here would thus name the social-performative power of modern fiction understood as 'displaced' into that fiction from the supernatural narratives of an earlier age exactly as it does in Frye, and this is accordingly the version of Julia's letters suggested by Ian Duncan. In Julia's letters we get a thematics of romance equivalent and opposed to the thematics of science in the story of her father and his friends. It is this thematization of romance that allows Duncan to class Julia's correspondence as itself an instance of romance agency (see Introduction, p.31).

Now, Julia's discourse certainly has a power, analogous to Meg's, to generate human relationships: her letters to Matilda constitute the relation between them, though this is a purely *intersubjective* one rather than the wider social and hierarchical bonds constituted by traditional narrative. Denotative phrases are subordinated to this function. Even her relationship to young Bertram is primarily constructed in her letters to Matilda, to the point where his story becomes a sign of the women's mutual devotion: '—But to my tale—let it be, my friend, the most sacred, as it is the most sincere pledge of our friendship' (I.xvii.274). Similarly, in the first extract we are given, Julia is ready to turn her father into the hero of a gothic or oriental tale (I.xvii.267). One of the things shared by the general narrator and Mannering, Pleydell and Mervyn is precisely their recognition of the performative power of

Julia's discourse which, within their own, incommensurable, cognitive discourse, must be presented as mere invention, as when her father tells her, 'You have a genius for friendship, that is, for running up intimacies which you call such [...]' (I.xviii.294). Mervyn writes to Mannering, concerning the colony of poets and artists across the lake from his house, '[...] were Julia my daughter, it is one of those sort of fellows that I should fear on her account. She is generous and romantic, and writes six sheets a-week to a female correspondent; and it's a sad thing to lack a subject in such a case, either for exercise of the feelings or of the pen' (I.xvi.263). And this serves by way of introduction to the first batch of extracts from that correspondence in the chapter immediately following. Julia's writing has priority over the subject matter of that writing and intervenes in the world to constitute that matter, where scientific discourse is constrained to merely report that which already exists. By maintaining her correspondence with Matilda, Julia is the author of her own identity; because such correspondence mirrors the relationship between the female author and her readers, Julia is also a figure for the female author as such, in her problematic autonomy from patriarchal culture.

As we might expect, on the model of *Evelina*, Julia's autonomous correspondence does not last; and as we might expect, on the same model, Julia longs to regain the confidence of her father-mentor: 'I was taught to look up to him with more awe than confidence. Would to heaven it had been otherwise! It might have been better for us all at this day!' (I.xvii.268–9); 'I have thought upon it, Matilda, till my head is almost giddy—nor can I conceive a better plan than to make a full confession to my father' (I.xviii.283). However, unlike Burney's novel, the reconciliation to the father does not *consist in* the abandonment of that autonomous discourse. A whole volume separates the disappearance of Julia's letters from the novel's discourse and Julia's submission to her father within the story. The disappearance of the correspondence is clearly not an effect of that submission: some other submission, to some other determining influence, must take place, which will indicate just what is at stake in the performative function of Julia's correspondence. The reconciliation does not involve the recognition of any female-quixotic error on Julia's part: significantly, this possibility is displaced onto Julia's mother, now conveniently dead, '[...] who called her husband in her heart a tyrant until she feared him as such, and read romances until she became so enamoured of the complicated intrigues which they contain, as to assume the management of a little family novel of her own, and constitute her daughter, a girl of sixteen, the principal heroine' (I.xviii.279). This was the affair with Brown/Bertram in India that Mannering suspected was his wife's but was in fact his daughter's. Instead, the reconciliation, similar to the confession and reconciliation between Evelina and Villars, occurs when she confesses the continuation of this affair and gives him the letters which reveal her mother's part in its initiation (III.xii.240–1) as she had previously refused to do: 'shall her daughter, who inherits all her weakness, be the first to withdraw the veil from her defects?' (I.xvii.270). But the effect of thus scapegoating the late Mrs Mannering is to keep this issue quite distinct from that of Julia's correspondence with Matilda: the condemnation of the former does not extend to the latter: 'There is great apology for you, Julia, as far as I can judge from a glance at these letters—you have obeyed at least one parent' (III.xii.240–1). The reconciliation proceeds without Julia's friendship with Matilda being mentioned.

At this point we therefore need to consider the circumstances under which this correspondence *does* disappear from the text. The second and last set of epistolary extracts occupy three chapters in the centre of the second volume. The first (chapter viii) describes the Mannerings settling down in their new home at Woodbourne, near Ellengowan, with the orphaned Lucy Bertram. Julia does indeed experiment with 'the management of a little family novel' by teasing Hazlewood into paying her more attention than Lucy, and hinting to her father that he might be thinking of marrying Lucy himself; but this line of 'coquetry' (II.viii.129) he immediately silences.

> '"[...] [A]ttend at least to the sacred claims of misfortune; and observe, that the slightest hint of such a jest reaching Miss Bertram's ears, would at once induce her to renounce her present asylum, and go forth, without a protector, into a world she has already felt so unfriendly."
> 'What could I say to this, Matilda?—I only cried heartily, begged pardon, and promised to be a good girl in the future. And so here am I neutralized again [...]. So I burn little rolls of paper, and sketch Turks' heads upon visiting cards with the blackened end [...] and I jingle on my unfortunate harpsichord, and begin at the end of a grave book and read it backward.—' (II.viii.133–4)

Julia's scope for the feminine creativity implicit in her whole correspondence up to this point and explicit in this episode is drastically reduced to the listless exercise of conventional feminine 'accomplishments': drawing, music, improving reading. Such activities constitute the same restricted version of femininity which Lady Honoria complains is all that men know of women while they are single.[54] The stage might seem to be set for the reconciliation with her father, but this is long delayed by the developments that will occupy the second half of the novel. The world of social change and class conflict from which, as Mannering reminds Julia, it is Lucy's refuge, now lays siege to the house, in the form of the smugglers' raiding party. This will reshape Julia's correspondence just as Mannering's verbal warning circumscribes her actions: the description of this violence takes over her letters, rather as Mannering's drawings of Indian costume get imposed on Lucy's needlework-patterns, giving them a new, anthropological function beyond their original feminine-creative one (II.viii.128–9). From constitutive of a friendship, patterns on which Matilda can work her reply, Julia's letters are transformed to purely denotative utterance, in which she is just a point of view on a reality beyond her management, like the eye that she puts to a gap between the books barricading the windows at Woodbourne.[55] From volume II chapter xi, her discourse disappears from the text altogether, and the novel reverts to omniscient third-person narration. Julia's voice first adopts the denotative, specular priorities of scientific discourse, then is replaced by it: her autonomous discourse is silenced not by the restitution of the father-figure as moral guide, but by the reassertion of the narrative discourse with which, as we

---

54 *Cecilia* X.x.934–5; quoted above at p.138.

55 Julia only says that she 'arranged a loop-hole for myself, from which I could see the approach of the enemy' (II.x.145) and not what it was a loophole in; but she has already told us about 'the windows were almost blocked up with cushions and pillows, and, what the Dominie most lamented, with folio volumes, brought hastily from the library, leaving only spaces through which the defenders might fire upon the assailants' (II.x.143–4). If one imagines her peering at the assault through piles of old books, however, one has a perfect image of what is happening to her as a narrator: she is no longer a writer of fiction, looking within the house, but an endangered observer of the world beyond both. In any case, the analogy with her father's situation with regard to Meg at I.iv.63 is clear.

have seen, he is identified.[56] Julia submits not to the father, but to the language of the father.

Julia's writing, then, gives her (albeit temporarily) the power to construct her own identity in just the way that Clarissa's does, and as Evelina's does not. On the other hand, unlike Clarissa's or, at a different narrative level, Meg's, Julia's performative utterance does not have a particular function in working out the plot. Indeed, it is the romance plot which marshals the historical energies of pirates and smugglers and what not and throws them against Woodbourne to eventually silence Julia in the manner we have seen above. We are thus obliged to disinter agency as a distinct category from the concept of romance in which it was buried by Northrop Frye. The meaning of Julia's discourse, it seems, consists entirely in its opposition of moral autonomy, its capacity for intersubjective self-invention, to the denotative discourse of the rest of the novel. I alluded earlier to Meg's dual status as object of scientific knowledge and carrier of a power that cannot be recognised by that science. Julia's autonomous narrative discourse means that she is never reducible to an object of the enlightened gaze in this way. Julia's discourse is never shown to be somehow *erroneous* or female-quixotic, that is, subject to the master-discourse of science: she is a cause which cannot be explained as also an effect, because she is an effect of a rival sort of *novel* to that which Scott is writing here. As such, her performative discourse is not subsumed by the romance plot, but suppressed by it; and this is a suppression with which Duncan, and the Frye/Jameson model of romance, is complicit, in its subsumption of *all* agency under romance plot. This novel evokes a particular sort of actually existing moral agency (that of the feminine author/reader), only to efface it as inconsistent with the denotative claims of the new, social-realist text.

When Meg finally returns for Brown in volume III chapter xiv, Julia herself makes a connection between Meg's agency and the affective nature of the stories she described in volume I chapter xvii, which is thus also a connection with her own self-conception as an autonomous agent: 'It [...] almost reminds me of the tales of sorceresses, witches, and evil genii, which I heard in India. They believe there in a fascination of the

---

56   As Julia is also a figure for female authorship more generally, the disappearance of her own discourse is also Scott's way of acting out the replacement of the feminine novel with his new historical novel as the dominant mode of prose fiction: see the discussion of Ina Ferris in the Introduction, pp.32–3.

eye, by which those who possess it controul the will and dictate the motions of their victims' (III.xiv.269). Just as Julia's fictive autonomy from their cognitive discourse was recognised by her mentors, so they recognise Meg's. When he receives her warning of the raid by Glossin's pirates on the prison where 'Brown' is languishing after shooting Hazlewood, Mannering says of her, 'Many of her class set out by being impostors, and end by being enthusiasts, or hold a kind of darkling conduct between both lines, unconscious almost when they are cheating themselves or when imposing on others—' (III.viii.141). Despite these misgivings, he follows her advice and sends the carriage that will rescue Brown and bring him to Woodbourne. Mannering's judgement of Meg is echoed by Pleydell when he reads the same letter: 'This woman has played a part till she believes it; or, if she be a thorough-paced impostor, without a single grain of self delusion to qualify her knavery, still she may think herself bound to act in character' (III.x.189–90). This is a perfect example of the incomprehension of science in the face of other cognitive regimes that Lyotard notes.[57] Within the denotative discourse of these men, Meg can only be either an imposter or a fool: either she knows that her prophetic role is a put-on, but maintains it for her own ends, or she really believes that she has supernatural powers, but in either case it is inconceivable that she might really have those powers. What the enlightened gentlemen cannot admit is that Meg's self-perception might be sufficient to *constitute* her powers, that her self-allotted role might allow her to do things others are incapable of. However, it is also an exact parallel to their jokes about Julia's self-invention in her letters. They cannot admit such self-invention, for it is incompatible with their model of the subject as purely cognitive: as the knower of the world, not its creator. Meg's discourse is incommensurable with theirs for exactly the same reasons as Julia's.

However, where the external world, the known world, the world of social conflict and violence, lays siege to Julia's discourse at Woodbourne and overcomes it, Meg's in turn achieves what neither a purely cognitive discourse, nor Julia's, can. Meg gives the story its ending, and in doing so, enacts that conservative ideology with which we began: that is, she succeeds in realising moral categories within the empirical world of the narrator. After the accidental shooting of

57   Lyotard 27.

Hazlewood by a man she identifies as her lover, Julia indeed presents herself as a free cause, but a cause of effects that have run out of her control: 'I feel the terrors of a child, who has, in heedless sport, put in motion some powerful piece of machinery [...]' (II.x.162–3). In fact the reader knows that the plot as such has always been out of Julia's control, and it is at just this point that the plot calls up another woman to claim authority over it and steer it to its proper end. Meg Merrilies identifies 'Brown' in a different way, as Bertram of Ellangowan, when he stumbles upon her and his dying pirate foster-father in volume II chapter vii, immediately before the epistolary chapters viii–x in which events overtake Julia's usual capacity to write them. Meg thenceforth takes Bertram under her wing, and makes two decisive interventions in the second half of the novel: the first time when she alerts the residents at Woodbourne by letter of the smugglers' planned attack on the jail where Bertram is a prisoner (III.vii–x); the second when she leads him back to the scene of his kidnapping (III.xiii–xvi). Meg shares with Julia's writing a free causality; yet Meg retains this authority, and uses it to intervene successfully in the material world to restore a threatened set of social relations.

I earlier pointed out that Julia's use of the term 'romance' in association with her own discourse did not identify a particular type of narrative structure, but rather figured her intersubjective self-authorship. However, while it lasts, Julia's discourse does open up a gap at the level of discourse *analogous to* that between Meg and the enlightenment gentlemen at the level of *récit*. In fact, I suggest that Meg *takes the place* within the plot of *Guy Mannering* that Julia occupies in its narrative discourse. Meg, and the romance plot of which she is the agent, no longer appears as the other to the enlightenment discourse of the novel: it is Julia's agency which is radically unassimilable to that discourse, and Meg appears as a substitute for that agency, one who owes her efficacy in bringing the romance plot to its conclusion precisely to the fact that she *is* assimilable to that discourse as its object. Oral culture is already there in the social-realist novel as available sociological subject-matter: if it must be assimilated from outside at the level of form (e.g. the level of Meg's authority over the plot) it is because it is carrying a capacity for fiction taken over from elsewhere, from another sort of novel much more dangerously other than a non-novelistic genre could ever be. Duncan's account of the negotiation between realism and romance in effect repeats Scott's homogenizing move in the second half of *Guy Mannering*, missing the more radical opposition that makes this negotiation necessary.

Further, the freedom that Meg and Julia share means that they are both *moral* subjects in a way that the male characters are not. Julia's 'genius for friendship' and the sentimental bonds it creates constitute, in their very freedom from material causation, the space of the ethical within this novel; the ethical, that is, as it is understood in a commercial society, as inward qualities and private relationships, rather than the public virtue of the citizen-orator of the republican tradition. The eloquence of the statesman has been displaced rather into Meg, who as we have seen, shares the orator's ability to summon a community into being; but this sort of social agency appears in the modern world only in the realm of romance, only in a utopian fantasy of restored hierarchical social order, only, that is, in the realm of the aesthetic. Julia and Matilda do not only provide a model of the female author and her reader; in their moral autonomy from historical determination within the limited sphere of personal intercourse they constitute a paradigm case of ethical subjectivity in its characteristically modern form.

I ended part 2 of this chapter by suggesting that the romance plot of *Guy Mannering* might function to legitimate scientific knowledge in terms of its opposite, traditional knowledge. However, the fragmentation of language, definitive of modernity, into discrete cognitive and ethical language games allows for no master-discourse in this sense. Now we can see that, while this fragmentation is overcome at the level of discourse by the simple erasure of Julia's voice, it reappears as a split between discourse (now uniformly denotative) and *récit*. Indeed, we might note that the incommensurability of these discourses, of objective science and ethical subjectivity, repeats in slightly different terms the 'great gulf' that Kant identifies between Understanding and Reason in the *Critique of Judgement*. For while the model of ethics deployed in female-authored fiction is very different from Kantian Reason, they are both sundered from science by precisely the problem we have been exploring: the incompatible conceptions of causality presupposed by each. It now appears that the role of romance plot in *Guy Mannering* is nothing less than the co-ordination of these two discourses, of objective science and ethical subjectivity; the task, that is, that Kant set himself a quarter-century before in the third Critique.

To thus locate the meaning of romance in this novel in its ability to co-ordinate these various discourses is not to deny its ideological function within its specific historical moment. Clearly, such a feudal–restoration plot does significant cultural work in consolidating the British conservative settlement in the immediate aftermath of the defeat of Napoleonic France: the date of publication alone alerts us to this. However, as I hope I have demonstrated, Scott exploits this particular historical moment to negotiate the place of the novel within the new discursive landscape created by the Enlightenment. Romance here functions, not only to legitimate the return to power of aristocracies all across Europe, but also to legitimate the novel form itself in the late-enlightenment context: to produce the novel, that is, as that aesthetic space in which scientific description of a society could be combined with a plot that deployed a conservative political ideology. Indeed, since what we find in *Guy Mannering* is not only the construction of analogies between incommensurable discursive spheres, but also a legitimation of the novel in opposition to science and its challenge to the autonomy of the subject, this necessarily inscribes a new discursive division, between literature and the human sciences as such.

3 *Rob Roy,* gender, and modernity

In our move from Smollett to Scott in the last two chapters we seem to have repeated the move made by Smollett within *Roderick Random,* by shifting our attention from party politics to the ideological function of the family. *Guy Mannering* is indeed itself a turning away from the portrayal of party conflict in Scott's first novel, *Waverley,* which I will be examining in chapter 4: the history which provides the master-narrative of *Guy Mannering* is driven by economic modernisation, not by the squabbles of princes. It is eminently possible to read *Rob Roy* in the same way. While it is set, like *Waverley,* at a time of Jacobite unrest, the rebellion itself only breaks out when the hero is already on his way home to England. Its underlying plot centres around letters of credit stolen by a Jacobite agent, ostensibly to hasten a rising; but he is revealed late in the novel to have been following a personal agenda in doing so, and when the theft fails to serve this purpose, betrays the planned rebellion to the government. The novel instead explores the ways in which the economic foundations of societies shape their manners. The boundary between highland and lowland Scotland functions here as in *Waverley* as the geographical equivalent of the border between two stages in enlightenment conjectural history; while the political plot which accompanies the exploration of these two cultures is a mere epiphenomenon to a much greater extent in *Rob Roy.* Ian Duncan's introduction to the Oxford World's Classics edition argues convincingly that *Rob Roy* goes much further than this, indeed, to the point of deconstructing this opposition between historical stages to show their mutual implication in each other. For the Highlands here are not the site of the immediate predecessor of commercial society, namely an agricultural economy underpinning a feudal system of manners, as in *Waverley*; rather, it is the site of a yet older (nominally, at least) type of social organisation, the tribal, 'savage', or 'primitive'. The 'savage' status of Rob and his clan-followers is revealed here, argues Duncan, as a modern category, the discursive product of a commercial society:

> Far from signifying a resurgence of ancient clan loyalties, in this novel the Jacobite and clan risings turn out to be determined by the fluctuations of a modern, imperial economy. [...] Economics seems to be the definitive discourse of the historical novel as well as history itself.[1]

> If feudalism and Jacobitism together constitute the British nation's socio-economic past, the Highlanders evoke a different order of ancestral relationship to modernity: the order of the primitive. The object of a nascent science, anthropology, the primitive signifies an origin still structurally present within modernity, rather than a superceded developmental form. The primitive, charged with 'original' virtues—courage, loyalty, pathos, but also violence—belongs to the present as well as to the past. (xxiv)

In this disengagement of the 'feudal' from the values represented by the Highlanders one might note that Scott is once again following Smollett, for Matthew Bramble too locates Highland society in the more primitive category of the patriarchal rather than the feudal, and for just the same reason: to make those values available for appropriation within commercial society where the more recent ancestor order, feudalism, had to be simply rejected.

While Duncan's reading is a satisfying sophistication of the critical commonplace that Scott takes conjectural history as his master-narrative, it leaves in place the totalizing claims of an enlightenment science which can make both the commercial and the primitive objects of knowledge. As in *Guy Mannering*, I want to suggest that this mode of discourse is not the only one at work in this text, that Scott has an alternative version of modernity to that offered by political economy, and that the status of scientific discourse itself is thus one of the features of modernity called into question here.

The status of discourse is already an issue in Frank's conversation with his merchant father on his return from France at the beginning of the novel. Frank's father is characterised at once by his taciturnity ('he never wasted words in vain'), but in fact he dominates the dialogue with his son. The bulk of their first conversation consists in his reading back Frank's last letter home, refusing his father's plan for his future as a partner in the company. This letter, 'to the penning of which there had gone, I promise you, some trouble', is a rhetorical exercise designed to 'work compassion, if not conviction': that is, to appeal to the emotions

---

1   Ian Duncan, 'Introduction' to Sir Walter Scott, *Rob Roy*, ed. Ian Duncan (1818; Oxford: Oxford University Press, 1998) xvii–iii.

rather than the cognitive faculties. But Frank glimpses it bundled up 'amongst letters of advice, of credit, and all the common-place lumber, as I then thought them, of a merchant's correspondence' (I.i.12; I.68).[2] This physical location of the letter reflects its reader's interpretive strategies, for the elder Osbaldistone's understanding of language does not extend to the sentimental, but rather seems at least congruent with that of any reader who understands truth in referential, and specifically economic, terms:

> 'For, after all, Frank, it amounts but to this, that you will not do as I would have you.'
> 'That I cannot, sir, in the present instance; not that I will not.'
> 'Words avail very little with me, young man', said my father, whose inflexibility always possessed the air of the most perfect calmness and self-possession. '*Can not* may be a more civil phrase than *will not*, but the expressions are synonymous where there is no moral impossibility.' (I.i.13–14; I.69)

What Frank's father says here amounts but to this: 'civility' avails very little, within language understood in its baldly referential function; that is, separated from moral categories. And Frank's 'will' is indeed understood here outside of moral categories; that is, as a fact about the world, rather than as the self-possession of an autonomous subject.

Now, while the possibilities for self-possession are clearly infinitely wider for a young man in a patriarchal society than for a young woman, we might note that a parallel here with Burney's novels discussed in previous chapter. I noted there that in *Cecilia*, for example, one of the villain-mentor Monckton's ways of controlling his ward was by narrating back to her the truth of her own experiences from an apparently moral, but in fact self-interested, point of view. So that when Cecilia complains that Mrs Harrel, an old school-friend, is in the high-road to fashionable ruin, and that 'I have ever since felt ashamed of my own want of discernment in having formerly selected her for my friend', Monckton describes what she was actually doing when she conferred this role on Mrs Harrel, and what she means by the term 'friend' *now*:

2　All references to *Rob Roy* give volume, chapter, and page numbers to the first edition (Edinburgh: Archibald Constable and Co., 1818), which is the text used for quotations, followed by chapter and page numbers for Duncan's edition, which follows the 'Magnum Opus' edition of 1829.

'When you gave her that title', said Mr. Monckton, 'you had little choice in your power; her sweetness and good-nature attracted you; childhood is never troubled with foresight, and youth is seldom difficult [...]. But now you meet again the scene is altered; three years of absence spent in the cultivation of an understanding naturally of the first order, by increasing your wisdom, has made you more fastidious [...].'[3]

In *Rob Roy* we get a very similar display of paternal authority expressed in second-person narration like this: but the content of that narration is not the experience of the vulnerable youth translated into the mentor's terms, but his *language* itself. The power of the father-figure here appears, not as the origin of its own privileged discourse, but as the place from whence the speech of the son returns to him judged, altered, corrected, according to the requirements not of civility, but of empirical reference. Objectivity is Frank's father's criterion as moral survival is, ostensibly, Monckton's.

The immediate effect of this strategy in the Osbaldistone household is to silence the son altogether: at dinner, 'I was unable to take that active share in the conversation which my father seemed to expect from me' (I.i.15; I.69). In miniature, one might argue, this encounter between Frank and his father acts out the fate of Julia Mannering, where submission to the rules of discourse represented by the father, rather than to his will *per se*, shut down her own discursive autonomy. In *Rob Roy*, the situation is repeated in the following chapter, where Frank's father reads aloud from Frank's commonplace book Frank's notes on the Bordeaux trade (and miscellaneous historical notes), again with his own comments and corrections. Out of this book then falls some poetry of Frank's, and it too is read back to him with his father's critical gloss. The place from which these verses fall, as much as the reception they receive, makes concrete the space of the aesthetic in a commercial society, alien to both the registers, moral and factual/financial, to which Frank's father is prepared to grant recognition.

Indeed, finance provides a model for discourse, as, at first glance, economics generally does for everything else in this novel:

My father never quarrelled with a phrase, however frequently repeated, provided it seemed to him distinct and expressive; and Addison himself could not have found

---

3   *Cecilia* III.iii.197.

expressions so satisfactory to him as 'Yours received, and duly honoured the bills inclosed, as per margin. (I.i.22; I.72)

The invocation of Addison at this point is curious, for the monologic professional discourse of commercial men, or of any other group, that prevented them from entering into improving conversation with others, was precisely what the polite discourse of the *Spectator* was designed to replace, and so reminds the reader of how Frank's father does *not* speak, as well as how he does. I shall return to this point. In the meantime, let me note that the distinguishing feature of commercial discourse as it is described here is that its expressions can be repeated without any alteration of meaning that reflects the place from which they are returned. In the dialogue (if one can call it that) between Frank and his father, on the contrary, Frank's words come back to him marked by the place of their repetition, and thus by the authority of the one repeating them. On one occasion only does Frank's father forget that this is the rule, and commercial discourse the exception. 'Knowing [...] very well what he desired me to be', he takes his French partner's assurance that his son is 'all that a father could wish' as a perfect return of his own desire (I.i.22; I.72); but of course Dubourg has desires of his own, an interest in this case in not disturbing their commercial relationship with the truth of Frank's truancy from the Bordeaux counting-house.

All of this fits well enough with Duncan's observation that economics seems to be the 'definitive discourse' of this novel as writers like Smith and Ferguson had made it the master-discourse of history itself. The plot concludes with Frank's reconciliation not only to his father, but to a career as a merchant, as if his personal story represented the inescapability of the commercial in a modern society. What resists this reading of *Rob Roy* is the role of Diana Vernon. Duncan places Diana within the economic master-discourse of the novel by assimilating her independence and energy to that of the savage and the sublime:

> The ordeal of masculinity beset by eloquent Amazons—the lovely Die Vernon, the terrifying Helen MacGregor—culminates not in any clarity of action or self-possession but in a remarkable fit of hysteria, as an archaic feminine energy overwhelms the hero from within. (xvii)

But this is a very unsatisfactory equation, for apart from their sex, the only thing Duncan is able to identify as shared by Diana and Helen is their 'eloquence.' Now, Helen MacGregor's speech certainly partakes of that spontaneous sublimity that eighteenth-century poetics located in the primitive origins of poetry, most influentially a treatise that Duncan cites, Hugh Blair's *Critical Dissertation on the Poems of Ossian* (1763), and of which Scott's readers had had a taste from Meg Merrilies in *Guy Mannering*. But Diana's language is clearly in another category altogether, as is the threat that she poses to Frank.

For unlike Helen, Diana herself is able to spell out her connection both with savages and with commerce.

> 'I must inform you at once, Mr Osbaldistone, that compliments are entirely lost upon me; do not, therefore, throw away your pretty sayings—they serve fine gentlemen who travel in the country, instead of the toys, beads, and bracelets, which navigators carry to propitiate the savage inhabitants of newly discovered lands. Do not exhaust your stock in trade—you will find natives in Northumberland to whom your fine things will recommend you—on me they would be utterly thrown away, for I happen to know their real value.' (I.vi.122; I.112)

Duncan quotes this passage in his introduction as a summary of the new imperial economy and the uncertainty, financial and otherwise, that it brings. However, this is to miss, on the one hand, that Diana's speech adopts the terminology of commerce and the 'savage' to describe her own *gendered* discursive situation in relation to Frank; and on the other, that the historical/economic comprehension that Duncan grants Diana in this speech raises her to a position of understanding greater than Frank himself ever explicitly achieves, and on a par with the novel's other explicator of progress, Baillie Nicol Jarvie. As such, Diana's own discourse eludes capture by the discourse of conjectural history as the object of its knowledge. These two aspects of Diana's speech mean that she transcends the distinction between the knower and the known that we saw in the previous chapter was so crucial to enlightenment science: for she is not simply an uninvolved spectator of cultural practices, nor an unknowing object of such observation, but rather turns her gaze on the discursive practices in which her own identity is constructed. And that which prompts this self-consciousness, that which makes this transcendence of the categories of enlightenment science necessary, is the *gender* of that identity. In the immediate context of her dialogue with Frank, this thematization of their discursive situation is designed to preempt the language of courtship that would reduce her to the passive

156

object of an active male desire. The effect of this is to render Frank the passive object of her own linguistic dissertation, and, significantly, to silence him just as his father's previous analysis of his writing had silenced him: 'I was silenced and confounded', he notes, immediately after the passage quoted above. This is a silence which Diana explains by continuing her commercial metaphor: 'I have cried down and ruined your whole stock of complimentary discourse by one unlucky observation'(I.vi.122; VI.112–3).

Nor is this an isolated assertion of discursive power on Diana's part: throughout her dialogue with Frank, she adopts exactly the same tactic as his father, the same tactic as Monckton in *Cecilia*, that of repeating back to Frank his thoughts in her own authoritative second-person version of them.

> 'I will tell you what you think of me. [...]
> '[...]You think me a strange bold girl, half coquette, half romp; desirous of attracting attention by the freedom of her manners and loudness of her conversation, because she is ignorant of what the Spectator calls the softer graces of the sex; and perhaps you think I have some particular plan of storming you into admiration. I should be sorry to shock your self-opinion, but you were never more mistaken. All the confidence I have reposed in you, I would have given as readily to your father, if I thought he could have understood me.' (I.vi.123, 124; VI.113)

Diana's language is not an instance of the Amazonian sublime to which Duncan assimilates her; it is rather a usurpation of the language of the father, or the lover-mentor, by a woman in order to exert its authority over a young man. The difference with Frank's father is simply that Diana remembers what Osbaldistone senior forgets: that language cannot be returned to its origin without being marked by the site of its repetition; that speech, like money, is not the medium of a perfectly reciprocal exchange. This is what is at stake in Diana's rejection of Frank's 'complimentary discourse'. To simply return the conventional replies to Frank's conventional niceties would not be to be to trade like for like, for the gentleman's compliment is an investment of desire on which he expects a return, and to proffer that return is then to be implicated in that desire. The link that Diana makes between the savage and the female (herself excluded) is not their common sublimity, but their common ignorance of the power-relations written into such exchanges.

In her ability to resist inscription in such power-relations, Diana's speech constitutes her mode of agency, her (however limited) ability to exert power over the world around her. In this we might link her with Julia Mannering, and before her Lydia Melford and Clarissa, heroines who maintain their authority within a correspondence with a sympathetic female friend. But Diana's achievement is clearly more impressive than this, for she maintains her authority, not in a discourse autonomous from that of patriarchy, but by appropriating the terms of patriarchal discourse and turning them to her own ends. Indeed, one of the types of language which she deconstructs is precisely that appropriated from fiction for the purposes of generating amorous intrigues of the sort that tempted Julia in *Guy Mannering*: when, later in the novel, Frank discovers an unknown rival, and reminds Diana that 'a beautiful young woman can have but one male friend', she replies

> 'You are, of course, jealous, in all the tenses and moods of that amicable passion. But, my good friend, you have all this time spoke nothing but the paltry gossip which simpletons repeat from play-books and romances, till they give mere cant a real and powerful influence over their minds. Boys and girls prate themselves into love, and when their love is like to fall asleep, they prate and teaze themselves into jealousy. (II.iv.79; XVII.221)

Diana's power is clearly not that of the female quixote, the female romance reader, tropes for feminine interpretive autonomy deployed in the other novels we have examined.

Where are we to place the speech of Diana Vernon in the discursive landscape of the early realist novel as we have mapped it so far? I think the clue to the function of Diana lies in her self-cancelling denial, quoted above, that she 'is ignorant of what the Spectator calls the softer graces of the sex.' In fact, this novel gives her precisely that civilising and 'polishing' role that Addison and Steele give to the lady in polite society. On the one hand, the very expression of discursive self-consciousness in commercial metaphors is strikingly suggestive, for 'commerce', understood broadly as free exchange between autonomous individuals, is used to signify both economic and conversational intercourse in the *Spectator* and elsewhere.[4] Diana's metaphor indeed goes to the heart of Scott's project as Kathryn Sutherland describes it:

> Scott [in his prefaces] presents the imagination itself as a model Smithian economy, a thriving commercial enterprise, and in so doing he elides Smith's distance between the real and the fancied [...] their equivalence grounded in the purchasing power, or exchange value, of words.[5]

If this is correct, then I suggest that Scott in *Rob Roy* is historicizing his own practice, by identifying a historical moment, the early eighteenth century, when such an equivalence first became possible.

Yet the *Spectator*'s agenda for a polite culture, while it understands conversation on the model of free trade, depends on the removal of professional jargons, including that of the merchant or financier, from that conversation. Frank, of course, has been pursuing such a course independently, to the point where he is ready to reject the commercial life altogether: on his journey North, he adopts the pose of the Spectator himself, inclined to seek out 'all scenes where my knowledge of mankind could be enlarged'; he first meets Rob at a County Durham equivalent of the Spectator's Club, Sunday dinner at the inn in Darlington, where

> The guests, assembled from different quarters, and following different professions, formed, in language, manners, and sentiments, a curious contrast to each other, not indifferent to those who desired to possess a knowledge of mankind in all its varieties. (I.iv.70; IV.92)

including the various professional types one would expect: the curate, the apothecary, the exciseman, and so on.

However, as I have already noted in the introduction (see pp.22–4 above), conversation with women is given a central role in the

---

4   'A man who is but a mere Spectator of what passes around him, and not engaged in Commerces of any Consideration, is but an ill Judge of the secret Motions of the Heart of Man', *The Spectator* 76 (May 28, 1711) 326. The equivalence of trade and conversation is an eighteenth-century commonplace that Frank has learned to parrot, assuring his father that he respects the 'commercial character' as being 'to the general commonwealth of the civilized world what the daily intercourse of ordinary life is to private society' (I.ii.30; II.75).

5   Kathryn Sutherland, 'Fictional Economies: Adam Smith, Walter Scott, and the nineteenth-century novel', *ELH* 54 (1987): 110.

socialisation of men by Addison and Steele. So, for Addison, it is women who have the specific task of maintaining the politeness of conversation:

> As Vivacity is the Gift of Women, Gravity is that of Men. They should each of them therefore keep a Watch upon the particular Biass which Nature has fixed in their Minds, that it may not *draw* too much, and lead them out of the Paths of Reason. This will certainly happen, if the one in every Word and Action affects the Character of being rigid and severe, and the other of being brisk and airy.[6]

The qualities that make a woman a useful corrective to the vices of men can themselves become vices if unchecked; but 'vivacious', 'brisk', 'airy', seem exactly to describe Diana's 'raillery' and 'good humor' in conversation with Frank, and these are qualities necessary to refine gentlemen out of a vulgarity natural to them.

This function of conversation with women is one that the English moralists inherit, notes Klein, from seventeenth-century French feminism.[7] And one might note that Diana conforms more closely to the type of the lady of the *salon*, transposed uncomfortably to Northumberland, in her learning and her wit. In the pre-revolutionary *salon*, writes Joan Landes, a 'novel pattern of interchange existed between educated men and literate, informed women who functioned not just as consumers but as purveyors of culture.'[8] This was a space for women that was lost in the French Revolution, when women were re-categorised in domestic terms as mothers first and foremost. In England, the persisting importance of exclusively masculine public spaces such as the club and the coffee-house meant that such mixed-gender spaces never achieved the centrality they did in France:[9] yet the common ground that Diana is

---

6   *Spectator* 128 (Friday, July 27, 1711) 8.

7   See Lawrence Klein, 'Gender, Conversation and the Public Sphere'.

8   Joan B. Landes, *Women and the Public Sphere in the Age of the French Revolution* (Ithaca: Cornell University Press, 1988) 22.

9   Coffee-houses, if not always masculine spaces, seem at least to have been homosocial: Lydia Melford complains from Bath, 'Hard by the Pump-room, is a coffee-house for the ladies; but my aunt says, young girls are not admitted, inasmuch as the conversation turns upon politics, scandal, philosophy, and other subjects above our capacity; but we are allowed to accompany them to the booksellers shops, which are charming places of resort; where we read novels, plays, pamphlets, and news-papers' (*Humphry Clinker* 40). Note how Tabitha's distinction separates a bluestocking culture, which has appropriated masculine

able to find with Frank in their shared enthusiasm for renaissance Italian poetry is clearly a recreation in miniature of something like the culture of the salons of the English Bluestockings.[10] For given Diana's refusal to implicate herself in Frank's fatuous gallantry, the library of Osbaldistone Hall provides 'a sort of public-room, where man and woman might meet as on neutral ground' (II.i.22; XIV.198), and here the two spend their time translating Ariosto. For Diana has been given a classical rather than a typically feminine education, by her one 'rational' cousin, Rashleigh:

'Rashleigh, who is no contemptible scholar, taught me Greek and Latin, as well as most of the languages of modern Europe. I assure you, there has been some pains taken in my education, although I can neither sew a tucker, nor work cross-stitch, not make a pudding, [...].

I wanted, like my rational cousin, to [...] make complete my approach to the tree of knowledge, which you men-scholars would engross to yourselves, in revenge, I suppose, for our common mother's share in the great original transgression.' (I.x.229; X.154)

Scott clearly feels obliged to raise the issue of the morality of this effacement of gender-difference: for this site of mutual self-improvement is also the site of Rashleigh's attempted seduction of his pupil. The motivation behind Rashleigh's tutorship was from the start this assault on the virtue of his cousin: Scott thus reassures his nineteenth-century novel-readers that knowledge cannot provide a de-sexualised space within society, where the 'unlucky sex' of half its members might conveniently be forgotten (I.vi.122; VI.113). Yet apart from its ultimate motive, and in distinction to the recurring concern over the effects of female romance- or novel-reading, it is the impolite nature of the philosophy that Rashleigh teaches Diana, a quality of these texts that inheres in these texts irrespective of the gender of their reader, that Frank sees its danger:

---

topics for its own, from the more innovative productions of an expanded print-culture aimed at or at least freely available to women, including the novel itself. Diana Vernon would clearly have belonged in the coffee-house, when Julia Mannering would have headed for the booksellers'.

10 Such an enthusiasm seems to function in these texts as the epitome of polite learning: it is Roderick's knowledge of Ariosto that first impresses Narcissa.

> Neither can I conceive with what view he should have engaged Diana in the gloomy maze of casuistry which schoolmen called philosophy [...] unless it were to break down and confound in her mind the difference and distinction between the sexes, and to habituate her to trains of subtile reasoning, by which he might at his own time invest that which is wrong with the colour of that which is right. (I.xiii.318–9; XIII.189)

I quoted the *Spectator* above on the mutually improving relation between feminine 'vivacity' and masculine 'gravity', qualities that would be coquettish or vulgar respectively if they were not kept in check by the other. Writing much later in the century, however, Frank notes here that what Diana misses is not a father-figure or husband who can keep her in check, but a female confidant, for 'she was sequestered from all female company, and could not learn the usual rules of decorum, either from example or precept' (I.xiii.319; XIII.189). Similarly, at Osbaldistone Hall, masculine vulgarity takes the form, not of philosophical or religious or commercial 'gravity', but of the unregenerate, unsociable masculine manners of her cousins, the Osbaldistone brothers, who are incapable of speaking in other than the jargon of hunting, drinking, or gambling.

> My cousins were mere cubs, in whose company I might, if I liked it, unlearn whatever decent manners, or elegant accomplishments I had acquired, but where I could attain no information beyond what regarded worming dogs, rowelling horses, and following foxes. [...] My father considered the life which was led at Osbaldistone Hall as the natural and inevitable pursuits of all country gentlemen [...]. (I.vii.142; VII.120)

Of all country gentlemen who have not yet been won over by Joseph Addison's scheme for their improvement, that is. Unlearn his decent manners Frank goes on to do in chapter xii, if only temporarily, by getting hopelessly drunk, punching Rashleigh, and getting into a fight with the eldest, Thorncliff. Such behaviour on the part of a gentleman must inevitably fall under the jurisdiction of the polite lady, and sure enough, when Frank finds her seated in the library next morning, 'like a judge about to hear a cause of importance', she 'signed to me to take a chair opposite to her, (which I did, much like the poor fellow who is going to be tried,) and entered upon conversation in a tone of bitter irony' (I.xii.293; XII.179).

Duncan incorporates Osbaldistone Hall into the stadial history of the Scottish Enlightenment by making it stand for the missing third term between savagery and commerce missing from Frank's experience in Scotland: the feudal organisation of an agrarian society. The very amount of space devoted to this stage Duncan explains as representing the 'legal stagnation' of feudalism (xx). Yet the reader's experience is not of stagnation, but of a decaying space filled with an vivacious feminine voice: feudalism is only half the story, for Osbaldistone Hall encloses Diana Vernon as well as her cousins. Duncan comments that '[s]peech, brilliantly stylized, lovingly crafted, rich in inflections of generic register and dialect, takes the place of action for much of the novel' (xiv), yet does not observe that speech is itself thematized in the discourse of Diana and Frank at Osbaldistone Hall: 'I am in this happy family as much secluded from intelligent listeners as Sancho in the Sierra Morena, and when opportunity offers, I must speak or die' (I.vi.124; VI.113). If Frank represents the type of the self-cultivating city man, one engaged in an Addisonian project of acquiring a culture that both consists in and makes possible conversation with other social types, then what he finds at Osbaldistone Hall, in the difference between Diana and her cousins, is not a past or passing stage of society, but a caricature of his own discursive situation; not 'the feudal' *per se*, but the feudal in its constitutive opposition to politeness. Osbaldistone Hall represents modernity as an unfinished project. That is, Frank's two experiences, of Diana at Osbaldistone Hall and of Scotland, constitute two different versions of modernisation: one economic, the other discursive. And modernity in Northumbria, like the letters of credit in the Highlands, are in the gift of a young woman.[11]

In chapter 2, I discussed *Guy Mannering*'s representation of modernisation in exclusively economic terms, yet one should note that

---

11 If the discursive politics of the novel are taken to encompass both Diana's effect on Frank and Frank's effect as narrator on the reader, as I shall go on to argue, then they can be seen to exemplify precisely the 'two criteria of modernity' identified by Jerome Christensen in Hume: 'the ascendancy of the woman as sovereign and the emergence of the man of letters as the successor of the classical orator.' But these criteria of modernity are clearly distinct from the foundationally economic ones deployed by Adam Smith and, following Smith, Ian Duncan: *Rob Roy* represents the juxtaposition of these two versions of modernity, the former in Northumbria, the latter in Scotland. Christensen, *Practicing Enlightenment* 105.

there too, the identity of the enlightenment gentleman is established not only by his cognitive position with respect to the society around him, but also by his ability to hold a rational conversation, in contrast to those inarticulate others that the young Mannering first meets at Ellengowan in the second chapter, the elder Bertram and Abel Sampson. Sampson has been unable to get a place as a minister because of his inarticulacy in the pulpit. Bertram senior's speech in contrast is fluent enough, but totally without order. 'Mr Bertram never embraced a general or abstract idea' (I.v.75), and, for example, can only conceive of the law in terms of its officers. Scott in *Guy Mannering* thus associates conversation with the ability to grasp and communicate abstract ideas, and thus with the ability to deploy abstract categories in the understanding of society demanded by an enlightenment science of man. 'General or abstract ideas' in each case supply 'ordinary social beings' with 'a mechanism for distancing themselves from themselves [...] which would allow them to see themselves in the context of other selves' that Klein identifies with politeness.[12] But if there is a continuity between science and politeness in *Guy Mannering*, it has been pulled apart in *Rob Roy*. I suggested earlier that the equivalence of money and words in the speech of Diana locates that speech in a specific historical moment, that of the *Spectator*, the rise of polite culture, and of the financial system that underpins it. One could argue that the understanding of social inter-action represented by Diana is then replaced, once Frank goes to Scotland, with another, that of Scottish Enlightenment sociology, representing a later historical moment than that in which the action of the novel itself is set.

However, there remains one aspect of the conversation that passes between Diana and Frank unaccounted for: and that is the way in which it is built around a third term, the 'mystery' (Frank's phrase, oft-repeated) of Diana's presence at Osbaldistone Hall in the first place. In chapter ix, Diana lists the disabilities under which she labours: her gender, her religion, and finally that very 'frank and unreserved disposition' that make the perfect Addisonian conversant (I.ix.219; IX.150). Yet this latter is only possible if certain subjects are left out of

---

12   Lawrence Klein, 'Property and Politeness in the early eighteenth-century Whig moralists', in John Brewer and Susan Staves, eds., *Early Modern Conceptions of Property* (London: Routledge, 1995) 228.

their conversation altogether: 'I must settle signals of correspondence with you, because you are to be my confident and my counsellor, only you are to know nothing whatever of my affairs', she explains to Frank (I.ix.223; IX.152). At points like this, indeed, rather than their conversation being carried on without the particular content that must be suppressed, the fact of its suppression provides their conversation with its content.

Frank increasingly believes that Diana's secret is a sexual one, as one might expect from an instance of 'nineteenth-century masculine subjectivity in full, proto-Freudian flood', as Duncan calls him, or at least from a proto-Freudian *analyst* of that troublesome thing, *feminine* subjectivity (xiii). He presumes that the shadowy figure who meets Diana in the library after dark is her husband, or at least her lover. When Diana falters in explaining the presence of this other, Frank 'filled up the blank in my own way. "Whom she *loves*, Miss Vernon would say"' (II.iv.75; XVII.219). This is perhaps the only instance in the novel of Frank turning the tables and repeating Diana's speech back to her, not so much improved, as completed. As narrator, his vocabulary here also echoes the marriage contract as described to Frank by Rashleigh: 'A dispensation has been obtained from Rome to Diana Vernon to marry *Blank* Osbaldistone, Esq.' (I.xi.270; XI.170). Frank will end the novel by revealing that he did indeed fill this blank also in his own way, by marrying Diana.

But the blank that shapes their conversation at Osbaldistone Hall is not, we have already learned by then, some sexual commitment on Diana's part. It is her political commitment to the Jacobite cause. The 'third party unknown and concealed' turns out to be her father, wanted by the government for his involvement in assassination attempts on William III (II.iv.79; XVII.221): it is he who is introduced by his daughter once the 1715 rising has collapsed, with the words 'You now understand my mystery' (III.xi.312; XXXVIII.438). It is almost all she does say; in his presence she is reduced to the same silence as Frank was in the opening chapters by *his* father, or as Julia Mannering is by the discourse of hers. Diana's relationship with her father has indeed been characterised in this way from the beginning: 'Their league, if any subsisted between them, was of a tacit and understood nature, operating on their actions without any necessity of speech' (II.ii.43; XV.206).

Party politics, in other words, partisan conflict in the public realm, is that which must be suppressed in order for the polite conversation between Diana and Frank to take place. In this too Diana's library functions as a microcosmic version of the *salon*; for, notes Habermas, debate in the coffee houses

> was soon extended to include economic and political disputes, without any guarantee (such as was given in the *salons*) that such disputes would be inconsequential, at least in the immediate context. The fact that only men were admitted to coffee-house society may have had something to do with this, whereas the style of the *salon* [...] was essentially shaped by women.[13]

But more broadly, the Whig periodicals also worked to suppress partisan loyalty with 'a style of journalism that was designed to control the fragmentation of opinion rather than exacerbate it'; to generate a cross-party alliance of monied and landed groups, they emphasised the 'social complexity' that Frank claims to relish on his journey North, 'rather than social dichotomy, so that the distinction [...] became a source of value in the civil order, not of disruption.'[14] And the importance of women to conversation is precisely that their presence precludes partisan argument: 'discussion among men on their own was too unsociable, whether because it wound down into pedantic concern with detail or because it exploded into an uncontrolled storm of controversy': a storm of the sort that temporarily engulfs the inn at Darlington during Frank's (all-male) dinner there, but from which Rob Roy himself stays aloof.[15]

In chapter 1 we saw Smollett's novels acting out the separation of the aesthetic from the party-political realm, a move made possible, or necessary, by the advent of a polite culture in which party-political questions were to some extent taboo. One might note that Diana's comment in chapter vi that, when opportunity offers, she 'must speak or die' is an echo of *Waverley*'s epigraph from *Henry IV part II*: 'Under which King, Bezonian? Speak, or die!' That which named the fatal division of a kingdom between two incompatible political loyalties in the earlier novel, is here enclosed within the polite realm to name the

---

13   Jürgen Habermas, *The Structural Transformation of the Public Sphere*, trans. Thomas Burger (Cambridge: Polity, 1989) 33.

14   Nicholas Phillipson, *Hume* (London: Weidenfeld and Nicolson, 1989) 24; Klein, 'Property and Politeness', 223–4.

15   Klein, 'Gender, Conversation and the Public Sphere', 105.

social necessity of polite conversation. The contrast between the speech of Helen MacGregor and that of Diana Vernon is indeed that between eloquence, now understood as originating in the savage rather than the classical past, and politeness.

However, it is not only polite culture that is based on the suppression of the political; for we have already seen how Scottish Enlightenment conjectural history withdraws historical agency from statesmen. While it is true that in *Rob Roy*, as in Adam Smith's *Lectures on Jurisprudence* and *The Wealth of Nations*, the important economic unit is the region, a trading city and its hinterland, rather than any political unit like the state, Smith is doing this in part, writes Phillipson, to *avoid* 'words with narrowly political associations like "province" or "country".'[16] Christensen sums this up by commenting that 'Smith's economics silently represses the antagonist political order.'[17]

Party politics thus appears in *Rob Roy* as the repressed other of *both* the master discourses of modernity: polite conversation and political economy. It is the eruption of party politics in the revelation that this is Diana's secret that places this novel most firmly in Scott's own post-revolutionary culture. Ian Duncan notes elsewhere that the Scottish Enlightenment's understanding of the institutions of civil society, that is, those outside of the state, as 'apolitical' was thrown into crisis by the French revolution: 'Traditional intellectuals in Britain, Whigs as well as Tories, interpreted the Revolution as a catastrophic saturation of the whole of social life by a repressed, volcanic force of politics.'[18] The *Edinburgh Review*, with which Scott enjoyed a long if not always easy association, set itself the task of pre-empting this process precisely by bringing a political, rather than a polite, criticism to bear on culture and society. One can understand *Rob Roy* as engaged in a very similar project: the representation of that shocking re-emergence in order to defuse it.

Given the continuing exclusion of women from most types of political debate, then, the revelation that Diana is a political agent perhaps reflects the unsettling of the gender-relations of polite culture in

16 Nicholas Phillipson, 'Adam Smith as Civic Moralist', 194.
17 Christensen, *Practicing Enlightenment* 105.
18 Ian Duncan, 'Edinburgh, Capital of the Nineteenth Century', in James Chandler and Kevin Gilmartin, eds., *Romantic Metropolis: Cultural Productions of the City, 1770–1850* (Cambridge: Cambridge University Press, forthcoming).

the aftermath of 1789. Even before he has discovered the true character of her mysterious male companion, the scene in which Diana appears by the road at night in the Trossachs in order to hand back the letters of credit before taking a final farewell, acts as a little allegory of the delivery of commercial society by the agency of that which it necessarily suppresses: political struggle. Duncan's characterisation of Frank's response to this encounter as 'hysteria' in fact fits Frank very nicely, not into a nineteenth-century proto-Freudian archetype, but an eighteenth-century commercial one:

> Economic man [...] was seen on the whole [in the eighteenth century] as a feminised, even an effeminate being, still wrestling with his own passions and hysterias and with interior and exterior forces let loose by his fantasies and appetites [...].[19]

The recurrence of party-politics in feminine form does of course allow it to be defused in the characteristic manner of novels of this period: by marrying Diana off to Frank. And yet the revelation that Diana became Frank's wife is reserved for the very end of the novel and the same paragraph as the discovery that she is, at the time of Frank's writing, dead:

> How I sped in my wooing, Will Tresham, I need not tell you. You know, too, how long and happily I lived with Diana. You know how I lamented her. But you do not—cannot know how much she deserved her husband's sorrow. (III.xii.346; XXXIX.452)

The novel makes no attempt to imagine Diana as a wife, subject to the authority of a husband as she had been before to a father. The novel does not silence her within the story, by subjecting her to such authority: but rather removes her as quickly as possible from the narration. In this way *Rob Roy*, alongside its other demystifications, reveals as a disjunction what the domestic ideology offers as a continuity: namely, the restoration of virtue within the domestic sphere under feminine authority as a replacement for the political virtue now impossible in the public sphere.

The return of Diana as political agent is not the only way in which the nightmare return of politics after the French Revolution marks this text. For as I suggested in the Introduction, another effect of the political

---

19   J.G.A. Pocock, *Virtue, Commerce, and History* 114.

anxieties raised by the conflict with revolutionary France, combined with an ever-increasing market for books, was the unpredictable political consequences of widening literacy. The exclusion of politics from the Addisonian project was from the start, as I have suggested, motivated by the need to establish common cultural ground for the 'middling sort', an ideology that could be shared by landed and trading classes alike and thus prevent the middle classes throwing in their lot with the poor and rising against oligarchy. This was just what had happened in France. The unchallengeable cultural hegemony of landed and trading interests in the United Kingdom before 1789 might be looked back on with some nostalgia by the Tory Scott, and this nostalgia finds expression in the romance plot of *Rob Roy*, where a merchant's son contrives both to inherit the ancient family seat, but also to continue his father's business empire; where an otherwise Jacobite gentry, in the shape of Diana and her father, complete a quest into the wild wood of the Highlands, not on their own behalf, but in order to return credit to where credit is due, to the heroes of a new national epic, the financiers. But nostalgia for this alliance is driven by the fear that it was breaking down in the face of popular unrest, an unrest in which the mass market for books could be implicated.

This anxiety appears in the text of *Rob Roy* as a set of questions surrounding, not the action, but Frank's retrospective first-person narration of it. Frank's depiction of Scottish society, highland and lowland, gains its authority from its deployment of the categories and vocabulary of conjectural history. But unlike the third-person narrator of *Guy Mannering*, Frank is narrating events in which his younger self was not a distanced scientific observer: the gap between Brown as ethnographer among the farmers of Liddesdale and Bertram as destined subject of gentry restoration is here to some extent repeated and reversed in the difference between Frank as narrator and Frank as protagonist. In the latter capacity, he endures the passivity in the face of events usual for a Scott hero. Only on one occasion does he implicate himself in those events, and then, revealingly, his agency is purely verbal. Falling in with Morris, the government courier, on his journey North, Frank remains completely ignorant of the contents of Morris's jealously-guarded saddle-bags; yet the combination of Morris's terror of losing them, and Frank's boredom, means that they dominate the conversation between them, as Frank allows Morris to suspect that he may be a highwayman: 'Neither was I offended. On the contrary, I found much amusement in alternately exciting, and lulling to sleep, the suspicions of my timorous companion' (I.iii.65; III.89). Frank, that is, simply acts as a mirror to Morris's fears, reflecting them back without knowing what they are. The gold itself draws him into adopting the position of thief, and Morris the position of victim, without it ever actually entering their speech. Money here is not *like* speech, but shapes it from without.

In this it functions in a similar way to the letters of credit whose theft and return constitute the narrative frame of the action. These letters draw the characters into the relationships that link them in the second half of the book, although their recovery from Rashleigh by Diana is never narrated. When Diana returns them to Frank, at the point where he must bid farewell to Diana for ever (not for the first time, nor the last), the transaction is marked by a simile of execution.

> I could neither return Miss Vernon's half embrace, not even answer her farewell. The word, though it rose to my tongue, seemed to choke in my throat like the fatal *guilty*, which the dilinquent who makes it his plea knows must be followed by the doom of death. (III.vi.178; XXXIII.386)

The return of his own is accompanied here by just that effect that earlier accompanied the return of language from his father or Diana: his own silence. What makes the difference in this instance is its accompaniment with the sensation of guilt. In this, it connects, not to the political plot in which the letters of credit are ensnared, but to Diana's gift of politeness at Osbaldistone Hall. For on the morning following his lapse into vulgarity, Frank follows Diana to the library 'like a criminal [...] to execution' (I.xii.292; XII.179). The expression on both occasions cannot help but bring to mind those two real, if extra-judicial, 'executions' in the novel. Morris is flung into Loch Ard with a rock tied round his neck by Helen MacGregor, and Rashleigh is despatched by Rob himself. Both of the victims, that is, are those who carried the wealth of others and were relieved of it. The authority wielded by Diana is imagined by Frank as the discursive equivalent of the violence meted out by the summary justice of the MacGregors, at once its replacement, and its continuation. In this way, the novel raises the question of Frank's ownership of his own speech, for the parallel with Morris and with Rashleigh would suggest that Frank's words are not only returned to him from elsewhere (his father, Diana) but originate somewhere other than himself; or rather, that their meaning, like that of money, consists in the power relation-ships that they mediate, rather than in any putative origin one might ascribe. What the novel adds to this routinely post-structuralist observation is the *guilt* that seems to afflict Frank when the contingency of his own discourse is brought home to him by the judgement of Diana.

This position of Frank in relation to his own language within the story reflects, I want to suggest, the position of Frank as the novel's narrator. For that narration is itself located by its opening and closing chapters within a very particular and intimate relationship: it is addressed to the elder Frank's friend and business associate, Will Tresham, the son of his father's sleeping partner. This intimacy, Frank suggests, raises a problem for him as story-teller: for Will has already heard this story, or most of it, many times before. One way of addressing this problem is to turn the novel into a sociological or historical treatise of the sort whose meaning, as I suggested in the introduction (pp.25–6 above), can claim to survive interpretation by *any* reader. And, despite the fact that less than half of the novel is set in the Highlands, Frank is clearly tempted by this option:

> you have often affirmed, that the incidents which befel me among a people singularly primitive in their government and manners, have something interesting and attractive for those who love to hear an old man's stories of a past age (I.i.4; I.65)

Yet Frank also concludes his introduction by promising to 'endeavour to tell you nothing that is familiar to you already' (I.i.9; I.67). Frank's problem is this: he knows that his story is guaranteed an interested readership for exactly the same reason that telling that story seems redundant: namely, that his readership knows the story very well already. One might go so far as to say that, in its *oral* form, this story forms a bourgeois equivalent of the folk-culture narrative discussed in the previous chapter, not the one-way transmission of information, but the maintenance of social (here, merely inter-subjective) bonds: 'The tale told by one friend, and listened to by another, loses half its charms when committed to paper' (I.i.4; I.65). This story is one that is already in Will Tresham's possession. The difference that its commitment to writing makes is figured by Frank instead in terms of power: the writer's power over his reader ('I have you in my power') and the power of writing over the writer ('The seductive love of narrative' that tempts him

171

to indulge his power over the reader: I.i.6; I.66). Frank and Will as writer and addressee are inscribed in the same discursive power relations as Frank and his father, as Frank and Diana. The difference is, that the elder Frank is now in the position of power previously occupied by Diana and his father; a position that he has been granted, not by his paternal relation to his addressee, nor by his gender, but by writing itself.

As an image of this power Frank then adds an anecdote: the French statesman the Duc de Sully had, says Frank, his own memoires read back by his secretaries to him in the second person. As a result, what Sully hears from others is an unaltered repetition of his own good opinion of himself, rather than the judgement returned by the younger Frank's interlocutors. The effect of the Sully anecdote is to align Frank's power as narrator with the political power of the statesman; Frank thus positions himself, a modern 'man of letters', as 'the successor of the classical orator' in just the way that Christensen suggests (see above note 11).

In what, one might then ask, does Frank's power of narration consist? What is it about writing that lends it the authority wielded by the statesman, or by the father, or by his substitute in a commercial society, the polite lady? Frank offers us an intriguing answer to this question: his writing has this power in so far as it can never be returned to him from its addressee judged and altered as his speech was as a young man. This will be made impossible, not by any extra-discursive power he wields over that addressee, but by the fact of his own death: 'Throw, then, these sheets into some secret drawer of your escritoire till we are separated from each other's society by an event which may happen at any moment, and which must happen within the course of a few,—a very few years' (I.i.5; I.65). It is this anticipation of death that allows Frank's narration to escape the contingent position his earlier speech endured in relation to the reply of others. Frank will never have to listen to this story being recited back to him with Will's, or anyone else's, comments and criticisms.[20]

I want to finish this chapter by suggesting that this resort to death as guarantor of Frank's narrative authority returns us to the situation of the

---

20 One might note that Frank's other potential reader with an even greater intimacy with the story told, namely Diana, is already dead at the time of narration.

novel in post-revolutionary culture. It is tempting to generalise from this chapter some truth about first-person narration that inheres simply in its grammatical structures, of the sort offered by Paul de Man in his later work on apostrophe and prosopopeia. In an essay on Wordsworth's *Essay Upon Epitaphs*, de Man comments,

> Writers *of* autobiographies as well as writers *on* autobiography are obsessed by the need to move from cognition to resolution and to action, from speculative to political and legal authority. Philippe Lejeune, for example [...] stubbornly insists [...] that the identity of autobiography is not only representational and cognitive but contractual, grounded not in tropes but in speech acts.[21]

This, it seems to me, is just what happens in Frank's narration of his own life in *Rob Roy*. De Man's implication is, characteristically, that the distinction between tropes and speech acts is in itself a kind of illusion, that speech acts on examination will always collapse into tropes, and that the imposition of the figures of language on reality is itself a type of (indeed, our *only*) agency. Frank encloses his representation of primitive manners and government within a narration that gives him a power over his reader understood on the model of the political or the legal. Further, de Man's discussion of Wordsworth's critique of prosopopeia, that is, the trope whereby the inscription on a tomb claims to be the voice of the dead, seems to me startlingly relevant to Frank's use of death to empower his own narrative voice.

> The latent threat that inhabits prosopopeia, namely that by making the death speak, the symmetrical structure of the trope implies, by the same token, that the living are struck dumb, frozen in their own death. [...] [Wordsworth] knows that the advocated 'exclusion' of the fictional voice and its replacement by the actual voice of the living in fact reintroduces the prosopopeia in the fiction of *address*.[22]

We are now in a position to explain how this works in *Rob Roy*, and in doing so, to historicize de Man's insight, to understand this mechanism not as hard-wired into the structures of language itself, but a tactic

---

21   Paul de Man, 'Autobiography As De-Facement', *The Rhetoric of Romanticism* (New York: Columbia University Press, 1984) 71.
22   Ibid. 78.

adopted within the discursive politics of a particular historical moment.[23] For we already know why the narrator of a Scott novel might require a 'fiction of address', might wish to imagine a reader from whom no critical interpretation, no worrying reply, might be returned: namely, the rise of a mass-readership consequent on the industrialisation of the book trade, and the resulting anxiety on the part of the elite, of which Scott was a part, concerning the political effects of such a fragmented and unpredictable audience. Frank speaks from beyond the grave, but does so in order to strike his reader dumb, to freeze him in his own death, in order to pre-empt any possible appropriation of the history figured in his own text as a mode of agency on the part of his reader. Frank, in other words, acts out the anxieties inherent in the role of author in Scott's own time. Seen in this light, Diana's feminine discursive agency now appears as the sort of authority that both Frank and Scott would dearly like to enjoy, an agency made available by the imaginable correspondent of a homogeneous republic of letters. But imagining such a correspondent is now impossible, and narrative authority can only be gained at the price of the imagined death of the author himself.

---

23 '[In autobiography] the specular moment is not primarily a situation or an event that can be located in a history, but [...] the manifestation, on the level of the referent, of a linguistic structure.' De Man 70–1.

4 Gender, domesticity, and the state in the Waverley novels

I concentrated in the previous chapter on the private narrative of Frank Osbaldistone: his relationship to his father, to Diana Vernon, and to his reader. This is the narrative that is resolved by Diana's recovery of the letters of credit, Frank's reconciliation with his father, and by his own imminent demise. But there is, of course, behind this private history, a public history, which Frank's narration only occasionally refers to, and from which his Scottish expedition functions as a distraction, rather than as an opportunity to witness great events at first hand: the 1715 rising. This is a narrative which is resolved by the bloody intervention of the British state. The two narratives are of course interrelated, but one might note that where Rashleigh's attempt to use the private affairs of the Osbaldistone family to further the Jacobite cause fails, the British state makes a successful, indeed decisive, intervention in the affairs of the Osbaldistone family, killing or fatally wounding the two sons who get as far as the battle of Preston and opening the way for Frank's restoration to the ranks of the gentry. Distinguishing between the two plots in this way, Diana's agency in retrieving the letters for Frank, despite the benefits they may offer her political cause, appears less as an instance of private love overcoming party interest, than as a means of keeping the two realms strictly separate. Diana's agency, that is, is concerned not with public politics as such, but with policing the border between the political and the private. Ultimate agency in the public sphere of a commercial society lies, not with a woman, but with the state.

In this chapter I want to suggest that at this point and in subsequent novels Scott goes beyond the categories of enlightenment human science to invest the state itself with the sort of historical agency that enlightenment thought had withdrawn from the individual statesman. To enjoy such agency, however, the state must escape from history understood as a determining causal force; and in doing so, I will suggest, takes up just that liminal position occupied in *Rob Roy* by

Diana Vernon. To understand how the state comes to take this position, it is necessary to examine the changing role of feminine agency in relation to politics and the aesthetic in Scott's work.

1. *Waverley*, domesticity, and closure

Diana's liminal position between the realm of privacy and politeness on the one hand and public politics on the other is one she inherits from her predecessor as Jacobite *femme fatale,* Flora Mac-Ivor in *Waverley.* However, in the earlier novel, that policing role is separated out from any real agency in the plot itself. The young woman who makes the decisive intervention in the plot is instead Rose Bradwardine. In *Waverley*, the Mac-Ivors are placed in a unique relation to the stadial history underpinning Scott's portrayal of the 1745 rising. They straddle the feudal manners of an agricultural stage, which legitimates the fractious self-rule we heard mocked by the narrator of *Guy Mannering*, and its modern version, party politics, and the polite culture into which the gentry had been corralled by a commercial society:

> Had Fergus Mac-Ivor lived sixty years sooner than he did, he would, in all probability, have wanted the polished manner and knowledge of the world which he now possessed; and had he lived sixty years later, his ambition and love of rule would have lacked the fuel which his situation now afforded. (I.xix.292; xix.91–2)[1]

---

1   All references to *Waverley* give volume, chapter, and page numbers to the first edition (Edinburgh: Archibald Constable and Co., 1814), which is the text used for quotations, followed by chapter and page numbers for Sir Walter Scott, *Waverley*, ed. Claire Lamont (Oxford: Oxford University Press, 1986), which follows the 'Magnum Opus' edition of 1829. 'Ambition' has here the quite particular connotation of party-political commitment that it is given in the sentimental discourse that displaces satire as a discourse from the mid-eighteenth century, as discussed in chapter 1. Sitter notes that in Gray's *Elegy*, for example, '"Ambition" is virtually synonymous with public history and with the "Pomp of Power" which lures the Cromwells and Hamdens of the world onto its high stage. [...] [Similarly,] from the Castle of Indolence the motive of Ambition is what leads men – and Ambition is usually a male problem in these poems – into the series of civil disturbances making up the history of nations" (Sitter 104).

Similarly, the narrator notes of Flora, although 'highly accomplished' (I.xxi.321; xxi.100), 'yet she had not learned to substitute the gloss of politeness for the reality of feeling' (I.xxi.321; xxi.101). This opposition of politeness and real feeling acts out, I think, the abandonment of an early- and mid-century rhetoric designed to include both landed and monied classes within a new cultural hegemony that excluded the poor, and its replacement by a rhetoric of nature, of spontaneous social 'feeling' and not cultivated sophistication, designed to include a whole nation in its address. The abandonment, that is, on the part of Scott and his generation; Scott posits this type of 'feeling' in Flora as a survival from the cultural past, not an anticipation of the future. This is the equivalent in the feminine sphere of the opposition projection into 'feudal' times of an account of liberty only in fact current after 1688 that we discussed in chapter 1. That is, if Flora represents an historical moment as her brother does, it is one much closer to Scott's own time, but it is a moment curiously reversed in order to locate in the society's origins what was in fact a recent innovation.

At the same time however, Flora's gender makes her liminal position here, not only a feminine equivalent to, but also fundamentally different from, that of her brother, precisely because 'politeness' excludes party-politics as a proper realm for women at all. While his two available sets of manners offer Fergus two different types of political agency, that of feudal baron and modern statesman, the virtues juxtaposed in his sister's person are not two modalities of the political, but the political as a whole and the polite. The narrator begins the passage quoted above by expanding at length on Flora's selfless devotion to the Stuart cause; but after describing her use of her diplomatic skills to prevent a quarrel between her brother and Bradwardine, the chapter concludes, 'To this young lady, now presiding at the female empire of the tea-table, Fergus introduced Captain Waverley, whom she received with the usual forms of politeness' (I.xxi.326; xxi.102). 'Politeness' here involves the effacement of political ambition altogether, and the substitution, in exactly the trope that Hume uses in 'On Essay Writing', of the tea-table for the British Empire that Flora so wants to seize. Flora's 'feelings', on the other hand, 'so different from those usually ascribed to young women at my period of life', as she admits to Edward, are the springs of her political commitments (II.iv.68; xxvii.135). 'Feeling' *here* carries with it the worrying associations of radical political ardour familiar to Scott's generation from debates over the French Revolution. Flora reveals the worrying continuity between the 'feeling' that guarantees sincerity in private conversation, and the 'feeling' invested in political principles, to be exercised in public life. Precisely insofar as feeling, as an inclusive principle of natural openness, invokes a *national* audience, as I suggest it does, then it also generates an anxiety that it might represent a threat to the political *status quo*.

It is this ambiguous figure, however, who identifies for us the virtues and destinies of both Edward and Rose, and not the narrator; who distinguishes those virtues from her own commitment to public politics; and who disavows any claim on Edward in order to ensure their separation. The virtues of Rose and Edward go beyond the manners of one historical era or another; their destiny lies in a third realm, beyond the 'feeling' of archaic political loyalties (although participating in the same sincerity), and the 'polish' of modern 'politeness' (although sharing the importance it grants to women). That realm is the *domestic* space of the companionate marriage, now understood, post-1789, as a bulwark against any revolutionary enthusiasm that enlightenment grand-narratives *might* appear to justify. We have seen, in *Humphry Clinker*, political problems turned into family problems that can then be resolved by the coincidences and comic resolutions of the plot. In *Waverley*, we find the emotional authenticity of the companionate marriage understood as the replacement for an imagined 'feudal' social order, whose immediate human connection between master and servant guaranteed a social order untroubled by the threat of revolution. The new emphasis on the family in post-revolutionary culture is in part due to Burke, as Claudia Johnson notes:

> To Burke, the family and its immediate environs in the neighbourhood [...] is not simply a metaphor for or microcosm of the estate, but a basic political unit in its own right. Because it establishes a network of mutual interests and nurtures such civilizing and affiliating affections as fond solicitude and trusting dependency, unselfish benevolence and grateful submission, [...] [the patriarchal family is defined] not simply as the linchpin of generational continuity but also as the locus of socialization and hence the object of revolutionary subversion.[2]

---

2   Claudia Johnson, *Jane Austen: Women, Politics, and the Novel* (Chicago: University of Chicago Press, 1988) 5–6.

However, Scott also inherits from pre-revolutionary sentimentalism the idea of the domestic space as an emotional refuge from a public world irreversibly atomised by *capitalism*. The bonds that Burke imagines maintained on behalf of the state by the patriarchal family are imagined by the man to whom *Waverley* is dedicated, Henry Mackenzie, as *impossible* elsewhere, and *only* preserved in the domestic sphere. Harley's one constructive act of charity in *The Man of Feeling*, in a commercial society portrayed as a heartless wasteland, is to restore the Edwards family to something like domestic union by relocating them to his estate as tenants.[3] This is exactly the 're-establishment of a kind of nostalgic feudalism, making ties out of patronage and loyalty rather than out of the emerging capitalist order' only possible as domesticity as it is constructed in the novel.[4] In the post-revolutionary context, however, as the threat shifts from modernity itself to its particular manifestation in Jacobin politics, the domestic as a bulwark against destructive social forces takes on a new importance.

The comparison with *Humphry Clinker* highlights this new centrality of the 'domestic' as a category of virtue. There, the political problem of luxury, and the corresponding breakdown in status distinctions, was displaced into the figure of the fashionable lady, represented by Mrs Baynard and her rivals. Lydia Melford represented an alternative, positive, version of femininity in her rejection of the fashionable world for domestic felicity. But this rejection is peripheral to the plot of *Humphry Clinker*, whereas in Burney's novels the young woman's choice of domesticity over fashion becomes central. In *Cecilia*, for example, Mr Delvile is described by his mother as '[f]ormed for domestic happiness', and Cecilia recognizes him as one 'whose turn of mind, so similar to her own, promised her the highest domestic felicity.'[5] Monckton on the other hand aspires to a life of fashionable pleasure:

> Having thus sacrificed to ambition all possibility of happiness in domestic life, he turned his thoughts to those other methods of procuring it, which he had so dearly purchased the power of essaying. [...] The little knowledge of fashionable manners

---

3   *The Man of Feeling* (1771; Oxford: Oxford University Press, 1967) chs. xxxv–vi.
4   Janet Todd, *Sensibility: An Introduction* (London: Methuen, 1986) 96.
5   *Cecilia* VI.viii.500; VI.x.520.

and of the characters of the times of which Cecilia was yet mistress, she had gathered at the house of this gentleman [...].[6]

In the post-revolutionary context, an oppressive emphasis comes to be placed on feminine domestic propriety: but some women writers counter this with a counter-emphasis on its masculine equivalent, embodied not just in potential husbands like Delvile but also in the family patriarchs themselves.

We can see this by comparing one of Maria Edgeworth's early novels, *Belinda* (1801) with one contemporary with *Waverley*, *Patronage* (1814). In the earlier text, domesticity is, as in *Humphry Clinker* or *Evelina*, one of two alternatives within the world of an upper-class woman. *Belinda* argues for the home and the family as the morally nurturing place for a woman to live, in opposition to the 'fashionable world' of loveless ostentation and feminine display. This is a lesson that its eponymous heroine learns fairly early on: the real conversion from the ball to the hearth is of Lady Delacour.

> 'O, no', said lady Anne, 'you must not give her up yet. I have been informed, upon *the best authority*, that lady Delacour was not always the unfeeling dissipated fine lady that she now appears to be. This is only one of the transformations of fashion—the period of enchantment will soon be at an end, and she will return to her natural character. [...] [W]hen she is tired of the insipid taste of other pleasures, she will have a higher relish for those of domestic life, which will be new and fresh to her.'
> 'And so you really think, my dear lady Anne, that my lady Delacour will end by being a domestic woman [...].'[7]

In *Patronage*, in contrast, the domestic sphere is defined not in opposition to the world of fashion but to the world of politics. Lord Oldborough, a minister of state, remarks upon Mr Percy's preference for the home over the chance of a political career:

> [H]e asked Mr. Percy some questions about his family, and turned the conversation again to domestic affairs;—expressed surprise, that a man of Mr. Percy's talents should live in such absolute retirement, and seeming to forget what he had said himself but half an hour before, of the pains and dangers of ambition, and all that

---

6   Ibid. I.i.8.
7   Maria Edgeworth, *Belinda* (Oxford: Oxford University Press, 1994) viii.105. References to this edition give chapter and page numbers.

Mr. Percy had said of his love of domestic life, appeared to take it for granted, that Mr. Percy would be glad to shine in public, if opportunity were not wanting.[8]

Note how the subject making this choice here is a man, not a woman. It is no surprise that the novel defines female virtue in terms of the home: 'Count Altenberg, in common with every man of sense and knowledge of the world, knew that it is in her own family, in domestic life, he should judge a woman's real disposition and temper.'[9] More surprising is that male virtue should be defined in identical terms. Mrs. Hungerford announces the imminent arrival of her son, a colonel in the army, returning with commendations from his commander for gallantry in the field against the French, with the words: 'I am proud that you, my friends, should see what a sensation the first sound of his return makes in his own *home*.—There it is, after all, that you may best judge what a man really is.'[10] This difference between *Belinda* and *Patronage* exemplifies perfectly Nancy Armstrong's observation that domestic virtue, although at first a uniquely feminine one, became in the early nineteenth century modern morality itself:

> Men were no longer political creatures so much as they were the products of desire and producers of domestic life [...]. [T]he difference between male and female was understood in terms of their respective *qualities of mind* [...] that had formerly determined female nature alone.[11]

Edward Waverley is described by Flora in a strikingly similar way to Colonel Hungerford:

> 'You seek [...] a heart whose principal delight should be in augmenting your domestic felicity, and returning your affection, even to the height of romance [...]. [Y]ou, Mr Waverley, would for ever refer to the idea of domestic happiness which your imagination is capable of painting.' (II.iv.69–70; xxvii.135)

Later she compares him to her brother:

---

8   Maria Edgeworth, *Patronage* (London: J. Johnson and Co., 1814) I.ii.41–2. References to this edition give volume, chapter and page numbers.
9   Ibid. III.xxix.169.
10   Ibid. II.xviii.111.
11   Armstrong 4.

> She was by no means blind to his faults, which she considered as dangerous to the hopes of any woman, who should found her ideas of a happy marriage in the peaceful enjoyment of domestic society, and the exchange of mutual and engrossing affection. The real disposition of Waverley, on the other hand, notwithstanding his dreams of tented fields and military honour, seemed exclusively domestic. (III.v.67–8; lii.248)

His marriage to Rose and the nature of his settlement at Tully Veolan proves Flora's estimation of Edward correct, as does Edward's behaviour seen from other points of view, for example his mistaking the Jacobites' white cockades for bridal favours (II.iii.49; xxvi.129). Rose is the domestic woman who makes possible a proper domestic settlement for the hero, just as Clarence Hervey or Lord Orville or Mr Knightley are domestic men that can provide a proper home for the heroine of a courtship novel. 'Her very soul is in the home, and in the discharge of all those quiet virtues of which home is the centre', Flora observes to her brother. The governing opposition here is not between one type of politics and another, but between politics and domesticity; and as in *Patronage*, that opposition no longer coincides with a gender division, for domestic virtue is now as proper to the male as to the female.[12]

Understanding the domesticity enjoyed by Edward and Rose at the end of the novel in this way undercuts one of the common interpretations of the marriages that usually end Scott's novels: that is, as allegories of national reconciliation, of actual or potential historical development. Such an interpretation has a long pedigree;[13] but has

---

12   David Brown has made a connection between the domesticity ascribed to Waverley and the 'proper novel' of Edgeworth *et al*: 'She [Flora] is quite right: Waverley's future position is not that of the feudal aristocrat – it is nearer to the way of life of Jane Austen's leisurely, upper-middle-class world' (Brown 22). From this perspective, the whole text of *Waverley* begins to look like the generic diversion of its hero from the sort of novel that is his proper home into an alien world of politics and military action; a diversion which is however necessary to teach him the true value of domesticity, the value that the heroine of a Burney novel learns from the equally dangerous world of balls, carriage-rides and Vauxhall Gardens.

13   Gordon is quite explicit about what the marriage symbolizes: 'Edward not only marries the Baron's daughter, he also marries the estate, where he may breathe the air of the Highlands and participate in a life that preserves feudal virtues and pleasures without the physical and moral perils of feudal violence'; 'their marriage [that of the Scott hero and heroine in general] [...] must symbolize a reconciliation between the opposing political currents that make the pageants of history so

received new life from recent discussions of the roots of Scott's historical novel in the contemporary Irish national tale. For these critics, the 'happy bourgeois family' into which hero and heroine disappear 'becomes the model for colonizer-colonized relationships' in the novels of Edgeworth or Owenson or Maturin; 'Each national tale ends with the traveller's marriage to his or her native guide, in a wedding that allegorically unites Britain's "national characters".'[14] This, it is argued, is one of the principal features Scott takes over in his own work, extended to other ideological areas of conflict within and without the United Kingdom. The meaning of Scott's endings is then embraced by the meaning of the text as a whole, an allegorical representation of the history narrated realistically elsewhere in the novel. The marriage can thus be assimilated to the novel's social-realist representation of historical process.

However, we have seen that Scott's enlightenment historical determinism locates different cultures not just in space, as the expressions of different nations, as does the national tale, but along a common historical line, where one will necessarily replace another, as the economic modes that caused them evolve. There is no political compromise between the feudal and the commercial: if feudal emotional authenticity survives at all, it is within the domestic sphere *alone* as a category of commercial society. The marriage now figures a resolution not in history, but in spite of history. Thus Edward's marriage to Rose makes possible the survival of emotional 'feudal' ties within a new economic order that makes them impossible in the outside world. The ending of a Waverley novel asserts fiction rather than history as producing this resolution, the end point of a plot that deploys a set of tropes discontinuous with those of Scott's historiography: the tropes, that is, of romance. The work of romance is thus, as we saw in chapter 2, essentially conservative, asserting the continuation of ties of sympathy inside the family even within a social world transformed by capital into the site of competing material interests. Scott's present is outside of history, not because the processes of historical change have

---

bloody.' Robert C. Gordon, *Under Which King? A Study of the Scottish Waverley Novels* (Edinburgh: Oliver and Boyd, 1969) 24; 60–1.

14 Anne K. Mellor, *Romanticism and Gender* (London: Routledge, 1993) 80; Katie Trumpener, *Bardic Nationalism* (Princeton: Princeton University Press, 1997) 141.

somehow ground to a halt with the production of the imperial and early-industrial United Kingdom, but because that present has been safely locked away within a domestic space isolated from (even if dependent on) the convulsions produced by capitalism and empire. And the key that turns in that lock is the romance plot.

What is crucial for my argument here is that along with Rose's domestic virtue goes a particular type of *agency*. Flora, despite, or rather because of the fact that she is working in the political-historical sphere, is powerless to prevent the defeat of the Jacobites. The historical retrospective and enlightenment historiography of the novel reveal that defeat as inevitable given that determining economic forces no longer render feudal institutions tenable. Rose's agency is in contrast crucial to the progress of the novel. It is Rose who orchestrates Edward's rescue from government troops, and she who cares for and protects him at Janet's cottage on the Tully Veolan estate. This action is central both in the discourse of the novel – it occupies volume II chapter xiv (chapter xxxvii) the mid-point of the novel – and the story, since it is only Rose's intervention here that prevents Edward's imprisonment and thus allows him to function as eye-witness to the rebellion that fills the text in the next 23 chapters. Unlike Frank in *Rob Roy*, Edward functions as the reader's point-of-view on momentous political events, but it is Rose's action that makes this possible.[15]

Further, Rose's action here provides the novel with a type of closure quite distinct from her marrying the hero. For neither the reader nor Edward know that Rose is his carer during his illness. Because this action is itself narrated from Edward's point of view, Rose's responsibility for it can be excluded from the discourse of the novel until volume III, chapter xviii (chapter lxv): there the narrator explains

---

15 Until, that is, he is left behind by the rebel army in Cumbria. It is clearly important that Edward does not follow the Jacobites to their defeat at Culloden, a piece of real history that would overshadow Waverley's escape from history into the arms of Rose. A.O.J. Cockshut explains this omission in terms of the novel's underlying enlightenment historiography instead: '[Scott] wished to show us the inherent collapse of the old Highland values, and not to derive the false impression that a mere military defeat was the cause.' This is true too: it is important for *this* novel that the state's responsibility for the defeat of the Jacobites is played down and displaced onto deeper economic forces. *The Achievement of Walter Scott* (London: Collins, 1969) 115.

that Rose's action, and the location of Edward's concealment, were 'such points of our narrative as, according to the custom of story-tellers, we deemed it fit to leave unexplained, for the purpose of exciting the reader's curiosity' (III.xviii.263–4; lxv.308–9). In other words, the identity of Edward's saviour was suppressed in order that its later revelation could provide the text with what one might call (after Barthes) *hermeneutic* closure.[16] As in *Guy Mannering*, as in *Old Mortality*, a plot-structuring device is both associated with autonomous feminine agency and then denied or deminished.

Rose's action thus makes this novel possible, by both maintaining Edward's participation in events, and adding to that historical representation a vestigial hermeneutic structure, in her role as that which is obscured by the narrator until the end of the novel. Rose's agency, one might say, is thus at the service of the structure of this novel, of its necessary combination of historical reference and narrative form. Yet she is also Edward's domestic destiny as understood by Flora. The two are linked: Edward's ignorance of his own domestic nature and his ignorance of the identity of his protectress are the same misrecognition of Rose.

This is clearly a similar sort of feminine authority, combining the moral and the aesthetic, to that which we saw at work in *Guy Mannering*. But Julia Mannering represented the ethical in that novel only in her autonomy from the historical determinism embodied in the discourse of her father and the general narrator. And that autonomy had to be closed down, and Julia's narrative agency transferred to a carrier of a folk-culture available for assimilation to just that social-historical discourse. In *Waverley*, Rose appears to be acting off her own bat to quite the same extent, despite the Baron's claim that 'She had never a will but her old father's' (III.xx.287; lxvii.316). But this autonomy never appears at the level of the narrative discourse itself. Instead, as we have seen, Rose's agency is effaced as much as possible from the text; this, and its being directed to domestic ends, renders it unthreatening to the patriarchal values of the text as a whole. Rose's position thus repeats that of women novelists like Burney, who win a certain authority as novelists only by using their novels to preach (on the surface at least)

---

16   Roland Barthes, *S/Z* trans. Richard Miller (1973; Oxford: Blackwell, 1990) x. 17 and *passim*.

the necessity of self-effacement. The moral autonomy of women is legitimated only by the particular type of morals that they adopt, and those morals involve the effacement of their own agency: yet it is on such agency that the action of *Waverley* depends. I noted in the introduction how *Waverley* is seen by Ina Ferris as replacing the tradition of women's writing that made this authority possible:[17] we can now see that it rather appropriates or absorbs it as part of the mechanics of its own plot.

2. The domesticity of Jeanie Deans

Rose's agency is effaced, Julia's agency is replaced. In the first case the state intervenes to guarantee the permanence of the hero's escape from history; in the latter a happy ending is brought about by the intervention instead of a member of the rural poor. It is a brilliant combination of these two scenarios that allows Scott to imagine a young female heroine whose autonomy from her father-figure can be both the focus of the narrative discourse, and driven to a successful conclusion, by making her a carrier of domestic values, like Rose, but also a member of the folk, like Meg; and by making her autonomous action a direct appeal to the British state itself. I am referring of course to Jeanie Deans in *The Heart of Midlothian.*

This suggestion that the cow-keeper's daughter from St. Leonard's should be understood in relation to the young ladies of *Guy Mannering* and *Waverley* may seem far-fetched. In fact the narrator of *The Heart of Midlothian*, in his efforts to make Jeanie comprehensible to the reader, repeatedly makes comparisons between her attitudes and those of other women, both upper- and lower-class. Generally speaking, the effect is the effacement of the class distinction and its replacement with the distinction between Jeanie's rigorous morality and the dissipation of the rest of her sex. She is a young woman, he tells us, 'to whom nature and the circumstance of a solitary life had given a depth of thought and force

---

17   Ferris 78: see above, pp.32–3.

of character superior to the frivolous part of her sex, whether in high or low degree' II.ii.39; xiv.143–4).[18]

> The very hour which some damsels of the present day, as well of her own as of higher degree, would consider as the natural period of commencing an evening of pleasure, brought, in her opinion, awe and solemnity in it [...] (II.ii.48; xiv.147)

The narrator also conflates the fashionable woman in search of a good marriage with the female quixote as Jeanie's defining feminine other, as she gazes on the house of the Laird of Dumbiedikes:

> She was no heroine of romance, and therefore looked with some curiosity and interest on the mansion-house and domains, of which, it might at that moment occur to her, a little encouragement, such as women of all ranks know by instinct how to apply, might have made her mistress [...]. But Jeanie Deans [...] never for a moment harboured a thought of doing the Laird, Butler, or herself, the injustice, which many ladies of higher rank would not have hesitated to do to all three, on much less temptation. (III.i.6–7; xxvi.251)

Jeanie, that is, is constructed from just the same oppositions as the virtuous heroine of a novel by Burney, Edgeworth, or Austen.

What separates her from them is her social status: not only because it changes the social spheres in which she can move, but also because her virtue, unlike theirs, is historically located. That is, it is understood as part of a set of manners produced by particular historical developments in her society: namely the Covenanting resistance to the Stuart state in the seventeenth century, represented by the historical memory and theological rigour of her father, Davie. The gentry heroines we have been discussing so far have not been understood in this way: Julia's autonomy from her father is made possible by a type of writing made available by eighteenth-century culture, certainly, but not conceived as its necessary consequence: the essential fact of Julia's correspondence is that it *escapes* the patterns of cause and effect in which the historical world is trapped. Similarly, Flora Mac-Ivor's

---

18   All references to *The Heart of Midlothian* give volume, chapter, and page numbers to the first edition (in *Tales of my Landlord* Second Series; Edinburgh: Archibald Constable and Co., 1818), which is the text used for quotations, followed by chapter and page numbers for Sir Walter Scott, *The Heart of Midlothian*, ed. Claire Lamont (Oxford: Oxford University Press, 1982), which follows the 'Magnum Opus' edition of 1830.

passion for the Stuarts is explained in terms of her upbringing in particular social circles at a particular historical moment: but Rose Bradwardine's contrasting domestic virtue is not presented to us as historically determined in this way, for it is the displacement, not the outcome, of her father's old-fashioned landlordism. And it is because Jeanie's virtue is understood as historically located in this way that she can provide the narrative focus of the novel, where Julia and Rose are sidelined or silenced.

This historical location of Jeanie's virtue then makes possible its integration in the particular historical circumstances of the new United Kingdom. By way of introduction to her interview with Queen Caroline, Scott describes in some detail the (factual) rivalries and alliances of the court of George II (III.xii; xxxvii). Jeanie gets this chance to put her case, not by the benign intervention of a fairy-godmother, but because the Duke of Argyle saved the Brunswick regime in the 1715 rising, and because they continue to depend upon, and indeed to fear, his authority in Scotland. He also has more personal forms of leverage with the Queen, despite their public differences over the Porteous affair:

> Lady Suffolk lay under strong obligations to the Duke of Argyle, for reasons which may be collected from Horace Walpole's Reminiscences of that reign, and through her means the Duke had some occasional correspondence with Queen Caroline [...]. (III.xii.304; xxxvii.361–2)

Jeanie's enjoys the agency she does in part because a whole set of documented historical circumstances work in its favour.

Indeed, as I have described it, it begins to sound as if Jeanie is submerged in her historical circumstances, and cannot really be said to represent the possibility of free agency despite them in the way that Julia Mannering does. From the opening description of the Porteous Riot, often picked out for special praise for its historical accuracy, through the novel's sympathetic understanding of the cultures of the whole range of social classes, to a story which works as an allegory of a historical process whereby the fractious, fundamentalist Scotland of the seventeenth century (David Deans) became a progressive partner in the Hanovarian United Kingdom (Argyle), it seems a definitive example of a social-realist text.

Problems only arise over volume IV. Most critics have seen the last chapters of the novel as a sad falling-away from the standard of what has gone before, and, or rather because of, an abandonment of the previous volumes' social realism. As social realism, the neo-feudal idyll that the newly-wed Butlers enjoy on Argyle's estate seems like a fairy-tale in comparison with what has gone before. R.C. Gordon is typical when he calls these chapters 'a sad and boring affair, full of irrelevant characters and a totally unrecognisable Effie (now Lady Staunton), and garnished with an excess of melodrama and a fake morality.'[19] Even if, given the romance model for Jeanie's quest and hence for the allegory, a fairy-tale ending is needed as her reward, it is surely unnecessary to drag that ending out over 14 chapters. Other critics, however, seem to think that it is, especially if the novel's allegory of Scottish history is seen to centre on the figure of Argyle. F.R. Hart, for example, argues that it is necessary to see just the sort of progress that Argyle stands for in practice, and this is what the Roseneath episode gives us:

> Jeanie wins Argyle's [support] through a [...] complex set of appeals. Thereafter, Argyle embodies the hope for reconciliation toward which the book moves. It is Jeanie's triumph to bring into play the force for which he stands. [...] To see the outcome, we must have the final chapters, the final pastoral image of a new world in which Butlers and Deanses are reconciled in marriage and progeny.[20]

In other words, Jeanie's settlement at Knocktarlitie constitutes an allegory of history in just the same way as Rose's marriage to Edward.

What both these estimations of the fourth volume of *The Heart of Midlothian* presume is that whatever meaning it might have must be in terms of its historical content. Gordon thinks it has none and is therefore worthless; Hart thinks it has lots and therefore casts further light on the novel's social and political themes. Neither argument considers the possibility that volume IV might contribute to the novel in some other way. We saw how Waverley was rewarded after *his* historical ordeal

---

19   Gordon 95.
20   Francis R. Hart, *Scott's Novels: The Plotting of Historical Survival* (Charlottesville: University Press of Virginia, 1966) 144. Similarly Tom Crawford: 'The Duke's Roseneath [...] is allegorical; it stands for the organized domains of the improving landlords, the leading class in enlightenment Scotland [...] [T]he final pastoral is a counter in what has, in the book's progress, become a historical fable.' *Scott* (Edinburgh: Scottish Academic Press, 1982) 96–7. More generally, 'the development of Jeanie's individual character proceeds in step with a development of the social character of Scotland' (113).

when marriage to Rose finally pulled him out of history altogether and into the domestic world for which he was always more truly suited. Jeanie's final victory places her outside history in a similar way, and this outside of history is similarly constructed on the model of feminine fiction.

To complain of the final chapter's lack of realism is for one thing to ignore as irrelevant to the novel's cognitive task the plot, whose central question remains unanswered by the end of volume III, namely the survival or otherwise of Effie's child. In particular, it is to miss the significance (as R.C. Gordon does in the quote above) of Effie's return from London as Lady Staunton. Speaking to her sister in the Tolbooth, and expanding on a line from Job, 'And mine hope hath he removed like a tree', Effie sounds like this:

> 'I thought o' the bonny bit thorn that our father rooted out o' the yard last May, when it had a' the flush o' blossoms on it; and then it lay in the court till the beasts had trod them a' to pieces wi' their feet. I little thought, when I was wae for the bit silly green bush and its flowers, that I was to gang the same gate mysel.' (II.viii.199; xx.204)

Writing four years later to her sister about an encounter with the Duke of Argyle at the opera in London, where he tells her the affecting story of Jeanie Deans in total ignorance of his listener's real identity, she sounds like this:

> '—I fainted; and my agony was imputed partly to the heat of the place, and partly to my extreme sensibility; and, hypocrite all over, I encouraged both opinions—any thing but discovery. Luckily he [Staunton] was not there. But the incident has led to more alarms. I am obliged to meet your great man often; and he seldom sees me without talking of E.D. and J.D., and R.B. and D.D., as persons in whom my amiable sensibility is interested. My amiable sensibility ! ! ! —And then the cruel tone of light indifference with which persons in the fashionable world speak together on the most affecting subjects! To hear my guilt, my folly, my agony, the foibles and weaknesses of my friends—even your heroic exertions, Jeanie, spoken of in the drolling style which is the present tone in fashionable life—Scarce all that I formerly endured is equal to this state of irritation—then it was blows and stabs—now it is pricking to death with needles and pins.—' (IV.xi.226–7; xlviii.455)

The values implied here (the cheerful admission of hypocrisy, the equation of awaiting execution in the Tolbooth with hearing others make light of your relatives without being able to reply); the vocabulary ('sensibility', 'fashionable life'); the very punctuation of this letter, are all those of the anti-heroine of a novel by Burney or Edgeworth.

Jeanie's reaction is of course partly a moral judgement, particularly disliking 'a smothered degree of egotism' (IV.xi.230; xlviii.456), but she also checks in herself a latent feeling of envy: 'surely I am no sic a fule as to be angry that Effie's a braw lady, while I am only a minister's wife?' (IV.xi.231; xlviii.456). One of the effects of Effie's letter is indeed to emphasize by contrast the exact nature of Jeanie's position as a minister's wife.

> Mrs Butler, whom we must no longer, if we can help it, term by the familiar name of Jeanie, brought into the married state the same firm mind and affectionate disposition,—the same natural and homely good sense, and spirit of useful exertion,—in a word, all the domestic good qualities of which she had given proof during her maiden life. She did not indeed rival Butler in learning; but then no woman more devoutly venerated the extent of her husband's erudition. She did not pretend to understand his expositions of divinity; but no minister of the presbytery had his humble dinner so well arranged, his clothes and linen in equal good order, his fireside so neatly swept, his parlour so clean, and his books so well dusted. (IV.x.207–8; xlvii.447–8)

This is one of the few points in the Waverley Novels in which life after marriage is explored in any detail. It is the only place in the Waverley Novels where the basis of a happy marriage is discussed in terms of a separation of spheres between man and wife, as a contract in which the woman receives authority in the home in exchange for a surrender of the public world to her husband. It is from this domestic situation that Jeanie must now write a reply to Effie. This is not easy, for she does not know to whom she is writing, whether to Effie Deans the cowkeeper's daughter, or Lady Staunton of Willingham, the famous wit and beauty.

> In entering into her own little details of news, chiefly respecting domestic affairs, she experienced a singular vacillation of ideas; for sometimes she apologized for mentioning things unworthy the notice of a lady of rank, and then recollected that every thing which concerned her should be interesting to Effie. (IV.xi.237–8; xlviii.458)

We misunderstand Jeanie's content in the fourth volume of *The Heart of Midlothian* if we read it only as her reward for what has gone before. It must also be read in contrast with the life that her sister is simultaneously living. The structuring opposition of the first three volumes was between truth as defined by the law, and truth as understood by the individual, between the authority of the state and the integrity of the individual: the structuring opposition of a social-realist novel. In the last volume the structuring opposition is between Jeanie and Lady Staunton, between bourgeois domestic virtue and aristocratic display: the structuring opposition of the domestic novel.[21]

This is not to say that Jeanie herself changes as a character: her virtues remain the same.[22] But that in opposition to which those virtues are defined, and hence their meaning, changes. It could be similarly argued that Effie too is at the beginning of the novel the same thoughtless party-goer that she is at the end, but her change of dialect changes what that character means with regard to others and to the story. While retaining her speech and manners, Jeanie ceases to be the object of narratorial ethnographic exposition as she was in the earlier volumes. One can even identify the point at which the narrator himself admits the fact. When a chest is delivered to David Dean's new cottage at Auchingower for Jeanie, who is staying there until her marriage to Reuben, the narrator abdicates his responsibility as an antiquarian for describing its contents to his female interlocutor from the 'Conclusion' to *Old Mortality*.

---

21   In categorizing the Roseneath chapters as a *domestic* idyll I am not necessarily denying that they are also a pastoral one (as most other critics classify it). Insofar as the domestic comes to be opposed to the public and political world in the early nineteenth century it takes on the role played by pastoral in earlier periods. Hence we find Mr Percy in Edgeworth's *Patronage* explicitly replacing the one with the other: 'He hated Delias and shepherdesses, and declared that he should soon grow tired of any companion, with whom he had no other occupation in common but '*tending a few sheep*'. There was a vast difference, he thought, between pastoral and domestic life. His idea of domestic life comprised all the varieties of literature, exercise, and amusement for the faculties, with the delights of cultivated society' (*Patronage* IV.xxxix.186). Jeanie's life in Argyle, read in the context of the public events of the previous chapters, is domestic in the way constructed in *Patronage*; seen in the context of Effie's contemporaneous life in London society, it is domestic in the way constructed in *Belinda*.

22   For example, in the last chapter: 'It was in such a crisis that Jeanie's active and undaunted habits of virtuous exertion were most conspicuous' (IV.xiv.355; lii.501).

To name the various articles by their appropriate names, would be to attempt things unattempted yet in prose or rhyme; besides, that the old-fashioned terms of manteaus, sacks, kissing-strings, and so forth, would convey but little information even to milliners of the present day. I shall deposit, however, an accurate inventory of the contents of the trunk with my kind friend, Miss Martha Buskbody, who has promised, should the public curiosity seem interested on the subject, to supply me with a professional glossary and commentary. (IV.viii.174; xlv.435)

The division of responsibilities between the sexes seems to have affected antiquarians, too. Miss Martha has taken on herself the same mediation of historical detail to an anonymous public that the narrator has fulfilled in the previous volumes; here he admits that there are limits to his sphere of knowledge, and that Jeanie's new situation is beyond those limits. So a different approach on his part is called for.

The shift that we saw between Edgeworth's *Belinda* and *Patronage* is here, within this novel, reversed. The other which defines Jeanie's domestic virtue within volume IV is not history or politics, but fashionable life, an opposition internal to the domestic novel itself. That this is the nature of Jeanie's reward must change not only our understanding of volume IV, but also of the previous three volumes in which that reward is won. When we look back at those volumes, what we find is that the fashionable is already figured there, but parodied and subverted in the figure of Madge Wildfire, who 'dropped a curtsey as low as a lady at a birth-night introduction' (II.iv.90; xvi.163).[23] This is our first meeting with Madge in person, as opposed to the singing voice that warned Robertson to escape from his meeting with Jeanie in volume II chapter iii (chapter xv) and which demanded this flashback, to her interrogation before the magistrates, in explanation. Later, as she brings Jeanie to Staunton/Robertson's home village in England, a purblind beggar woman

dropped as deep a reverence to Madge as she would have done to a countess. This filled up the measure of Madge's self-approbation. She minced, she ambled, she smiled, she simpered, and waved Jeanie Deans forward with the condescension of a noble *chaperone*, who has undertaken the charge of a country miss on her first journey to the capital. (III.vi.154–5; xxxi.306)

---

23 The connection with Effie, but also with Jeanie, is made in Jeanie's reaction to hearing of Effie's introduction to the royals: 'A birth day! and at court!—Jeanie was annihilated, remembering well her own presentation, all its extraordinary circumstances, and particularly the cause of it' (IV.xi.239; xlviii.459).

Where the comparisons of Jeanie with upper-class women tended to replace the class-distinction with a moral one, here the class-distinction is grotesquely emphasized in order to abolish any claim to moral superiority on behalf of the rich. George Staunton is a nobleman, and has fathered two illegitimate children by women well below him in rank: Madge Murdockson and Effie Deans. Madge goes mad where Effie is ultimately rewarded with marriage and a rise in social status, but Madge's madness takes the form of a parody of the terms of Effie's reward.[24] Madge's parody of the pretentions of fashionable life prefigures the moral contrast between Jeanie and Effie in the last chapters of the book, a contrast that carries with it the moral concerns of domestic fiction. Madge's tragedy is that she appropriates the wrong side of the domestic novel's moral dialogue, as she actually recognizes at one point. Talking to Jeanie she finds herself describing her life in biblical terms, as Effie did in the Tolbooth (and as she does *not* in her later incarnation):

> '[F]or I have been burning bricks in Egypt, and walking through the weary wilderness of Sinai, for lang and mony a day. But whenever I think about mine errors, I am like to cover my lip for shame.'—Here she looked up and smiled.— 'It's a strange thing now—I hae spoke mair gude words to you in ten minutes, than I wad speak to my mother in as mony years. It's no that I dinna think on them— and whiles they are just at my tongue's end, but then comes the Devil, and brushes my lips with his black wing, and lays his broad black loof on my mouth—for a black loof it is, Jeanie—and sweeps away a' my gude thoughts, and dits up my good words, and pits a wheen fule sangs and idle vanities in their place.' (III.v.132–3; xxx.298)

Madge carries within herself a grotesque version of the domestic heroine's dilemma. The opposition between domestic virtue and frivolous pleasure that we found in volume IV is thus implicit in the earlier volumes of *The Heart of Midlothian*, but parodied within a single figure, and a member of the folk at that.

---

24 With fine irony, the narrator also uses those terms to point out that, had she belonged to the class to which she is raised from the beginning, Staunton would never have got away with what he did: 'In the higher classes, a damsel, however giddy, is still under the dominion of etiquette, and subject to the surveillance of mammas and chaperones [...]' (I.x.254; x.101).

This suggests the equivalence between an autonomous feminine writing and the speech of the folk-outcast that we found in *Guy Mannering*. Where Meg Merrilies carried the creativity of feminine fiction into the social realism of the second half of her novel, Madge Murdockson prefigures the domestic nature of the last volume of hers. This similarity inevitably raises the question of whether Madge might be the repository of the sort of traditional knowledge that allowed Meg Merrilies to solve the central mystery of *Guy Mannering* and provide that novel with closure. In the context of volumes I and II, the fact of Jeanie's southern quest in volume III may, as we have suggested, function as a political allegory, a story that will end with Effie's release and Jeanie's settlement in Argyle. However, the story of that journey as it fills out volume III, chapters iii–ix (chapters xxviii–xxxiv) is the story of her encounter with Madge, and the gradual piecing together of the relationships between Staunton/Robertson, Madge, and Meg, and this is a story that connects her journey to volume IV and will only end with Staunton's death. The one piece of information that she does *not* acquire here is the ultimate fate of Effie's bairn. The text thus promises two sorts of closure, the completion of Jeanie's task, and the discovery of the truth about the child.

But although Meg Merrilies's good intentions, along with her 'twilight sort of rationality' (III.v.125; xxx.295) indeed seem deposited in Madge, she is unable to help Jeanie in the way that Meg helps Brown/Bertram. Volume III, chapter v includes a repetition of the scene in volume III, chapter vi of *Guy Mannering* where the hero is obliged, though half-terrified, to follow Meg Merrilies through the woods to the scene of the original crime, reliving it as they go. Except that the crime relived here for Jeanie is not the murder of Effie's child, but the murder of Madge's own.

> 'Do I ken the road?—Wasna I mony a day living here, and what for shouldna I ken the road?—I might hae forgotten too, for it was afore my accident; but there are some things ane can never forget, let them try it as muckle as they like.' (III.v.129; xxx.297)

Madge cannot help others discover the past, because she is trapped in her own. She cannot recover the truth of Effie's trauma because that is in many ways already a repetition of her own. In fact this confusion between Effie's situation and her own, combined with her frequent inability to accept that her own child is dead, is the mainspring of the story: for we later discover that she took Effie's infant out of Meg's hands, thinking it was her own. Madge has already relived her story, already exercised a feminine creativity to come to terms with the past, but she did so with Effie's baby.

Jeanie's journey into England ends with the sight of Meg hanged, and a last interview with a dying Madge in which she can get no further information (III.xv; xl). Jeanie travels north to her domestic destiny, leaving the folk culture hanging from a gibbet at Carlisle, but seems to have left the possibility of closing the novel behind her too. Yet Meg is the one character who *does* know what happened to Effie's child. As in *Guy Mannering*, the old gypsy woman is the repository of a knowledge which the law is unable to gain. But Meg withholds that information as a means of revenging herself on Staunton/Robertson for what he did to Madge, rather than help the protagonist discover the truth and bring the plot to closure. Just as the elision of feminine dialogue by social realism in *Guy Mannering* is reversed in *The Heart of Midlothian*, so too is the role of M.M.. The hermeneutic closure that her special knowledge can provide seems forgotten, unnecessary, in a novel where the triumph of domesticity itself gives the story its ending.

Meg's agency in fact lives on after her to reveal the child's fate and give the novel hermeneutic closure after all, but the mode in which it does so is significant. Archibald, Argyle's man given the job of looking after Jeanie on her way to her new existence, finds a seller of a broadsheet 'Last Speech and Execution of Margaret Murdockson [...] and of her pious Conversation with his Reverence Arch-deacon Fleming' (IV.iv.75; xli.398–9), and buys them all up to avoid getting Jeanie any more upset than she already is. He wants to destroy them, but domestic prudence intervenes in the shape of Mistress Dolly Dutton, a milkmaid going north to help run the model dairies on the estate,

> who said, very prudently, it was a pity to waste so much paper, which might crêpe hair, pin up bonnets, and serve many other useful purposes; and who promised to put the parcel into her own trunk, and keep it carefully out of the sight of Mrs Jeanie Deans [...]. (IV.iv.76; xli.399)

One of these broadsheets returns, wrapping a cheese sent by Mrs Dutton to Knocktarlitie: a protective covering for the domestic reciprocity of Jeanie's new life, a reminder of what lies outside it, of what must be removed before it can be enjoyed. Jeanie finds her little daughter playing with it, discovers from it that Effie's boy survived, and thus sets in motion the chain of enquires that will lead to Staunton's death at the hands of his only son and the end of the story. The fact that Meg's admission has its effect only after her death and in printed popular form perhaps reminds us that Scott finds his originals for characters like her in the old broadsheets and books that are the raw materials of the literary antiquarian. Meg ends up where she and Meg Merrilies actually began: memories of a folk tradition available for appropriation by print culture. Meg's intervention can provide closure, but only in a form that is already the raw material for a novel. Like Meg Merrilies, she is removed from the text, yet remains as a condition of its existence, its existence as a completed plot, and simply as a novel.

We have seen how Jeanie's success in her interview with Queen Caroline is partly ascribed at that point in the text to a set of documented historical facts concerning the relations between the Queen, Lady Suffolk, and the Duke of Argyle. Seen as the culmination of the sociological objectivity of the first three volumes, this description is a perfect example of the realism of Scott's historical novel. Seen from the perspective of the last volume, however, the intervention of the state, including the help she gets from Argyle immediately afterwards, seems totally different. 'The impression remains that some sort of miracle has occurred.'[25] And yet the agent of this miracle is not some folk carrier of traditional knowledge, but the British state itself. The political agency that enlightenment historiography tended to efface returns as the capacity of the state to work outside of the cause and effect laws of human science, that is, to work miracles.

The comparison with *Guy Mannering* is once more instructive here. There, Scottish legalism failed the hero because it understood the world as pre-existing, as an object of knowledge, and its own discourse as a way of gaining that knowledge. The feminine discourses of that novel, on the other hand, accepted that the world is shaped rather than known in language, and thus understood themselves as performative rather than

25   Gordon 95.

cognitive. In *The Heart of Midlothian*, we find the law in a different mood. Calvinism presented Jeanie's class with its own epistemological dilemma: how to distinguish the reprobate from the elect. In their struggle with the state, the post-1662 Covenanters used this to their moral advantage, by taking condemnation by the state as prima-facie evidence of sainthood. Law and rebels agree that the law is seen as discovering a pre-existing truth, but disagree about what that truth is. With the 1690 law on child-murder that condemns Effie, which presumes guilt on the basis of a lack of evidence to the contrary, the state seems to have trumped this rebellion, by abandoning the claim to be *discovering* the truth at all. The law takes upon itself the ability to *constitute* the truth by which its subjects must live.[26] Understood thus, the 1690 law is not a legal freak, exploited as a mere pretext for the action of *The Heart of Midlothian*, but a metonym for the claims of the state, or at least the modern nation-state, in general. And in thus placing the law outside the boundaries of an enlightenment discourse of society, the state takes on the feminine, performative role of the women of the earlier novels.

When the law is understood thus, Jeanie's rebellion against it appears in a new light. The law will declare Effie Deans innocent, if Jeanie declares in court that Effie told her of her pregnancy. If Jeanie says that, on oath, then that will be the truth as far as the law is concerned. And the law, or at least its officers on this occasion, expect Jeanie to lie. She does not, because she cannot accept the law's ability to constitute the truth. The truth exists prior to its discovery by the law, and lies cannot be made truth by the mere fact of having the seal of the law put upon them. Jeanie's rebellion is less one of Calvinism than of epistemological realism. It is less in the name of her father that she rebels, but in that law of the father from which Julia Mannering temporarily escaped by writing her own fiction. The state's capacity to pardon is its ability to act irrespective of the truth, the obverse of the law's claim to constitute the truth. Fiction, authorship, is now the King's business.

---

26   Welsh makes this point central to his discussion of *The Heart of Midlothian*. See Alexander Welsh, *The Hero of the Waverley Novels: With New Essays on Scott* (Princeton: Princeton University Press, 1992) 93.

Or rather, the Queen's business. What is remarkable about Jeanie's interview with Queen Caroline is the extent to which politics, far from being the typical material of Scott's historical realism, appears within it to have been domesticated. The Queen's rule must be understood as much in terms of private, personal relationships as of public, party allegiances: 'It was a very consistent part of Queen Caroline's character, to keep up many private correspondences with those to whom in public she seemed unfavourable, or who, for various reasons, stood ill with the court' (III.xii.301; xxxvii.360). This subordination of the political to the personal even extends to her acquisition of her husband's mistress as her 'confidante' (III.xii.303; xxxvii.361). Effie is saved by the restitution of a performative female-female dialogue to her sister and its ability to bypass the problem of what really happened (albeit that one of the women in that dialogue is the state).

Enlightenment conjectural history sidelines state policy as an explanatory factor, and in consequence the state as such makes comparatively few direct interventions in the Scottish Waverley Novels: the history that Scott is interested in is more a matter of social and economic change than of acts of government. Even so, it is a surprise to find the state, as here, functioning in the text at the border of objectivity, as a semi-historical agency that takes the place of half-mad gypsy-women in previous novels. Jeanie Deans refuses to subordinate the literal truth to a performative speech that would get her sister out of jail. In doing so she repeats within the text the cognitive priorities of the novel at this point. But when a figure for the author must appear, as the one who can resolve the plot left by these priorities, that figure is a woman, a queen, and not a king. The allocation of all right to performative speech to the state seems to have made the inclusion of the domestic possible in a way which was not possible in Scott's earlier novels.

3. *Redgauntlet*, national culture, and the state

The Jacobite subject-matter of *Redgauntlet* and its use of a hapless young man as witness to its political and military content has usually led critics to group it with *Waverley* and *Rob Roy*, a return (after a gap of only six years, but comprising twelve, very different, novels) to a favourite subject and a final laying of it to rest.[27] Yet in setting and theme it has as least as much in common with *Guy Mannering* as with the Highland novels. Both stories are set in the second half of the eighteenth century, in Edinburgh, on the Dumfriesshire coast, and in Cumberland; both involve the lawyers of the first, and the salmon-fishers, smugglers and itinerants of the second. Both are obviously concerned with the power and limitations of systemized law much more than with party-politics narrowly defined. And of course, both follow the travels through these scenes of a young man who is ignorant of his own true identity, an identity that binds him to them in ways that he does not know. Ignorance of their family background is not a problem for Edward Waverley or Francis Osbaldistone; their identities are rather *over*-determined, their names forcing them into situations at odds with their real natures. *Redgauntlet* revisits the terrain of *Guy Mannering* just as the earlier novel revisited the terrain of *Humphry Clinker*.

However, by far the greatest coincidence between *Redgauntlet* and *Guy Mannering* lies in their use of epistolary technique alongside an omniscient narrator. The letters of the two heroes, Darsie Latimer and Alan Fairford, which make up the whole of the first volume of the original edition, constitute a correspondence of the type that we explored in the context of the earlier novel, but with young men rather than young women as the correspondents. Critics have often noted in passing that Scott is using the technique of another sort of fiction within his own in these chapters.[28] Our study up to this point provides a new

---

27 'Having written of the Jacobites in *Waverley* and *Rob Roy* [...] Scott returns to them once more' (Gordon 149); '[...] the last of three highly distinguished and beautifully contrasted meditations on the meaning of the Jacobite rebellions' (Cockshut 193).

28 For example, Cockshut says that the reader may 'be inclined to feel that in the first third of the book Scott was trying to be Richardson, and that a third of the way through he fortunately realized that he never could be' (194).

context for this observation, however, for Scott, as we have seen, has done this before. We must therefore begin with the extent to which the correspondence of Darsie and Alan repeats the female dialogues of the earlier texts.

Like Julia Mannering and Matilda Marchmont, Alan and Darsie constitute their reality in an intersubjective dialogue. This is indeed, in contrast to the epistolary chapters of *Guy Mannering* (or *Humphry Clinker* or *Evelina*, for that matter), a more properly Richardsonian correspondence, where we are given the letters of both friends; this makes more explicit the extent to which the subject-position of each with regard to the other is being constantly re-negotiated. Part of their subject matter in these letters is the difference between them:

> Why, what a pair of prigs hast thou made of us!—I plunging into scrapes, without having courage to get out of them—thy sagacious self, afraid to put one foot before the other, lest it should run away from its companion [...]. (I.iii.14)[29]

Their other subject matter is the stories that they tell each other about their respective lives. These stories are never authoritative versions of events: rather, they are always open to reinterpretation by the other, and are indeed written in the expectation of this alternative reading:

> [...] I am sure you will, as usual, turn the opposite end of the spy-glass on my poor narrative and reduce, *more tuo*, to the most petty trivialities, the circumstances to which thou accusest me of giving undue consequence. Hang thee, Alan! thou art as unfit a confidant for a youthful gallant with some spice of imagination, as the old taciturn secretary of Facardin of Trebizond. (I.iii.17)

Thus the stories themselves are means of establishing and re-establishing the nature of their relationship and their subjectivities as they are constructed within it. Darsie's complaint here that Alan is an unfit confidant should be taken ironically: Alan is of course the *perfect* confidant for Darsie, since the latter's self-understanding as romantic and daring is one that depends upon Alan's mocking responses to confirm it. Neither identity is possible outside the dialogue with the

---

29 Walter Scott, *Redgauntlet*, ed. G.A.M. Wood and David Hewitt (1824; Edinburgh: Edinburgh University Press, 1997. References give volume, chapter and page numbers to this edition.

other. Like Marianne and Elinor in *Sense and Sensibility*, this is a double-act consisting of an over-imaginative romantic, with a tendency to under-stand the world around them as if it were fiction, and their prosaic foil:[30]

> You smile, Darsie, *more tuo*, and seem to say it is little worth while to cozen oneself with such vulgar dreams; yours being, on the contrary, of a high and heroic character [...]. [S]incerely do I wish that thou hadst more beatings to thank me for, than those which thou dost acknowledge so gratefully. Then had I thumped these Quixotical expectations out of thee, and thou hadst not, as now, conceived thyself to be the hero of some romantic history [...]. (I.ii.12)

When we turn to the stories that they tell each other, we find Darsie justifying his more imaginative response to his experience in terms of its function within that correspondence: namely, that of entertaining Alan even while it confirms his version of Darsie's character:

> I continue to scribble at length, though the subject may seem somewhat deficient in interest. Let the grace of the narrative, therefore, and the concern we take in each other's matters, make amends for its tenuity. [...] And so, despite thy solemn smile and sapient shake of the head, I will go on picking such interest as I can out of my trivial adventures, even though that interest should be the creation of my own fancy; nor will I cease to inflict on thy devoted eyes the labour of perusing the scrolls in which I shall record my narrative. (I.xii.102)[31]

The governing role of their friendship within their story-telling is just one aspect of a general subordination of their other relationships and projects to this friendship. Darsie and Alan's friendship takes priority over their other commitments: 'All my exertions are intended to vindicate myself one day in your eyes' Alan tells Darsie (I.ii.13), and the exertions referred to are his legal studies, which constitute in large measure Alan's other important human bond, that with his father. This priority will be dramatized within the omniscient narrative when Alan abandons his first court-case to search for his vanished friend in chapter

---

30 'Scott's very success in capturing the tone of late adolescent banter may be deceptive, for their differences are no more to be taken lightly than those between Elinor and Marianne Dashwood or Elizabeth and Jane Bennet' (Gordon 152).

31 Note the echo of Julia's worry in her correspondence with Matilda in *Guy Mannering*: 'I write all these trifles, because you say that they amuse you, and yet I wonder how they should' (II.viii.135).

I. Their friendship similarly forces into second place the nearest thing that Darsie has to a vocation: 'my love for Alan Fairford surpasses the love of woman' (I.xii.113).

Alan's relation to Darsie gives him a mode of self-definition, then, independent from the identity that he has as his father's son within his 'hereditary' vocation (I.ii.11): that is, their correspondence functions for Alan in this respect just as it does for Julia Mannering or Lydia Melford or Clarissa Harlowe. The difference is that the boys' friendship is one that Alan's father not only tolerates but encourages. It is the appearance of a father-figure for *Darsie* that interrupts their correspondence in the way that the feminine discourse of *Guy Mannering* is interrupted by Colonel Mannering. The father-figure from whom this correspondence offers autonomy is Darsie's paternal uncle Hugh Redgauntlet. Yet even once communication with Alan is shut down, when Redgauntlet kidnaps Darsie, Darsie continues to write. He even continues to address Alan from time to time, sometimes in the second person and sometimes in the third, in the hope that his journal will eventually reach his friend's hands:

> The rage of narration, my dear Alan—for I will never relinquish the hope that what I am writing may one day reach your hands—has not forsaken me, even in my confinement, and the extensive though unimportant details into which I have been hurried, renders it necessary that I commence another sheet [...] (II.iii.152)

On one level, this writing can be seen as Darsie's mode of resistance to his kidnapping, as it is Clarissa's, enabling him to maintain an identity in his relation to an other independent of the identity being forced on him by his kidnapper.[32] At the same time as he addresses Alan, however,

---

32 Indeed, Darsie realises that 'the probability that my papers may be torn from me, and subjected to the inspection of one in particular, who, causelessly my enemy already, may be yet farther incensed at me for recording the history of my wrongs' (II.iii.145), i.e. that, as in *Pamela* and *Clarissa*, the kidnapper himself will become the reader of this writing. Darsie hopes that, as in *Pamela*, reading it might force the kidnapper to see the error of his ways: '[...] I have, as I have elsewhere intimated, had hitherto the comfortable reflection, that if the record of my misfortunes should fall into the hands of him by whom they are caused, they would, without harming any one, shew him the real character and disposition of the person who has become his prisoner—perhaps his victim' (II.ix.200). Instead, the plot is somewhat closer to *Clarissa*: reading Alan's letters gives Redgauntlet, if not the power over his ward that Lovelace gains from his epistolary interceptions, at

Darsie also addresses an anonymous reader, the unknown person who might find this journal after his death or disappearance or abduction abroad, and in doing so is obliged to build in a new aspect to his identity: loyalty, not to a friend, but to the British State:

> Those who read this Journal, if it shall be perused by impartial eyes, shall judge of me truly; and if they consider me as a fool in encountering danger unnecessarily, they shall have no reason to believe me a coward or a turncoat, when I find myself engaged in it. I have been bred in sentiments of attachment to the family on the throne, and in these sentiments I will live and die. (II.viii.198–9)

I will return to this point later. Meanwhile, it is important to note the difference between Colonel Mannering and Hugh Redgauntlet in their silencing of the autonomous voices of the young people in their power: that the former does so in the name of knowledge, of objectivity, of a discourse that records rather than creates, where the latter does so precisely as his mode of political agency. Redgauntlet kidnaps Darsie not to resign him to the impersonal forces of history, but to make him a tool of Redgauntlet's own autonomous agency *within* history. Redgauntlet's version of history remains the Tory-humanist one, where an individual statesman can rescue his *polis* with his own performative eloquence, his own decisive intervention in events.

The autonomy that Darsie gains from writing is thus important because Darsie's agency is otherwise abandoned. Writing is his only mode of action once he is in Redgauntlet's hands. Plans of future action are as pointless as expectations of a reply to his writing from Alan are unreal. The 'petty trivialities' of past incident that had previously provided the raw material for Darsie's exaggeration and Alan's deflating response are now a refuge from a future over which Darsie has no control at all:

> These particulars may appear trivial; but it is better, in my present condition, to exert my faculties in recollecting the past, and in recording it, than waste them in vain and anxious anticipations of the future. (II.iii.147–8)

---

least encouragement in his plans for the suggestible and romantic young man described there. Like *Clarissa*, *Redgauntlet* thematizes not only the power of intersubjective dialogue to resist coercion, but the liability of the text to be interpreted in different ways, and put to different uses, by an unforeseen readership.

In the absence of a reader whose response can be securely anticipated, Darsie retreats into the role of historian, the recorder of, and not the actor in, events.[33]

> In the meantime, there has stolen on me insensibly an indifference to my freedom—a carelessness about my situation, for which I am unable to account [...].
>
> Yet my inactivity is not the result of despondency, but arises, in part at least, from feelings of a very different cast. My story, long a mysterious one, seems now upon the verge of some strange development; and I feel a solemn impression that I ought to wait the course of events, to struggle against which is opposing my feeble efforts against the will of fate. Thou, my Alan, wilt treat as timidity this passive acquiescence, which has sunk down on me like a benumbing torpor; but if thou hast remembered by what visions my couch was haunted, and dost but think of the probability that I am in the vicinity, perhaps under the same roof with G. M., thou wilt acknowledge that other feelings than pusillanimity have tended in some degree to reconcile me to my fate.
>
> Still I own it is unmanly to submit with patience to this oppressive confinement. My heart rises against it, especially when I sit down to record my sufferings in this Journal; and I am determined, as the first step to my deliverance, to have my letters sent to the post-house. (II.v.163–4)

Note the bathetic culmination of Darsie's summoning-up of his powers of self-determination: he really has no conception of what his own agency might consist in here except more writing. Here we find one type of context in which Darsie addresses Alan directly after his kidnap; that is, any context that requires reference to 'G.M.', Greenmantle, the young woman (actually Darsie's sister) whose unexplained interest in Darsie's situation has led her to appeal in person to both of them. She is a sign of the continuing uniqueness of Darsie's relationship with Alan, a secret that they share, despite Darsie's now general address to an unknown reader, rather as Brown functions in the Julia-Matilda correspondence of *Guy Mannering* as a sign of the uniqueness of their friendship. But she also functions here as a justification for Darsie's unwillingness to attempt escape, and as such, acts in unknowing complicity with their uncle's political schemes. Greenmantle is the truth

---

33 Insofar as Darsie's journal is a formal continuation of his correspondence with Alan, narrative form here is at odds with the authority of the one who writes: for Darsie no longer has the power to make up his story in a collaborative effort with Alan as he did before. Darsie as narrator is thus in exactly the position of Julia Mannering as narrator in II.ix–x of *Guy Mannering*, after she is rendered powerless by the siege of Woodbourne, but before her writing disappears altogether.

of Darsie's identity in ways that he does not understand (as Rose is the truth of Edward's); but as she is figured in Darsie's writing, she represents both the possibility of resistance to, and the temptation of acquiescence in, the authority of their nightmarish patriarch.

We find this same paradoxical position of Greenmantle in the conflicting advice that she gives Darsie on different occasions. When Darsie first meets Greenmantle at the dance at Brokenburn, she berates him for his passivity and for drifting into low company, unaware that her presence itself is Darsie's main motive for remaining in the area:

> 'Is it manly to wait till fortune cast her beams upon you, when by exertion of your own energy you might distinguish yourself?—Do not the pursuits of learning lie open to you—of manly ambition—of war? —But no—not of war, that has already cost you too dear.'
>
> 'I will be what you wish me to be,' I replied with eagerness—'You have but to choose my path, and you shall see if I do not pursue it with energy, were it only because you command me.'
>
> 'Not because I command you,' said the maiden, 'but because reason, common sense, manhood, and in one word, regard for your own safety, give the same counsel.' (I.xii.109–10)

Even this exhortation to take his fate in his own hands leaves a problem in what exactly Greenmantle means by 'manly' and 'manhood.' For the traditional mode of grasping one's fate for a gentry male in a situation like Darsie's is just the one that Greenmantle stumbles over and then retreats from: violence. The reference to 'ambition' gestures at another traditional version of masculinity, namely that of the citizen-orator of renaissance political thought. But in any case, after Darsie's kidnap by his uncle's politics of violence, Greenmantle's advice makes no such appeal to Darsie's gender, and she recommends exactly the sort of passivity that he has adopted anyway as the best way of coping with Redgauntlet's coercion. She leaves a poem in the room to which he is confined:

> 'As lords their labourers' hire delay,
> > Fate quits our toil with hopes to come,
> Which, if far short of present pay,
> > Still owns a debt and names a sum.
>
> Quit not the pledge, frail sufferer, then,
> > Although a distant date be given;

Despair is treason towards man,
And blasphemy to Heaven.'

(II.ix.204)

And later she is able to give the same advice face-to-face:

'But you may temporize,' said Lilias, upon whom the idea of her uncle's
displeasure made evidently a strong impression,—'you may temporize, and let the
bubble burst of itself, as most of the gentry in this country do [...]' (III.v.310)

When, shortly after, his uncle begins pressuring him to commit himself
to the cause, this is the tactic that Darsie adopts: 'He therefore
concluded the enterprize would fall to pieces of itself, and that his best
way was, in the meantime, to remain silent [...]' (III.vi.178; chapter
xix.341). And Lilias gives Alan exactly the same advice (III.x.302;
chapter xix.390). Alan, like Darsie, does as she says, despite his earlier
resolution to 'counterplot' the Jacobites (III.iii.75; chapter xvi.300), and
despite the fact that this implies a complete reversal of the gender-roles
set up just four paragraphs before:

The relative situation of adviser and advised, of protector and protected, is so
peculiarly suited to the respective condition of man and woman, that great progress
towards intimacy is often made in very short space [...]. (III.x.367)

This tactic of delay is, of course, successful, for the rebellion does
indeed fall to pieces of itself. Now, it would be going too far to say that
Lilias is thus responsible for the survival of the two young men and the
successful outcome of the plot, for Darsie, with the prospect before him
of his identity at last being revealed, tends to wait and see from the start,
and neither Alan nor Darsie are ever in any serious danger other than
that offered by the sea or a bad fever. But the fact that a young woman
advises delay rather than action, coupled with her own characterisation
of it as somehow not manly, genders the young men's survival strategy
as *feminine*.

This gendering of delay is confirmed by the circumstances of
Darsie's interview with Lilias in volume III chapter v, in which she
advises it: an appeal to Darsie's manhood here would indeed be
incongruous, for at this point Darsie is dressed in a skirt, perched on a

side-saddle and wearing what looks like a riding veil (but is in fact a mask). It is in this discussion that Darsie learns that Greenmantle, the object of his desire, is in fact Lilias, his sister, and that Hugh Redgauntlet is their uncle; she tells him how he was kept from the hands of the latter by their mother, who sent him to be raised in Scotland. In other words, Lilias brings Darsie's story, in so far as that story is the search for his origins, to an end. As Alan predicted, 'the Unknown She of the Green Mantle' proves able after all to 'read this, the riddle of thy fate, better than wise Eppie of Buckhaven, or Cassandra herself' (I.viii.72): she is equivalent, as one might expect by now, to the carrier of a traditional knowledge that ensures the continuity of the family line, that was filled in *Guy Mannering* by Meg Merrilies.

I will return shortly to the role of folk-culture proper in the restoration of Darsie's familial identity; but it is worth noting at this point that Lilias represents here, in contrast to Redgauntlet, an identity as a member of a gentry family shorn of its accompanying political role. She has been up until this point a love-object for Darsie, and the family bond that they now discover continues rather than abandons this private affective bond: their family tie will be understood, that is, in private and affective terms, rather than as a shared public, political role as envisaged by their uncle. Lilias represents a family identity which maintains sentimental roots in the past, but which has surrendered its political agency to the state. Like *Guy Mannering*, *Redgauntlet* deploys a gentry-restoration plot; like *Guy Mannering*, it figures the eighteenth-century's hegemonic alliance of gentry and bourgeoisie by having its hero raised in a middle-class profession (however restless both Bertram and Darsie are rendered in those professions by their gentle blood). But *Redgauntlet* is far more explicit than the earlier novel that the price of this alliance is the abandonment by the landed classes of their traditional political loyalties and social supremacy. In this it is much closer to the final movement of *Rob Roy*, where the abandonment of that role appears in Diana Vernon's silent reappearance as the contented wife of Frank Osbaldistone, merchant, of the City of London, even while Frank gains the dignity of restoration to his paternal estates.

The precedent of *Rob Roy* also helps us answer another question: why must Darsie discover all this while dressed as a woman? It is Redgauntlet's vicious sidekick, Cristal Nixon, of all people, who tells us why: '"Come, young ladies, you have had time enough for your chat this morning, and your tongues, I think, must be tired"' (III.v.312). Darsie's conversation with Lilias constitutes the restoration of the sort of dialogue that he had previously enjoyed with Alan; but it is now the civilizing, feminizing dialogue that virtuous ladies are supposed to supply in polite culture. Redgauntlet tells her that "'You may use my permission and authority, to explain so much of our family matters as you yourself know"' to Darsie (III.iv.294), but in fact she tells him a story quite different from the one that Redgauntlet would recognize. Lilias, like Rose before her, has performed a kind of miracle by acquiring and maintaining one set of values, domestic or 'polite', despite being raised in a household whose values worked in quite the opposite direction. Like Rose, it is this miraculous escape from historical determination is what facilitates the rescue from history of the male hero. Lilias is thus the mirror image of Diana Vernon: for where Diana Vernon hid her political commitment under a veil of politeness, Lilias has hidden her politeness under an apparent acquiescence in her uncle's politics. Lilias has Diana's freedom of speech, indeed, but Darsie's initial shock at her lack of decorum with a young unmarried male (identical to Frank's unease with Diana's liberties) evaporates with the discovery that she is his sister. This is a much more final suspension of sexual desire than that demanded by Diana as a condition of improving conversation, but it functions in the same way to facilitate that other feminine role, that of moral example to the impolite male.[34]

I have noted that Alan's comparison of Greenmantle to 'wise Eppie of Buckhaven' as the possessor of Darsie's true identity assimilates her to folk-figures like Meg Merrilies. We might also note that a similar opposition is in play here between the traditional knowledge of such figures and the law; for as in *Guy Mannering*, the law has an opposing claim to be able to constitute narrative truth:

---

34 Judith Wilt writes: 'To discover in place of a lady-love a practical sister, who has her whole life been temporizing with and cleverly evading in womanly fashion the tyranny of their uncle [...] is for Darsie to discover not a fantasy but a model' (Wilt 150). I think this is exactly right, except that the model that Lilias provides is not only for Darsie's behaviour, but also for his speech. At first he finds he cannot enter a dialogue in that speech, because sexual desire disrupts discourse just as it does between Diana and Frank.

> Turn, then, thy sharp, wire-drawing, lawyer-like ingenuity to the same task—make
> up my history as though thou wert shaping the blundering allegations of some blue-
> bonneted, hard-headed client, into a condescendence of facts and circumstances,
> and thou shalt be, not my Apollo—*quid tibi cum lyra?*—but my Lord Stair. (I.i.5)

writes Darsie. As in *Guy Mannering*, the law does not succeed in
recovering the hero's story; but the place of the wise woman has been
taken by the polite lady. Indeed, while the folk-culture of the Solway
coast does figure largely in *Redgauntlet*, it is hard to see it as part of a
social totality of the sort that Colonel Mannering, and the text itself, was
able to subject to the enlightenment gaze of the ethnographer. For all its
historical and political content, *Redgauntlet* does not build up a picture
of a society consisting of various social classes in their mutual inter-
dependence of the sort that we might expect. Its characters come from a
wide range of the social spectrum, indeed, and we discover something
of their social and historical circumstances: of the tensions between the
spear-fishermen who catch salmon on the estuary, and those who net
them at the Solway mouth; of the awkward social position of a man like
Provost Crombie, obliged by his position to proclaim loyalty to the
government despite having Jacobite friends and relations. However,
these tensions and characters never tell us very much about the structure
of their society as a whole, or an economic situation which has produced
it. Neither Joshua Geddes nor Redgauntlet, for example, represent any
sort of class norm in the way that Dandie Dinmont, or Bailie Jarvie, or
Davie Deans do, and as a result do not carry with them a general context
that gives meaning to their individual actions. Joshua Geddes, as a
Quaker, is not a typical southwest of Scotland Protestant, and
Redgauntlet is too exceptionally fanatical to be a representative Tory
gentleman. Similarly, both Tam Trumbull and Nanty Ewart are too
particularized to represent a way of life, with a shared culture and an
economics that ties them into the society around them, in the way that
Meg Merrilies, for all her individuality, does represent a way of life.
This is in part because the social groups that these people *do* belong to
are *all* marginalized: there is no peasantry, for example, or lower gentry
like the Bertrams, complicit in the acts of the smugglers, tolerant of the
travellers, borrowing money (perhaps) from the Quakers, to provide the
ground for these groups' mutual economic dependence. The society of
the Solway area as represented in *Redgauntlet* is all margins with no

linking core. Dumfiresshire in the 1760s seems as atomised as Smollett's England, but (more or less) contentedly so.

However, although *Redgauntlet* does not portray a complete society in the way that *Guy Mannering* does, Darsie is, like Mannering himself, an amateur antiquarian and folklorist.

> [...] I could not help taking the bottle in my hand, to look more at the armorial bearings, which were chased with considerable taste on the silver frame-work. Encountering the eye of my entertainer, I instantly saw that my curiosity was highly distasteful [...]. (I.iv.29–30)

> Black-letter, you know, was my early passion, and the tomb-stones in the Grey-Friar's Church-yard early yielded up to my knowledge as a decipherer what little they could tell of the forgotten dead. (I.vii.139; letter vii.53)

> [...] and, as you know, I like tales of superstition, and I begged to have a specimen of his talent as we went along. (I.xi.86)

In the latter case, of course, the novel itself shares Darsie's interest, since we get 'Wandering Willie's Tale' included in the text in its entirety. Here we can see a difference between the young Guy Mannering and Darsie, and between their respective novels, for where I.iv of *Guy Mannering* presents, not Meg's original song, but Mannering's paraphrase of it, 'Wandering Willie's Tale' is presented as it was told to Darsie by Willie himself. And just as *Redgauntlet* includes folk-culture without positing a narratorial intermediary, so Darsie does not just collect folk-culture, understanding and appreciating it from the distance produced by enlightenment science, he actually participates in it. He too is a musician, knows the tunes that Willie plays on his fiddle, and is able to join Willie as his accompanist at the dance at Brokenburn, where his playing meets the old man's qualified commendation. Willie's tale is one that we as readers participate in, on the model of Darsie's participation in Willie's music (as we do not, for example, participate in Meg Merrilies's fortune-telling or ban-saying). If, as I suggested in chapter 2, *Guy Mannering* produces society as a knowable organic whole only by at the same time dividing it between the knowers and the known, *Redgauntlet* seems concerned to do the opposite: to posit a unifying culture at work in what is otherwise a collection of isolated and economically self-interested individuals, and by extension to constitute such a culture in its own relation to a fragmented modern readership.

211

It constructs, that is, a *national* readership understood as unified not by any class or status position but by a common cultural inheritance that cuts across such politically-dangerous distinctions. Bourgeois writers like Scott appropriate the modes and genres of traditional culture, the culture of a peasantry on whose destruction the economic rise of their own class was predicated, as a way of asserting this continuity: what is lost through 'progress' is recuperated as bourgeois 'art' or 'literature' to form a national (British, Scottish, or the two in some essential interrelation) culture. The appropriation of folk culture within an aesthetic sphere as a figure for this historical continuity is acted out in this novel in the part of Wandering Willie. In comparison to *Guy Mannering*, *Redgauntlet* is anxious to promise the *survival* of this culture in domesticated form, rather than its destruction: Dr Dryasdust's Conclusion mentions Willie ending his days in Darsie's hall.[35] In comparison also, the gentry-restoration theme is muted here; the actual house that will contain both Darsie and Willie, unlike Ellengowan, unlike Tully-Veolan, unlike Osbaldistone Hall, only figures within the story as a *prison*. Perhaps simply because the war with France has been over for nine years by 1824, the restoration of the estate is emptied of its counter-revolutionary political meaning. What Yoon Sun Lee says of *The Antiquary* is true also of *Redgauntlet* (although perhaps not of all these novels), that Scott suggests 'that the inheritance of personal property bears no necessary relation to the ideological narrative of national continuity'.[36]

---

35 Interestingly, at just at this point, the dance at Brokenburn, a complaint finds voice against the social heterogeneity that this national culture legitimates, a complaint that we have already heard from grumpy middle-aged men like Mannering and, before him, Matthew Bramble. Yet here, bizarrely, the voice is that of a young woman, of Greenmantle herself: 'I would have gone on in the false gallop of compliment, but she cut me short. "And why," she said, "is Mr Latimer here, and in disguise, or at least assuming an office unworthy of a man of education?—I beg pardon," she continued,—"I would not give you pain, but surely making an associate of a person of that description—"' (I.xii.108–9). This is a very odd moment in the novel, because its complaint against the collapse of status distinctions is one that the novel does not follow through. Greenmantle's advice at Brokenburn, in this as in its urging Darsie to action, is simply dropped. The customary complaint against the breaking down of status distinctions is raised, only to be shown to be irrelevant to what follows.

36 Yoon Sun Lee, 'A divided inheritance: Scott's antiquarian novel and the British nation', *ELH* 64 (1997): 540

As a result, folk culture does not intervene in the action of this novel as Meg Merrilies does, indeed, but as a guarantor of continuity despite that action. Willie's story, for example, figures in Darsie's first sight of the hereditary horseshoe frown of the Redgauntlets on his captor's forehead. This happens in volume II chapter vi, when Darsie is called upon by an incompetent and corrupt English magistrate, as his only chance of escaping Redgauntlet's legal guardianship, to swear that he has never seen him before. Darsie realises that he has seen a man with that expression on his face before, and cannot so swear, and so remains in Redgauntlet's power. He had seen this man, he realises at this time, as an infant; that is, he subsequently learns from Lilias, when Redgauntlet had stormed their mother's garden to abduct her children. However, in the presence of Justice Foxley, this original trauma does not come immediately to mind. The memory of Redgauntlet's face is mediated by Wandering Willie's Tale: it was this story which first recalled the horseshoe frown, and the physical confrontation with it recalls this previous recollection at the same time as the content of the memory itself.

I had heard such a look described in an old tale of *diablerie*, which it was my chance to be entertained with not long since [...].

The tale, when told, awaked a dreadful vision of infancy, which the withering and blighting look now fixed on me again forced on my recollection, but with much more vivacity. [...] 'The young man will no longer deny that he has seen me before,' said he [Redgauntlet] to the Justice, in a tone of complacency; 'and I trust he will now be reconciled to my temporary guardianship [...].' (II.vi.174)

This horseshoe frown appears as that which is shared by Darsie and his uncle, and thus offers him another type of identity to that which he constructs in his letters to Alan: an identity at once historically determined and yet holding out the (illusory) promise of historical agency.

[...] I answered him by a look of the same kind, and catching the reflection of my countenance in a large antique mirror which stood before me, I started again at the real or imaginary resemblance which my countenance, at that moment, bore to that of Herries. Surely my fate is somehow strangely interwoven with that of this strange and mysterious individual. (II.vii.181)[37]

The role of Wandering Willie's Tale in this (mis)recognition of his identity suggests a duality in the role of folk culture, for it appears here as a threat in its ability to confirm inherited political loyalties, to mediate their passage across the generations. These songs and stories can be used to construct a homogeneous national culture if understood in strictly *aesthetic* terms; but they could also drag a nation back into the nightmare of partisan schism if they are used to legitimate the *political* institutions of the past. Darsie, as we have seen, is rescued from this fate by his own writing, and by the reclaiming conversation of a woman, both of which return him to the more provisional textual identities offered by modernity.

Redgauntlet, then, constructs a national community, united by an inherited culture, rather than a socio-economic totality that could be the object of scientific exegesis. I want to finish this study by noting how this refusal of the cognitive function given discourse by enlightenment thinking is figured in this novel by the rejection of knowledge as the function of discourse by characters within the text itself. Alan, to whose legalistic brain Darsie appeals for a knowable version of his identity, is obliged to abandon his cognitive capacities once he is on Darsie's trail. He is not the only lawyer to do this: Justice Foxley has been refusing to know who his neighbour Mr. Ingoldsby is for years, a use of words to remain ignorant that Peter Peebles's naming of Ingoldsby as Herries of Birrenswork nearly makes impossible (II.vii. 183–4). Tam Trumbull, too, conveniently keeps himself ignorant of the origins and destinations of the contraband in which he deals, by never allowing them to be named in his presence (II.xii.238–9). It is in company such as this that Alan refuses to recognize that the handwriting on the letter he is carrying is Nanty Ewart's (III.iii.279), and refuses to know that Father Buonaventure is the priest that he is pretending to be (III.iii.278).

---

37 Mirrors in this novel figure fixed, inherited identities as opposed to negotiable intersubjective ones: Alan's destiny as a lawyer also appears to him in this way when he tries to see how he must appear in Greenmantle's eyes: 'The mirror was not unnaturally called in to aid; and that cabinet-counsellor pronounced me rather short, thick-set, with a cast of features fitter, I trust, for the bar than the ball [...].' (I.viii.68–9).

This refusal to admit to speech facts that are actually perfectly well-known is in all of these cases a strategy to avoid them becoming objects of the discourse of the law. In other words, they are instances of the subordination of the cognitive function of discourse to a performative end. And the novel itself does something very similar with the Jacobites as a political party. Politics itself has now become a matter of creating in words a convenient reality. The government delivers the *coup de grace* to the Jacobites not with superior military force, or a more contemporary ideology, or better economics, or anything that this novel could choose to *know* within its enlightenment frame of reference. It rather does so with that performative use of language that is the tactic of smugglers and of lawyers in a tight spot: the *refusal* to know. This is Argyle, unarmed in the Jacobite's headquarters:

> 'I do not,' he said, 'know this gentleman'—(Making a profound bow to the unfortunate Prince)—'I do not wish to know him; it is a knowledge which would suit neither of us.' (III.x.372)

I argued above that Lilias represents an inherited family identity for Darsie, but one shorn of a political agency which it has been surrendered to the state. Here we discover the form that agency takes: precisely the autonomy from historical determination that both Scott and Smollett previously identified with women's writing.

As in *The Heart of Midlothian*, the allocation of the authority to bypass questions of truth and falsehood, to dictate that which constitutes the truth, to the *state*, guarantees a happy ending in which heroes and heroines can enter or remain in a world shaped by the conventions of feminine fiction. Jeanie and Effie can enjoy their rival versions of feminine happiness, Darsie and Alan and Lilias can go back to their rival versions of each other, can be, in other words, subjects of their speech rather than objects of someone else's; they can be this, because they are subjects of a state which is both at work within history, and can decide what history is; at once the Law, and at the same time a creator of fictions. In *Redgauntlet*, the modern novelist makes complete his claim to replace the orator, the political agent imagined by renaissance humanism, not by claiming a corresponding agency, but by appropriating the state itself as a figure for the novelist's own authority over his creation.

Bibliography

Allan, David. *Virtue, Learning, and the Scottish Enlightenment: Ideas of Scholarship in Early Modern History.* Edinburgh: Edinburgh University Press, 1993.

Armstrong, Nancy. *Desire and Domestic Fiction: A Political History of the Novel.* Oxford: Clarendon Press, 1987.

Ballaster, Ros. *Seductive Forms: Women's Amatory Fiction from 1684 to 1740.* Oxford: Clarendon Press, 1992.

Barthes, Roland. *S/Z* trans. Richard Miller. 1973; Oxford: Blackwell, 1990.

Battestin, Martin C. *The Providence of Wit: Aspects of Form in Augustan Literature and the Arts.* 1974; Charlotteville: University Press of Virginia, 1989.

Beasley, Jerry C. *Novels of the 1740s.* Athens: University of Georgia Press, 1982.

Bollingbroke, Henry St. John. *Historical Writings,* ed. Issac Kramnick. Chicago: University of Chicago Press, 1972.

—. *Political Writings,* ed. David Armitage. Cambridge: Cambridge University Press, 1997.

Bond, Donald S., ed. *The Spectator.* 5 volumes. Oxford: Clarendon Press, 1965.

Brown, David. *Walter Scott and the Historical Imagination.* London: Routledge and Kegan Paul, 1979.

Brown, Homer. 'The Institution of the English Novel: Defoe's Contribution', *Novel: A Forum on Fiction* 29.3 (Spring 1996): 299–318.

Burney, Frances. *Evelina, or the History of a Young Lady's Entrance into the World.* 1778; Oxford: Oxford University Press, 1968.

—. *Cecilia, or Memoirs of an Heiress.* 1782; Oxford: Oxford University Press, 1988.

Burtt, Shelley. *Virtue Transformed: Political Argument in England, 1688–1740.* Cambridge: Cambridge University Press, 1992.

Chitnis, Anand C. *The Scottish Enlightenment: a Social History.* London: Croom Helm, 1976.

Christensen, Jerome. *Practicing Enlightenment: Hume and the Formation of a Literary Career.* Madison: University of Wisconsin Press, 1987.

Christie, John. 'The human sciences: origins and histories', *History of the Human Sciences* 6.1 (1993): 1–12.

Cockshut, A.O.J. *The Achievement of Walter Scott.* London: Collins, 1969.

Colley, Linda. *In Defiance of Oligarchy: The Tory Party 1714–60.* Cambridge: Cambridge University Press, 1982.

Cook, Elizabeth Heckenhorn. *Epistolary Bodies: Gender and Genre in the Eighteenth-Century Republic of Letters.* Stanford: Stanford University Press, 1996.

Crawford, Thomas. *Scott.* Edinburgh: Scottish Academic Press, 1982.

Damrosch, Leopold. *God's Plot and Man's Stories: Studies in the Fictional Imagination from Milton to Fielding.* Chicago: University of Chicago Press, 1985.

De Man, Paul. *The Rhetoric of Romanticism.* New York: Columbia University Press, 1984.

Doody, Margaret Ann. *A Natural Passion: A Study of the Novels of Samuel Richardson.* Oxford: Clarendon Press, 1974.

Douglas, Aileen. *Uneasy Sensations: Smollett and the Body.* Chicago: University of Chicago Press, 1995.

Duncan, Ian. *Modern Romance and Transformations of the Novel: The Gothic, Scott, Dickens.* Cambridge: Cambridge University Press, 1992.

—. 'Edinburgh, Capital of the Nineteenth Century', in James Chandler and Kevin Gilmartin, eds., *Romantic Metropolis: Cultural Productions of the City, 1770–1850.* Cambridge: Cambridge University Press, forthcoming.

Edgeworth, Maria. *Belinda.* 1801; Oxford: Oxford University Press, 1994.

—. *Patronage.* London: J. Johnson and Co., 1814.

Epstein, Julia. *The Iron Pen: Frances Burney and the Politics of Women's Writing.* Bristol: Bristol Classical Press, 1989.

Fabel, Robin. 'The Patriotic Briton: Tobias Smollett and English Politics, 1756–1771', *Eighteenth-Century Studies* 8 (1974): 100–14.

Ferguson, Adam. *An Essay on the History of Civil Society*, ed. Duncan Forbes. 1767; Edinburgh: Edinburgh University Press, 1966.

Ferris, Ina. *The Achievement of Literary Authority: Gender, History, and the Waverley Novels.* Ithaca: Cornell University Press, 1991.

Fielding, Henry. *The History of Tom Jones*, ed. R.P.C. Mutter. 1749; Harmondsworth: Penguin, 1966.

Fleishman, Avrom. *The English Historical Novel.* Baltimore: John Hopkins University Press, 1971.

Forbes, Duncan. 'The Rationalism of Sir Walter Scott', *Cambridge Journal* 7 (1953): 20–35.

Foucault, Michel. *The Order of Things.* London: Tavistock, 1970.

Fox, Christopher, Roy Porter, and Robert Wokler, eds. *Inventing Human Science: Eighteenth-Century Domains.* Berkeley: University of California Press, 1995.

Frye, Northrop. *The Anatomy of Criticism: Four Essays.* 1957; Harmondsworth: Penguin, 1990.

Garside, P.D. 'Scott and the Philosophical Historians', *Journal of the History of Ideas* 36.3 (1975): 497–512.

Gerrard, Christine. *The Patriot Opposition to Walpole: Politics, Poetry and National Myth.* Oxford: Clarendon Press, 1994.

Goldsmith, M.M. 'Faction Detected: Ideological Consequences of Robert Walpole's Decline and Fall', *History* 64 (1979): 1–19.

Gordon, Robert C. *Under Which King? A Study of the Scottish Waverley Novels.* Edinburgh: Oliver and Boyd, 1969.

Green, Katherine Sobba. *The Courtship Novel 1740–1820: A Feminized Genre.* Lexington: University Press of Kentucky, 1991.

Habermas, Jürgen. *The Structural Transformation of the Public Sphere*, trans. Thomas Burger. Cambridge: Polity, 1989.

Harris, Robert. *A Patriot Press: National Politics and the London Press in the 1740s.* Oxford: Clarendon, 1993.

Hart, Francis R. *Scott's Novels: The Plotting of Historical Survival.* Charlottesville: University Press of Virginia, 1966.

Hill, Christopher. *Reformation to Industrial Revolution, 1530–1780*. The Pelican Economic History of Britain vol.2. Harmondsworth: Penguin, 1969.

Hume, David. A Treatise of Human Nature, ed. L.A. Selby-Bigge. 1739; Oxford: Clarendon Press, 1978.

—. *Selected Essays*. Oxford: Oxford University Press, 1993.

Jameson, Frederic. *The Political Unconscious: Narrative as a Socially Symbolic Act*. London: Methuen, 1981.

Jeffrey, David K. '*Roderick Random*: The Form and Structure of a Romance', *Revue Belge de Philologie et d'Histoire* 58 (1980): 604–14.

Johnson, Claudia. *Jane Austen: Women, Politics, and the Novel*. Chicago: University of Chicago Press, 1988.

Kant, Immanuel. The Critique of Judgement, trans. J.C. Meredith. 1790; Oxford: Clarendon Press, 1952.

Klancher, Jon. *The Making of English Reading Audiences 1790–1832*. Madison: University of Wisconsin Press, 1987.

Klein, Lawrence. 'Gender, conversation and the public sphere in early eighteenth-century England', in Judith Still and Michael Warton, eds., *Textuality and Sexuality: Reading Theories and Practices*. Manchester: Manchester University Press, 1993. 100–15.

—. *Shaftesbury and the Culture of Politeness: Moral Discourse and Cultural Politics in Early Eighteenth-Century England*. Cambridge: Cambridge University Press, 1994.

—. 'Property and Politeness in the early eighteenth-century Whig moralists: the case of the *Spectator*', in John Brewer and Susan Staves, eds., *Early Modern Conceptions of Property*. London: Routledge, 1995. 221–33.

Knapp, Lewis Mansfield. *Tobias Smollett: Doctor of Men and Manners*. Princeton: Princeton University Press, 1949.

Kramnick, Issac. *Bolingbroke and His Circle: The Politics of Nostalgia in the Age of Walpole*. Cambridge MA: Harvard University Press, 1968.

Landes, Joan B. *Women and the Public Sphere in the Age of the French Revolution*. Ithaca: Cornell University Press, 1988.

Lee, Yoon Sun. 'A divided inheritance: Scott's antiquarian novel and the British nation', *ELH* 64 (1997): 571–601.

Lennox, Charlotte. *The Female Quixote, or, The Adventures of Arabella*, ed. Margaret Dalziel. 1752; Oxford: Oxford University Press, 1989.

Levine, George. *The Realistic Imagination: English Fiction from Frankenstein to Lady Chatterley*. Chicago: University of Chicago Press, 1981.

Lyotard, Jean-François. *The Postmodern Condition: A Report on Knowledge*, trans. Geoff Bennington and Brian Massumi. Manchester: Manchester University Press, 1984.

MacCormick, Neil. 'Law and Enlightenment', in Campbell and Skinner, eds., *The Origins and Nature of the Scottish Enlightenment*. Edinburgh: John Donald, 1982. 150–66.

Mackenzie, Henry. *The Man of Feeling*. 1771; Oxford: Oxford University Press, 1967.

McKeon, Michael. *The Origins of the English Novel 1600–1740*. Baltimore: John Hopkins University Press, 1987.

McMaster, Graham. *Scott and Society*. Cambridge: Cambridge University Press, 1981.

Meek, Ronald L. *Social Science and the Ignoble Savage*. Cambridge: Cambridge University Press, 1976.

Monod, Paul. *Jacobitism and the English People 1688–1788*. Cambridge: Cambridge University Press, 1989.

Mullan, John. *Sentiment and Sociability: The Language of Feeling in the Eighteenth Century*. Oxford: Clarendon, 1990.

Paulson, Ronald. *Satire and the Novel in Eighteenth-Century England*. New Haven: Yale University Press, 1967.

Pettit, Alexander. *Illusory Consensus: Bolingbroke and the Polemical Response to Walpole, 1730–37*. Newark: University of Delaware Press, 1997.

Phillipson, Nicholas. 'Adam Smith as Civic Moralist', in Istvan Hont and Michael Ignatieff, eds., *Wealth and Virtue: The Shaping of Political Economy in the Scottish Enlightenment*. Cambridge: Cambridge University Press, 1983. 179–202.

—. *Hume*. London: Weidenfeld and Nicolson, 1989.

Pocock, J.G.A. *Politics, Language, and Time: Essays on Political Thought and History*. London: Methuen, 1972.

—. *The Machiavellian Moment: Florentine Political Thought and the Atlantic Republican Tradition*. Princeton: Princeton University Press, 1975.

—. *Virtue, Commerce, and History*. Cambridge: Cambridge University Press, 1985.

Potkay, Adam. *The Fate of Eloquence in the Age of Hume*. Ithaca: Cornell University Press, 1994.

Richardson, Samuel. *Clarissa; or The History of a Young Lady*. 1747–8; Harmondsworth: Penguin, 1985.

Richetti, John. 'The Old Order and the New Novel of the Mid-Eighteenth Century: Narrative Authority in Fielding and Smollett', *Eighteenth-Century Fiction* 2.3 (April 1990): 183–96.

—. *The English Novel in History 1700–1780*. London: Routledge, 1999.

Rogers, Nicholas. 'Popular Protest in Early Hanoverian London', *Past and Present* 79 (May 1978): 70–100.

—. 'Riot and Popular Jacobitism in Early Hanoverian England', in Eveline Cruickshanks, ed., *Ideology and Conspiracy: Aspects of Jacobitism, 1689–1759*. Edinburgh: John Donald, 1982. 70–88.

—. Whigs and Cities: Popular Politics in the Age of Walpole and Pitt. Oxford: Oxford University Press, 1989.

Rosenblum, Michael. 'Smollett as Conservative Satirist', *ELH* 42 (1975): 556–79.

Rothstein, Eric. 'Scotophilia and Humphry Clinker: The Politics of Beggary, Bugs and Buttocks', *University of Toronto Quarterly* 52.2 (Fall 1982): 63–78.

Rousseau, George. 'Smollett and Politics: Originals for the Election Scene in Sir Launcelot Greaves', *English Language Notes* 14 (1976): 32–7.

Scott, Walter. *Waverley, or 'Tis Sixty Years Since*. Edinburgh: Archibald Constable and Co., 1814.

—. *Guy Mannering, or The Astrologer*. Edinburgh: Archibald Constable and Co., 1815.

—. *Rob Roy*. Edinburgh: Archibald Constable and Co., 1816.

—. *Takes of My Landlord, Second Series* [*The Heart of Midlothian*]. Edinburgh: Archibald Constable and Co., 1818.

—. *The Heart of Midlothian*, ed. Claire Lamont. Oxford: Oxford University Press, 1982.

—. *Waverley*, ed. Claire Lamont. Oxford: Oxford University Press, 1986.

—. *The Tale of Old Mortality*, ed. Douglas S. Mack. 1816; Edinburgh: Edinburgh University Press, 1993.

—. *Redgauntlet*, ed. G.A.M. Wood and David Hewitt. 1824; Edinburgh: Edinburgh University Press, 1997.

—. *Rob Roy*, ed. Ian Duncan. 1818; Oxford: Oxford University Press, 1998.

Siskin, Clifford. *The Work of Writing: Literature and Social Change in Britain, 1700–1830*. Baltimore: John Hopkins University Press, 1998.

Sitter, John. *Literary Loneliness in Mid-Eighteenth-Century England*. Ithaca: Cornell University Press, 1982.

Skinner, Quentin. 'The Principles and Practice of Opposition: The Case of Bolingbroke versus Walpole', in Neil McKendrick, ed., *Historical Perspectives: Studies in English Thought and Society*. London: Europa Press, 1974. 93–128.

Smith, Adam. *Essays on Philosophical Subjects*. Strasburg: F.G. Levrault, 1799.

Smollett, Tobias. *The Adventures of Roderick Random*, ed. Paul-Gabriel Boucé. 1748; Oxford: Oxford University Press, 1979.

—. *Roderick Random*, ed. David Blewett. 1748; Harmondsworth: Penguin, 1995.

—. *The Expedition of Humphry Clinker*, ed. Lewis M. Knapp. 1771; Oxford: Oxford University Press, 1966.

Spector, Robert D. 'Smollett's Politics and the Briton, 9 October 1762', *Papers on Language and Literature* 26.2 (Spring 1990): 280–4.

Spencer, Jane. *The Rise of the Woman Novelist: From Aphra Behn to Jane Austen*. Oxford: Basil Blackwell, 1986.

Stein, Peter. 'Law and Society in Scottish Thought', in Rosalind Mitchison and Nicholas Phillipson, eds., *Scotland in the Age of Improvement*. Edinburgh: Edinburgh University Press, 1970. 148–68

Stephanson, Raymond. 'The (Non)Sense of an Ending: Subversive Allusion and Thematic Discontent in *Roderick Random*', *Eighteenth-Century Fiction* 1.2 (Jan. 1989): 103–18.

Sutherland, Kathryn. 'Fictional Economies: Adam Smith, Walter Scott, and the nineteenth-century novel', *ELH* 54 (1987): 97–127.

Swift, Jonathan. *Gulliver's Travels*. 1726; Harmondsworth: Penguin, 1967.

Todd, Janet. *Women's Friendship in Literature*. New York: Columbia University Press, 1980.

—. *Sensibility: An Introduction*. London: Methuen, 1986.

Troide, Lars E. And Stewart J. Cooke, eds. *The Early Journals and Letters of Fanny Burney*. Oxford: Clarendon Press, 1994.

Warner, John M. 'Smollett's Develoment as a Novelist', *Novel: A Forum on Fiction* 5.2 (Winter 1972): 148–61.

Weber, Max. *From Max Weber: Essays in Sociology,* ed. H.H. Garth and C. Wright Mills. 1948; Oxford: Oxford University Press, 1958.

Weinsheimer, Joel. *Eighteenth-Century Hermeneutics: Philosophy of Interpretation from Locke to Burke*. New Haven: Yale University Press, 1993.

Welsh, Alexander. *The Hero of the Waverley Novels: With New Essays on Scott*. Princeton: Princeton University Press, 1992.

Williams, Ioan, ed. *Sir Walter Scott on Novelists and Fiction*. London: Routledge and Kegan Paul, 1968.

Wilt, Judith. *Secret Leaves: The Novels of Sir Walter Scott*. Chicago: University of Chicago Press, 1985.

Zomchick, John P. 'Social Class, Character, and Narrative Strategy in *Humphry Clinker*', *Eighteenth-Century Life* 10 (1986): 172–85.

Index